The Chivalric Biography of Boucicaut, Jean II Le Meingre

The Chivalric Biography of Boucicaut,

Jean II Le Meingre

Translated with notes and introduction by
Craig Taylor and Jane H.M. Taylor

THE BOYDELL PRESS

First published 2016
The Boydell Press, Woodbridge
Paperback edition 2020

ISBN 978 1 78327 166 5 hardback
ISBN 978 1 78327 464 2 paperback

The Boydell Press is an imprint of Boydell & Brewer Ltd
PO Box 9, Woodbridge, Suffolk IP12 3DF, UK
and of Boydell & Brewer Inc.
668 Mt Hope Avenue, Rochester, NY 14620–2731, USA
website: www.boydellandbrewer.com

A catalogue record for this book is available
from the British Library

Contents

For Richard W. Kaeuper
And In Memory of Elspeth Kennedy
Ardent Enthusiasts for Medieval Chivalry

Preface

This book is the fruit of a fortuitous, and fortunate, conversation between the two of us at the International Medieval Congress at Kalamazoo in May 2014. Jane Taylor and Robert L. Krueger had just published a translation of Antoine de La Sale's *Le Petit Jehan de Saintré* (Philadelphia, 2014), and that naturally led us to discuss other late medieval French texts that deserved to be opened up to a wider audience. Within just a few minutes, we had agreed to collaborate on a translation of the early fifteenth-century chivalric biography of Jean II Le Meingre, known as Boucicaut, marshal of France.

This anonymous biography remains little used by Anglophone scholars, despite its fundamental importance as a source for chivalric culture, the study of France and Italy during the age of the Great Schism, the history of late medieval crusading and what modern scholars often refer to as 'vernacular humanism' – that is to say the impact of classical learning on vernacular writing and lay society. The biography recounts the life of Boucicaut from his youthful chivalric exploits to his crusading adventures in eastern Europe and the Mediterranean. It also offers a great deal of unique evidence regarding the politics of Italy in the first decade of the fifteenth century when Boucicaut was governor of Genoa and deeply involved in the rivalries between the great city-states and the attempts to resolve the Papal Schism. The final book of the biography steps back from the narrative account to offer the lessons to be learnt from the example of Boucicaut, and hence a thorough dissection of political leadership and knighthood comparable with better known chivalric manuals and mirrors for princes.

The biography of Boucicaut was most recently edited in 1985 by Denis Lalande in *Le livre des fais du bon messire Jehan le Maingre, dit Bouciquaut, mareschal de France et gouverneur de Jennes* (Geneva, 1985), and Lalande also published a scholarly biography of Boucicaut three years later. We have translated that edition but revised the scholarly apparatus that Lalande offered, correcting, where necessary, and developing his identification of geographical locations, individuals and especially the sources used by the biographer.

Acknowledgements

Dr Alan Murray (University of Leeds) kindly provided guidance on matters relating to the Teutonic Knights, and in particular the identification of the 'Chastel de Chevaliers' – that is to say a castle on an island half a mile from Kaunas in Lithuania. Professor Richard Unger (University of British Columbia) and Dr Susan Rose were good enough to provide invaluable information on ships, shipping and naval warfare in the Eastern Mediterranean in the late Middle Ages. Dr Ralph Moffatt, Curator of European Arms and Armour, Glasgow Museums, was a fount of information on armour and chivalric practices in the late Middle Ages. Dr Alan Wedgwood was most helpful on naval idiom and naval manoeuvres.

But finally, it would be churlish of us not to express our profound gratitude to the late Denis Lalande, for the accuracy of his edition, for his copious annotations, for his excellent introduction and critical apparatus; his work has made ours a pleasure.

Abbreviations

Arch. Nat.	Archives Nationales
BM	Bibliothèque Municipale
BNF	Paris, Bibliothèque Nationale de France
c.	chapter
DMF	*Dictionnaire du moyen français*: online only, see http://www.atilf.fr/dmf/
fr.	français
Livre des fais	*Le livre des fais du bon messire Jehan le Maingre, dit Bouciquaut, mareschal de France et gouverneur de Jennes*, ed. D. Lalande (Geneva, 1985)
MS	manuscript
n.a.f.	nouvelles acquisitions françaises

Glossary

à outrance	A chivalric combat that was fought until one participant was killed or captured
barque	A smaller open boat which could use oars or sail for propulsion
bascinet	A lighter-weight helmet, with visor, covering the head
bastille	A wooden tower on wheels, built for siege warfare
battle	One of the divisions of the army when arrayed for combat
bombard	A large-calibre, muzzle-loading artillery piece used to throw stone balls during sieges or naval battles
brigantine	A small galley with both oars and sails, perhaps with some room for cargo
condottiere	An Italian term for a mercenary
coronel (lance with)	Crown-shaped safety-head for a lance, used in tournaments to prevent injury
destrier	A war-horse, or charger
écu d'or	The principal gold coin in France by the start of the fifteenth century; 9 écus were worth around £2
emprise	A chivalric undertaking that was declared formally, such as a series of jousts to be held at a particular place or over a particular period of time
galee soubtille	A narrow, streamlined war galley designed to be fast and highly manoeuvrable
galiot	A smaller, lighter-weight galley, with fewer benches than the galley and hence with a smaller crew
galley	The workhorse of the Mediterranean, for trade or warfare: a flat-built single-deck sea-going vessel propelled by sails and oars, with twenty-five to twenty-eight benches for the rowers
grande galee huissiere	A great galley fitted out with a hatch for horse transport
great galley	A galley propelled by sails and oars and which was larger in order to have room for cargo

gripperie	A lateen-rigged oared vessel, smaller than a galley, whose name would be a variant of the Italian *gripos* used by Pietro Bembo in 1530–40 for a vessel used to carry soldiers for an amphibious operation
league	A league was the distance that a person could walk in an hour, usually defined as three miles
letter of marque	Letter to authorise an act of reprisal by individuals, to seize by force goods, chattels or even people as compensation for injuries that they had received
lettre d'armes	A document setting out a detailed statement of conditions and stipulations relating to an order of knighthood, or a particular chivalric undertaking
marshal	The highest-ranking military officer in France, below the constable
nave	A sailing-ship – that is to say, a ship not equipped with oars. They were usually broader and deeper than a galley, and would be used largely for the transport of cargo
Outremer	A general name given to the Crusader states established after the First Crusade, but by the end of the fourteenth century a term used more generally to refer to French-speaking regions lying across the Mediterranean
Prisoners' Base	A game involving two teams who stage a mock battle, the aim being for each side to accumulate prisoners
Reise	A crusading campaign into Lithuanian territory organised by the Teutonic Order
routier	An unemployed soldier. Routiers often organised themselves into free companies (*routes*)
varlet	A servant, page or attendant to a knight or other person of military importance
vidimus	The attested copy of a document

Introduction

The Book of the Deeds of My Good Lord Jean Le Meingre, Known as Boucicaut is a chivalric biography celebrating the life of one of the most prominent knights of the Middle Ages. This anonymous work was completed on 9 April 1409, thirteen years before the death of its subject, Jean II Le Meingre, known by the sobriquet Boucicaut (1366–1421).[1] It survives in just one manuscript, BNF fr. 11432,[2] a fine, large folio volume of 125 parchment leaves. It is written throughout in two columns, by the same neat early fifteenth-century hand. It is a handsome, expensively produced volume: initial letters have been decorated in gold, red, and blue, and the copyist has left space for eight miniatures, although these, unfortunately, were never completed. Might this have been the author's own presentation manuscript? There are in any case no other surviving manuscripts.

The biography presented Boucicaut as a flower of chivalry and the embodiment of the highest qualities expected of a knight. It recounted his life and career up until 6 March 1409, when he was still serving as governor of Genoa on behalf of the French king Charles VI (1380–1422),[3] and when his reputation, in France, was still high.

The first part of *The Book of the Deeds* narrated the origins of Boucicaut's career and his swift rise to prominence. He had followed in the footsteps of his father Jean I Le Meingre, also known as Boucicaut (d.1367), who had enjoyed a successful career as a soldier and diplomat, culminating in his appointment as one of the two marshals of France in 1356. As a young man, Jean II Le Meingre served in the company of Louis de Bourbon and Louis de Sancerre, fighting against both the English and rebels like Charles de Navarre and Philip van Artevelde. The younger Boucicaut was knighted at the age of sixteen on the eve of the battle of Roosebeke (27 November

1 See p. 213 below. For the life of Boucicaut, see D. Lalande, *Jean II le Meingre, dit Boucicaut (1366–1421): étude d'une biographie héroïque* (Geneva, 1988), together with N. Housley, *The Crusaders* (Stroud, 2002), pp. 139–72, and id., 'One Man and His Wars: The Depiction of Warfare by Marshal Boucicaut's Biographer', *Journal of Medieval History*, 29 (2003), pp. 27–40.

2 Described briefly in the *Catalogue général des manuscrits français de la Bibliothèque Nationale. Ancien supplément français*, vol. II (Paris, 1896), p. 301, and in much greater detail by Lalande, *Le livre des fais*, pp. xiii-xxi.

3 See pp. 97–100 below.

1382), where Artevelde was killed and his Flemish army defeated (**I, chapter 10**). Boucicaut later took part in Louis de Bourbon's expedition to Castile in 1386 to fight against John of Gaunt and the English (**I, chapter 15**). In 1391, Charles VI appointed Boucicaut, aged just twenty-six, to replace Jean IV de Mauquenchy as marshal of France (**I, chapter 19**).[4] Boucicaut was then dispatched at the head of an expedition to punish Archambaud V count of Périgord for his rebellion against the French crown (**I, chapter 29**).

Above all, the biographer underlined Boucicaut's commitment to crusading.[5] Taking advantage of lulls in the Anglo-French wars, he had joined the *reise* fought in Prussia by the Teutonic Order against the pagan Lithuanians (**I, chapters 11 and 18**). From 1387 to 1389, Boucicaut travelled to Hungary, Constantinople, the Ottoman court of the sultan Murad I and the Holy Land, and quickly rushed to the aid of Philippe d'Artois, count of Eu, following his arrest by the Mamluk sultan of Egypt while on pilgrimage (**I, chapter 16**). Most famously, Boucicaut was one of the commanders of the ill-fated Nicopolis expedition in 1396 (**I, chapters 22–8**).[6] The French army at Nicopolis was nominally led by the twenty-eight-year-old Jean de Nevers, son of Philippe duke of Burgundy, supporting King Sigismund in the defence of Hungary against the Ottoman Turks.[7] On 12 September 1396, the Christians laid siege to the city of Nicopolis but just two weeks later suffered a devastating defeat at the hands of the Ottoman sultan Bayezid. Many prominent French noblemen died in the battle, including the admiral Jean de Vienne, Philippe de Bar and Renaud de Roye. Worse, the sultan took revenge for earlier atrocities committed by the crusaders against his own men by killing almost all of the three thousand Christian prisoners taken during the battle. Only those aged under twenty were spared, to be sold as slaves, as well as the wealthiest nobles who could afford great ransoms such as Jean de Nevers, Philippe d'Artois, Henri de Bar, Enguerrand de Coucy and Guy de La Trémoïlle. Boucicaut himself was almost executed but Jean de Nevers

4 The biography did not mention that Boucicaut was present alongside the king near to Le Mans on 5 August 1392, and may even have been wounded, when Charles VI suffered his first attack of mental illness. R.C. Famiglietti, *Royal Intrigue: Crisis at the Court of Charles VI, 1392–1420* (New York, 1982), pp. 2–3 and 207–8, note 15.

5 Housley, *The Crusaders*, pp. 139–72, and J. Paviot, 'Boucicaut et la croisade (fin XIVe-début XVe siècle)', *La noblesse et la croisade à la fin du Moyen Âge (France, Bourgogne, Bohême)*, ed. M. Nejedlý, J. Svátek, D. Baloup, B. Joudiou and J. Paviot (Toulouse, 2009), pp. 69–83.

6 Intriguingly, the biographer did not mention the fact that Boucicaut was one of the members of the Order of the Passion, set up by Philippe de Mézières to encourage zeal for crusading, and which by 1396 included sixty-one prominent nobles and clerics, mainly from France and England. P. Contamine, '"Les princes, barons et chevaliers qui a la chevalerie au service de Dieu se sont ja vouez". Recherches prosopographiques sur l'ordre de la Passion de Jésus-Christ (1385–1395)', *La noblesse et la croisade à la fin du Moyen Âge (France, Bourgogne, Bohême)*, ed. M. Nejedlý, J. Svátek, D. Baloup, B. Joudiou and J. Paviot (Toulouse, 2009), pp. 43–67.

7 For the Nicopolis Crusade of 1396, see the special issue of *Annales de Bourgogne*, 68 (1996).

successfully pleaded for his life. Three years after the disaster at Nicopolis, Boucicaut was commissioned by the French king in 1399 to break the Turkish blockade on Constantinople, and to aid the Emperor Manuel II Paleologos against his nephew John VII, who was supported by the Ottoman sultan Bayezid (**I, chapters 30–7**).

The first part of the biography also celebrated Boucicaut's success in chivalric combats, such as his defeat of the great Gascon champion Sicart de La Barde at Châlucet in 1385 (**I, chapter 13**), as well the famous jousts held outside the abbey of Saint-Inglevert in 1390 (**I, chapter 17**).[8] The author delighted in the bravery and success of Boucicaut and his companions at Saint-Inglevert, who were celebrated in a popular proverb: 'If the devil comes out of hell to fight a duel, he will accept the challenge of a Boucicaut, a Renaud de Roye and a Sempy.'[9] In addition to these chivalric exploits, the biographer was also keen to underline Boucicaut's credentials as a courteous lover and a protector of women. Early in the narrative, the biographer argued that Boucicaut had been motivated to accomplish great deeds at the start of his career by his passion for a secret lover, a commonplace theme of chivalric romance; he also reported that Jean had been one of the authors of the *Cent ballades*, a long poetic debate about love and loyalty that was probably presented before King Charles VI and his court in October 1389 (**I, chapters 8–9**).[10] No mention was made in the biography of Boucicaut's marriage to Antoinette de Turenne in 1392, but the biographer did report that in the aftermath of the disaster at Nicopolis, Boucicaut founded a knightly order dedicated to the protection of the women who had been widowed and orphaned (**I, chapters 38–9**). This Ordre de la Dame Blanche en l'Escu Vert (order of the Enterprise of the White Lady of the Green Shield) was established on 11 April 1400, and its thirteen members promised to fight in the lists in order to aid and to protect the honour and property of women widowed or orphaned by the plague or as a result of the disaster at Nicopolis. The great advocate of women, Christine de Pizan, praised this knightly order and its defence of women.[11]

8 The list of such events recorded in the biography was far from complete. For example, no mention was made of the fact that Boucicaut was one of the winners at the two days of jousts held to celebrate the marriage of Jean de Montaigu and Jacqueline, daughter of the late Étienne, lord of La Grange on 24 July 1390. R.C. Famiglietti, *Tales of the Marriage Bed from Medieval France (1300–1500)* (Providence, RI, 1992), pp. 38–9.

9 *Le livre des proverbes français*, ed. A.J.V. Le Roux de Lincy, 2 volumes (2nd edition, Paris, 1859), II, p. 390, and E. Gaucher, 'Les proverbes dans une biographie du XVe siècle: *Le livre des fais de Bouciquaut*', *Le Moyen Âge: Revue d'histoire et de philologie*, 99 (1993), p. 61.

10 *Les cent ballades, poème du XIVe siècle composé par Jean le Seneschal avec la collaboration de Philippe d'Artois, comte d'Eu, de Boucicaut le jeune et de Jean de Crésecque*, ed. G. Raynaud (Paris, 1905).

11 Christine de Pizan, *Autres ballades* II, III, IV and XII, in *Les oeuvres poétiques de Christine de Pisan*, ed. M. Roy, 3 volumes (Paris, 1886–96), I, pp. 208–12 and 220–1. For the remarkable career of Christine (1364-c.1430) see N. Margolis, *An Introduction to Christine de Pizan* (Gainesville, FL, 2011).

The second part of *The Book of the Deeds* continued the narrative of Boucicaut's career in Italy from 1401 to 1404. After a period of great internal turbulence, the doge of Genoa, Antoniotto Adorno, had signed a treaty with King Charles VI on 25 October 1396, placing the city under the protection and sovereignty of the French crown.[12] Boucicaut was appointed as governor of Genoa on 23 March 1401 (**II, chapter 5**).[13] The biographer recounted the marshal's initial actions upon arriving in the city (**II, chapters 6–10**). The narrative then shifted to Boucicaut's expedition that set sail in April 1403 to rescue the Genoese-controlled city of Famagusta on the island of Cyprus (**II, chapters 11–12**), as well as the raids that this force made along the Anatolian and Syrian coasts, culminating in the sack of Beirut in August 1403 (**II, chapter 21**).[14] The biographer strongly denied the Venetian claims that Boucicaut's troops had robbed their merchants in Beirut, denouncing this justification for their subsequent attack upon the marshal's fleet at Modone on 7 October 1403 (**II, chapters 25–31**).

The third part of *The Book of the Deeds* continued the story of Boucicaut's governorship of Genoa from his return from the expedition to Beirut up until 6 March 1409. This was a complex narrative of the marshal's involvement in the murky politics of Pisa, Milan, Florence and Rome, and above all the Great Schism that divided the Church and Western Europe. In 1378, Pope Urban VI (1378–89) had been elected pope at Rome, but a rival, anti-pope named Clement VII (1378–94) was also elected four months later, shortly before returning to Avignon. Their successors continued to maintain their rival claims to be the one true pope.[15] The biographer discussed Boucicaut's efforts to persuade the Genoese in October 1404 to support the Avignonese pope Benedict XIII against the claims of the rival Roman pope Boniface IX (**III, chapters 3 and 5**), Boucicaut's role in a plan in 1407 by which the two popes would resign in order to allow a general council to elect a new pope who could unify the Church (**III, chapter 19**), and Boucicaut's efforts to seize Rome back from King Ladislaus of Naples after he had seized the city in April 1408 (**III, chapter 20**).[16] Woven into this narrative of papal politics was Boucicaut's involvement in an

---

12 S.A. Epstein, *Genoa and the Genoese, 958–1528* (Chapel Hill, NC, 2001), pp. 228–70, and also see E. Jarry, *Les origines de la domination française à Gênes (1392–1402)* (Paris, 1896) and C. Masson, *Des guerres en Italie avant les guerres d'Italie. Les entreprises militaires françaises dans la péninsule à l'époque du Grand Schisme d'Occident* (Rome, 2014).

13 C. Masson, 'Gouverneur royal ou chevalier croisé? Boucicaut à Gênes, une administration intéressée', *Faire la guerre, faire la paix. Approches sémantiques et ambiguïtés terminologiques* (Paris, 2012), pp. 181–91.

14 A. Fuess, 'Prelude to a Stronger Involvement in the Middle East: French Attacks on Beirut in the Years 1403 and 1520', *Al-Masaq*, 17 (2005), pp. 173–80.

15 *A Companion to the Great Western Schism (1378–1417)*, ed. J. Rollo-Koster and T.M. Izbicki (Leiden, 2009), and also see N. Valois, *La France et le Grand Schisme d'Occident*, 4 volumes (Paris, 1896–1902).

16 Ladislaus, king of Naples (1386–1414), had intervened in the complex politics of Rome since 1404, and almost certainly laid siege to the Roman port of Ostia on 25 April 1408 in order

uprising in Pisa against Gabriele Maria Visconti in July 1405 (**III, chapters 6–12**), as well as Visconti's treacherous efforts to seize Genoa in 1408 (**III, chapter 22**). In addition, the biographer reported in some detail on Boucicaut's failed efforts in 1407 to secure the support of the king of Cyprus for an expedition to capture Alexandria (**III, chapters 15–18**), and a minor success in a naval battle against four Moorish galleys in September 1408 (**III, chapter 21**).

The fourth and final part of *The Book of the Deeds* abandoned the narrative of Boucicaut's life and instead offered a celebration of the virtues and good habits of the marshal. This attempt to draw together the lessons offered by the life of Boucicaut was extremely unusual in chivalric biographies, and more closely echoed the didactic manuals of writers like Christine de Pizan and Antoine de La Sale.[17] Drawing heavily upon the Roman history and moral advice presented in a recent French translation of Valerius Maximus's *Facta et dicta memorabilia*, the biographer meticulously compared the virtues and qualities of Boucicaut with those of the most famous men of Antiquity. The author highlighted the marshal's piety, charity and devotion to God (**IV, chapters 2–3**), his discipline, restraint and leadership in war (**IV, chapter 4**), his bravery (**IV, chapter 5**), his lack of avarice (**IV, chapter 6**), his chastity and self-discipline (**IV, chapter 7**), his love of justice and mercy (**IV, chapters 8–9**), his eloquence (**IV, chapter 10**) and his diligence (**IV, chapter 11**). The author concluded by emphasising that Boucicaut was worthy of the highest honour, but also acknowledged that Fortune could be fickle and often failed to reward the just, especially when others were jealous of them (**IV, chapters 12–13**).

* * *

The account of the life of Boucicaut in *The Book of the Deeds* stopped on 6 March 1409, but that was far from the end of his career. On 30 July 1409, Boucicaut left Genoa with an army to assist the duke of Milan against King Ladislaus, and so was absent from the city when an uprising against his rule began on 2 September. Within ten days, the French garrison in Genoa had surrendered to the marquis of Montferrat who stripped them of all weapons, armour and money and exiled them from the city.[18] Meanwhile Raoul de Gaucourt brought military reinforcements from France to assist the marshal, joining Boucicaut at Moncalieri in Piedmont in

to undermine the negotiations between the two rival popes, fearing that a resolution to the Schism might lead to the election of a new pope who would support Ladislaus' rival for the throne of Naples, Louis II, duke of Anjou (1377–1417).

17 Christine de Pizan, *Le livre du corps de policie*, ed. A.J. Kennedy (Paris, 1998), and id., *The Book of Peace*, ed. and trans. K. Green, C.J. Mews and J. Pinder (Philadelphia, PA, 2008), and Antoine de La Sale, *Oeuvres complètes d'Antoine de La Sale*, ed. F. Desonay, 2 volumes (Liège/Paris, 1935–41).

18 For the uprising in Genoa against Boucicaut and his return to France, see Lalande, *Jean II le Meingre*, pp. 153–5.

October 1409. But even with this help, the marshal lacked the financial resources to pay for an attack upon Genoa, and on 10 November 1410 he was ordered to return to Paris, where he arrived on 10 October 1411.

Despite this enormous setback, Boucicaut continued to enjoy a prestigious career in French royal service and particularly in the tangled rivalries and power-struggles of the factions led by the great princes of the blood.[19] For example, in April 1411, Boucicaut and Jean de Thoisy, bishop of Tournai, were sent as royal emissaries to meet with the duke of Burgundy at Arras.[20] In November of the same year, Boucicaut led an expedition to secure Bonneval and Étampes during a counter-attack led by the duke of Guyenne against the Armagnacs. In February 1413, Boucicaut was commissioned to secure royal power over Languedoc and Guyenne, following the failures of the duke of Berry who had lost his lieutenancies. On 28 May 1413, Boucicaut arranged a truce until the following Christmas with the counts of Foix and Armagnac. In April 1414, Boucicaut was appointed Captain-General for Languedoc by the duke of Berry, who had been reinstated by the king. In the summer of 1414, the marshal put down a tax revolt in Carcassonne.

Boucicaut's career finally came to an end upon the battlefield of Agincourt on 25 October 1415.[21] He had been one of the French captains shadowing the English army of King Henry V as it approached the Somme. In the week before the battle, Boucicaut, Alençon and Richemont had drawn up a plan for how to tackle the invading enemy force in the field, perhaps intending to fight at or near Blanchetaque. In practice, events took a very different course and battle was joined at Agincourt, perhaps against the advice of Boucicaut and the more experienced commanders. Following the French defeat, Boucicaut was taken to England as a prisoner in November 1415 alongside other leading commanders such as the constable Charles d'Artois and Arthur de Richemont.[22] Negotiations over Boucicaut's ransom proved intractable, despite the attempted intervention of papal ambassadors, not least because of the English desire to retain control of such an important and experienced French commander while the war still raged in Normandy. He remained in English hands when his wife Antoinette de Turenne died in July 1416. Indeed, Boucicaut remained in custody, moving from Fotheringhay to Methely in Yorkshire where he

19 The severe mental problems affecting King Charles VI from 1392 until his death in 1422 created a fierce struggle for power between the leading members of the royal family, and in particular Louis, duke of Orléans who was assassinated in 1407, and Philip the Good, duke of Burgundy who was murdered in 1419. Famiglietti, *Royal Intrigue*, and for Boucicaut's career between 1411 and 1415, see Lalande, *Jean II le Meingre*, pp. 165–9.

20 F. Lehoux, *Jean de France, duc de Berri: sa vie, son action politique (1340–1416)*, 4 volumes (Paris, 1966–8), III, pp. 216 and 255–6, and Famiglietti, *Royal Intrigue*, pp. 101–2.

21 Lalande, *Jean II le Meingre*, pp. 169–70, together with C.J. Phillpotts, 'The French Battle Plan During the Agincourt Campaign', *English Historical Review*, 99 (1984), pp. 59–66, and A. Curry, *Agincourt: A New History* (London, 2005).

22 Lalande, *Jean II le Meingre*, pp. 169–70, together with R. Ambühl, 'Le sort des prisonniers d'Azincourt (1415)', *Revue du Nord*, 89 (2007), pp. 755–88.

probably died on 25 June 1421 at the age of fifty-six. His body was returned to France and buried at Tours, alongside his father and his wife.[23]

The biography

Chivalric biographies were a flourishing genre in the fourteenth and fifteenth centuries, as witnessed by Guillaume de Machaut's life of King Peter I of Cyprus (1372/3), Jean Cuvelier's biography of Bertrand Du Guesclin (1381) and the Chandos Herald's life of the Black Prince (1385).[24] Such works typically recounted the lives of well-known contemporary military leaders and presented them as the embodiment of knightly values. Their celebration of the adventures, heroism and courtesy of their subjects often echoed chivalric romance.[25]

Up until the end of the fourteenth century, chivalric biographies were usually written in verse in order to magnify the achievements of their subjects by echoing the style of the *chansons de geste* and romances that celebrated the greatest heroes of chivalry. But the author of *The Book of the Deeds* chose to write in prose, perhaps in part because of changing fashion, seen for example in a prose adaptation of Cuvelier's biography of Du Guesclin commissioned by Jean d'Estouteville.[26] The choice of prose may also have reflected the most unusual feature of the biography of Boucicaut, that is to say the fact that the subject was still alive when the text was written. The author claimed that he completed *The Book of the Deeds* by 9 April 1409.[27] He said that he had been commissioned to write the biography by the marshal's comrades, carefully denying that Boucicaut had played any direct role in the composition of the work in order to defend the marshal against the potential charge of self-aggrandisement.[28] Indeed the writer implicitly compared himself with past authors who had written

---

23 P. Nobilleau, *Sépultures des Boucicault en la basilique de Saint-Martin (1363–1490)* (Tours, 1873).

24 D.B. Tyson, 'Authors, Patrons and Soldiers: Some Thoughts on Four Old French Soldiers' Lives', *Nottingham Medieval Studies*, 42 (1998), pp. 105–20, together with Guillaume de Machaut, *La Prise d'Alexandrie (The Taking of Alexandria)*, ed. and trans. R.B. Palmer (London, 2002); Jean Cuvelier, *La chanson de Bertrand du Guesclin de Cuvelier*, ed. J.-C. Faucon, 3 volumes (Toulouse, 1990–3), and Chandos Herald, *La vie du Prince Noir [The Life of the Black Prince], by Chandos Herald. Edited from the Manuscript in the University of London Library*, ed. D.B. Tyson (Tübingen, 1975).

25 S. Ferris, 'Chronicle, Chivalric Biography and Family Tradition in Fourteenth-Century England', *Chivalric Literature: Essays on Relations Between Literature and Life in the Later Middle Ages*, ed. L.D. Benson and J. Leyerle (Kalamazoo, MI, 1980), pp. 25–38; W.T. Cotton, 'Teaching the Motifs of Chivalric Biography', *The Study of Chivalry: Resources and Approaches*, ed. H. Chickering and T.H. Seiler (Kalamazoo, MI, 1988), pp. 583–609; E. Gaucher, *La biographie chevaleresque. Typologie d'un genre (XIIIe-XVe siècle)* (Paris, 1994).

26 *Chronique de Du Guesclin, collationnée sur l'édition originale du XVe siècle, et sur tous les manuscrits, avec une notice bibliographique et des notes*, ed. F. Michel (Paris, 1830).

27 See p. 213 below.

28 See pp. 24 and 188 below.

books celebrating great men without their knowledge: Pompey and Scipio Africanus had been surprised and delighted to hear that poets like Theophanes and Ennius had commemorated their deeds, and so offered these writers generous rewards.[29] Of course, the efforts made by the biographer to deny Boucicaut's involvement in the writing of the book may have simply been a lie.

Authors of medieval chivalric biographies consistently presented their books as memorials to the fame and glory of their subjects; their works, they said, would serve as inspiration for future knights. So it is no surprise that these themes were repeated at the start of *The Book of the Deeds*, when Boucicaut's biographer championed the importance of learning and literary skill as the means by which the great deeds of a knight like Boucicaut could be preserved forever and thereby serve as an inspiration to others.[30] Throughout the biography, Boucicaut was presented as a flower of chivalry and a model of the highest qualities expected of a knight, qualities that were underlined in the unusual fourth and final book that provided a chivalric manual reflecting Boucicaut's particular virtues. It is no surprise, then, that Johan Huizinga said of *The Book of the Deeds* that 'it is not like a piece of contemporary history, but rather like the depiction of an ideal knight'.[31]

Yet the fact that the biography of Boucicaut was written while the marshal was still alive would suggest that the text was intended to serve a more immediate purpose than merely to offer a grand chivalric statement about his achievements or an inspiration to future generations. Indeed in truth, most chivalric biographies were written with more practical goals in mind, and in particular to advance the agendas of their subject. For example, Guillaume de Machaut's celebration of the life of Peter I of Cyprus was written shortly after the king's assassination on 17 January 1369 and inevitably served not just as a memorial for a man who had endured such a tragic end, but also as a rallying call for its subject's crusading ventures, aimed in particular at the families of the small group of French nobles who had served alongside him and at the great princes like Charles V who would be crucial to the achievement of Peter's dream.[32]

The anonymous author of the biography of Boucicaut offered a strong clue to the purpose of his text when he admitted that the marshal had acquired many critics

29 See pp. 211–13.

30 Pp. 23–4 below, where the entourage is said to have commissioned the work so that it might inspire others, together with p. 188 where the writer insists that the aim of this book is not vainglory but to present Boucicaut as a role model.

31 J. Huizinga, *The Autumn of the Middle Ages*, trans. R.J. Payton and U. Mammitzsch (Chicago, 1996), p. 78. Barbara Tuchman famously described Boucicaut as 'the epitome of chivalry' and 'knighthood's zealot'. Barbara Tuchman, *A Distant Mirror: The Calamitous Fourteenth Century* (New York, 1978), p. 556.

32 R.B. Palmer, 'Guillaume de Machaut's *La Prise d'Alexandrie* and the Late Medieval Chivalric Ideal', *Chivalry, Knighthood, and War in the Middle Ages*, ed. S.J. Ridyard (Sewanee, TN, 1999), pp. 185–204, and Daisy Delogu, *Theorizing the Ideal Sovereign: The Rise of the French Vernacular Royal Biography* (Toronto, 2008), pp. 92–123.

and enemies after a long and controversial career. *The Book of the Deeds* denounced those envious men who liked to attack virtuous figures like Boucicaut, calling upon his readers to be suspicious of popular opinion and to pray that the marshal might be protected from the envy of others.[33] It is therefore highly likely that the biography was written as a very careful defence of the actions and policies of Boucicaut, and a response to his critics.

Both Jean II Le Meingre and his father had been attacked as avaricious and power-hungry courtiers who had taken advantage of their king. In *Le songe du vergier* (1378), Jean Le Fèvre defined a Boucicaut as a man without scruples who put the desire for profit ahead of honour. He claimed that Jean I Le Meingre targeted the royal court as an arena to win royal patronage, and had a saying that there was no fishing except in the sea, a pun based upon the notion that the surname Boucicaut meant a fishing basket.[34] The same idea was invoked in *Le songe du vieil pelerin* (1389), when Philippe de Mézières denounced knights who flattered their lords in order to win reward, citing a proverb that he claimed originated with Jean I Le Meingre: just as one could only fish in the sea, so one could only receive a reward from the king.[35] In 1406, the anonymous *Songe véritable* identified Jean II Le Meingre as one of the greedy members of a regime profiting from and exploiting the generosity of King Charles VI.[36] It is therefore hardly surprising that the biographer of Boucicaut went to such lengths to highlight the marshal's lack of interest in wealth and personal status.[37]

Boucicaut was also the subject of criticism for other reasons. In the *Chronique du Religieux de Saint-Denis*, Michel Pintouin characterised the marshal as irascible, impetuous and hot-headed, as seen in particular in his part in the great disaster at Nicopolis in 1396.[38] Boucicaut's biographer turned such criticisms on their head in his account of the Nicopolis expedition. Admitting, for example, that Boucicaut and his knights had ridden through the night ahead of the main Christian army and plunged straight into the fray at Oryahovo, the biographer praised this as audacity and courage rather than ill-discipline. He also emphasised the self-control and bravery of the French during the battle of Nicopolis, preferring instead to blame the disaster on the failings of their Hungarian allies. Above all, the biographer blamed fickle Fortune for turning against Boucicaut and his men, as had happened to many other

33 See pp. 164–7 and 206–9 below.

34 *Songe du vergier: édité d'après le manuscrit Royal 19 C IV de la British Library*, ed. M. Schnerb-Lièvre, 2 volumes (Paris, 1982), I, pp. 236–7, and also see D. Lalande, 'La naissance d'un sobriquet: Boucicaut', *Revue des langues romanes*, 85 (1981), pp. 115–23.

35 Philippe de Mézières, *Le songe du viel pèlerin*, ed. J. Blanchard, 2 volumes (Geneva, 2015), II, p. 976.

36 *Le songe véritable, pamphlet politique d'un Parisien du XVe siècle*, ed. H. Moranville (Paris, 1891), p. 325.

37 For example, see pp. 24–5 below.

38 E. Gaucher, 'Deux regards sur une défaite: Nicopolis (d'après la *Chronique de Saint-Denis* et le *Livre des faits de Boucicaut*)', *Cahiers de recherches médiévales*, 1 (1996), pp. 93–104.

brave and good men of Antiquity including Hercules, Hector, Achilles, Alexander, Hannibal and Pompey.[39]

Above all, the biography offered a defence of Boucicaut's tarnished reputation following his controversial involvement in the murky politics of Genoa, Venice, Florence and Pisa. The book was completed just months before an uprising in Genoa on 2 September 1409 that brought an end to Boucicaut's inglorious rule. Throughout his term as governor, Boucicaut had faced resistance within the city because of the rigour of his justice, the dislocation of trade caused by his expensive military expeditions, and his controversial diplomatic policy towards other Italian cities. *The Book of the Deeds* reported on successive threats to his rule of Genoa, including a Ghibelline plot in 1401, a plot by Pisans and expatriate Genoese in 1406, and a conspiracy by Gabriele Maria Visconti and the *condottiere* Facino Cane in December 1408.[40] The biographer admitted that many of Genoese citizens disliked Boucicaut's rule but defended the administration of the marshal, denouncing the lack of gratitude on the part of the *popolari*, condemning their envy and jealousy. He pleaded with them to recognise what Boucicaut had really done for them.[41]

The Book of the Deeds also presented a very careful defence of Boucicaut's policies towards other powers in Italy and the Mediterranean. For example, the biography defended his actions on the controversial expedition against Muslim ports in 1403 that had undermined relations with the city of Venice. According to the Venetian version of events, Boucicaut's troops had seized property belonging to their merchants during the sack of Beirut on 10 August 1403. Using this pretext, Carlo Zeno and the Venetians had attacked Boucicaut's fleet at Modone on 17 October 1403, destroying all but five ships, killing six hundred men and capturing a number of prisoners including Châteaumorand.[42] In the aftermath, Boucicaut had wanted to declare war on Venice but had been constrained by the French court which prioritised negotiations for the release of the prisoners taken at Modone who were not freed until May 1404. The biographer reported that Boucicaut was frustrated at this interference and sent a personal letter of defiance to Michele Steno, doge of Venice, and the admiral Carlo Zeno on 6 June 1404. When Zeno refused to respond to this challenge, the biography itself remained as Boucicaut's last effort to defend his honour.

The Book of the Deeds also sought to explain Boucicaut's involvement in the politics of Pisa that had allowed Florence to seize control of that city.[43] On 20 July 1404, the Pisans had risen up against their ruler, Gabriele Maria Visconti, who had agreed to pay homage to the king of France just a few months earlier, in return for French protection for Pisa. So Boucicaut had been obliged to send troops to Pisa to aid Visconti, and after having failed to secure the city, the marshal ceded it to Florence

39 See pp. 63–4 below.

40 See pp. 102–3, 158 and 184–6 below.

41 See pp. 165–6, 200 and 206 below.

42 See pp. 137–8 below.

43 Lalande, *Jean II le Meingre*, pp. 127–40.

on 27 August 1405 in return for other concessions.[44] Strongly opposing this decision, the Pisans dispatched an embassy on 11 February 1406 to the dukes of Orléans and Burgundy at the French royal court, offering them joint lordship over their city. In July Burgundy sent troops to Pisa under the Picard captain Enguerrand de Bournonville, and also dispatched his counsellor Girard de Bourbon to meet with Boucicaut, calling upon the marshal to resist Florentine efforts to seize Pisa.[45] So again, *The Book of the Deeds* set out Boucicaut's version of this extremely controversial sequence of events. The biographer reported that Boucicaut had written to Paris, defending the deal that he had made with the Florentines and denouncing the treachery of the Pisan efforts to go behind Boucicaut's back in order to secure the support of the French royal court. The writer also denounced those at court who had been motivated by jealousy to deceive the royal dukes and turned them against Boucicaut.[46]

Finally *The Book of the Deeds* presented a defence of Boucicaut's actions in the context of the Great Schism. In 1378, a split amongst the cardinals led to the election of two rival popes, Urban VI (1378–89) at Rome and Clement VII (1374–98) at Avignon. The French crown had supported Clement and his successors as popes at Avignon until the start of the fifteenth century, when momentum grew for a resolution to the crisis. Yet Boucicaut had continued to support the Avignon pope Benedict XIII, against the French court's policy of withdrawal of obedience from Benedict and his Roman rival, Gregory XII (1406–17), in order to allow the election of a new pope to reunite the Church.[47] His biographer therefore took great pains to deny any responsibility on the part of Boucicaut for the unravelling of the plan for Benedict XIII and Gregory XII (1406–17) to meet at Savona in April 1407 in order to move towards a solution to Schism.[48] He also defended Boucicaut's failure to restore Pope Gregory XII to Rome after the city was seized by King Ladislaus of Naples in April 1408.[49]

In short, the biography of Boucicaut served as a highly detailed defence of the marshal's career, and in particular the decisions that he had made during his service as governor of Genoa. The obvious audience for this was the French royal court. Indeed, the author acknowledged as much when he denounced the envy motivating those at the court who were undermining Boucicaut and misleading the

44 See pp. 152–60 below.

45 B. Schnerb, *Enguerrand de Bournonville et les siens. Un lignage noble du Boulonnais aux XIVe et XVe siècles* (Paris, 1997), p. 85, and also C. de La Roncière, 'La domination française à Pise', *École française de Rome: Mélanges d'archéologie et d'histoire*, 15 (1895), pp. 240–4.

46 See pp. 161–4 below.

47 See pp. 146–50 above. The marshal's brother, Geoffrey Le Meingre, had laid siege to the papal palace at Avignon in 1398, for which he was pardoned two years later and performed a year-long penance. This may partially explain Boucicaut's support for Benedict XIII. Lehoux, *Jean de France, duc de Berri*, III, pp. 396–9.

48 See pp. 176–8 below.

49 See pp. 178–80 below.

royal dukes.[50] Such opposition posed a very grave risk to Boucicaut who had long depended upon the goodwill of the royal princes who effectively ruled France during the mental incapacity of King Charles VI.[51] Above all, the deteriorating situation in Genoa meant that Boucicaut was desperate for reinforcements and money to pay his soldiers. In the spring of 1409, Raoul de Gaucourt led a French expedition to reinforce Boucicaut that finally arrived in October.[52] Yet even with that help, Boucicaut lacked the financial resources to mount an effective recovery of Genoa. Therefore in March 1410 he sent three envoys to Paris to ask for more assistance. They brought with them copies of Boucicaut's accounts for the occupation of Genoa, highlighting the precarious financial situation.[53] Shortly before their arrival, the archbishop of Genoa, Pileo de Marini, had written to King Charles VI setting out a long justification for the opposition of the citizens of Genoa to their governor who had forced many, including the archbishop himself, to flee the city.[54] Therefore *The Book of the Deeds of My Good Lord Jean le Meingre, Known as Boucicaut* would have made a very useful counter to Marini's complaints, setting out a very careful defence of the marshal's involvement in the murky politics of Italy, the Mediterranean and the Church. The manuscript might have been intended for one of the great princes, most probably Jean duke of Berry who had commissioned the translation of Valerius Maximus that was a major source for the biography. Or alternatively, the biography would have armed Boucicaut's envoys with the detailed justification of all of his recent actions, especially those criticised by Marini.

If the biography was indeed written for this very specific context of negotiations at the French royal court in 1410, then that may explain one further unique feature of this particular chivalric biography. Unlike comparable works, the biography of Boucicaut survives in just one manuscript that was never finished.[55] Space was left on folio 3r, for example, for the armorial of the lord to whom it was to be presented, but this was never completed. Add this to the fact that the narrative within the biography stopped on 6 March 1409 at the end of book III, the only book which did not have an *explicit*, and there is a strong suggestion that the biography was completed in a rush.[56]

---

50 See p. 164 below.

51 Famiglietti, *Royal Intrigue.*

52 Lalande, *Jean II le Meingre,* pp. 153–6 and Schnerb, *Enguerrand de Bournonville,* pp. 89–90.

53 Arch. Nat. Kk40, *Comptes de guerre 1409–10.* These original accounts were entitled 'Dommages gros et menus et messageries faites pour ledit fait de Jennes'.

54 The letter was probably written in October or November 1409. D. Puncuh, 'Il governo genovese del Boucicaut nella lettera di Pileo de Marini a Carlo VI di Francia 1409', *Mélanges de l'École française de Rome. Moyen Âge, Temps modernes,* 90:2 (1978), pp. 657–87.

55 BNF MS fr. 11432. In contrast, there are five surviving manuscripts of Machaut's biography of Peter I of Cyprus, eight manuscripts of the life of Bertrand Du Guesclin, and two copies of the Chandos Herald's life of the Black Prince. See note 24 above.

56 The anonymous author also called for a future writer to complete the biography after the death of the marshal. See p. 210 below.

The author

The author of *The Book of the Deeds* did not reveal his identity, unlike the writers of most contemporary chivalric biographies.[57] Nevertheless, there are a number of clues within the text itself. The author was almost certainly male, and certainly not the famous contemporary writer Christine de Pizan (c.1364–1429).[58] He evidently had strong roots in Paris, given his wish that 'we had such a governor [as Boucicaut] in Paris'.[59] He was also familiar with not only the Bastille Saint-Antoine and the Cimetière des Saints-Innocents in Paris, but also the marketplace at Genoa and the nearby harbour at Darsena, suggesting that he had accompanied Boucicaut to Italy.[60] The biographer had been in Paris in 1396 when news of the disaster at Nicopolis arrived, and so had probably not been part of Boucicaut's immediate circle during the early stages of the marshal's career.[61] He may also have been slightly older than Boucicaut, given his call at the end of the book for others to complete his work in the future.[62]

The search for the identity of this anonymous author has focused upon the clerks and secretaries who worked for Boucicaut during his time as governor of Genoa. According to the surviving accounts for the period from 10 September 1409 to 3 February 1410, there were six such individuals: Jean d'Aunis, Michel Clément, Nicolas de Gonesse, Pierre de Nantron, Julien Panissar and Jacques de Valières.[63] Of these men, by far the most compelling candidate was Gonesse (1364?–142?).[64] Gonesse had completed his doctorate at Paris by 1403. He served as Boucicaut's confessor from at least December 1406, and as such enjoyed the perfect position from which to observe and comment upon the qualities of the marshal. Moreover, Gonesse shared Boucicaut's partisanship for Pope Benedict XIII and his mistrust of the Roman pope, Gregory XII. In March 1410, Boucicaut sent Gonesse to Paris as one of his envoys to secure additional funding for the recovery of Genoa following the rebellion of September 1409. After the marshal returned to France, Gonesse remained on very good terms with Boucicaut and his family, and Antoinette de Turenne named Gonesse as an executor of her will on 10 April 1413.

---

57 Tyson, 'Authors, Patrons and Soldiers', pp. 106–7.

58 Attempts to identify Christine de Pizan as the author of the *Livre des fais* have been demolished, as summarised by Lalande in *Livre des fais*, pp. xxiv–xxv and xlii–l.

59 See p. 190 below.

60 See pp. 104, 105, 156 and 188 below.

61 See pp. 70–2 below, and also pp. 65 and 68.

62 See p. 210 below.

63 See note 53 above.

64 H. Millet, 'Nouveaux documents sur Nicolas de Gonesse, traducteur de Valère-Maxime', *Romania*, 102 (1981), pp. 110–14, and id., 'Qui a écrit *Le livre des faits du bon messire Jehan le Maingre dit Bouciquaut*?', *Pratiques de la culture écrite en France au XVe siècle,* ed. M. Ornato and N. Pons (Louvain, 1995), pp. 135–50.

Gonesse was certainly qualified to write the biography of Boucicaut. Around 1400, he had composed a defence of poetry, the *Collatio artis poetice probativa*, that showcased his wide-ranging knowledge of learned authors from Aristotle, Augustine and Cicero to Boccaccio.[65] Gonesse was best known for completing a translation of and commentary on the *Facta et dicta memorabilia* originally written in the first century AD by the Roman author Valerius Maximus.[66] The French translation was entitled the *Dits et faits memorables* and had been started in 1375 by Simon de Hesdin, doctor of theology and commander of a house of the Hospitallers of St John at Éterpigny in Picardy.[67] By the time of his death in 1383, Hesdin had completed six and a half of the nine books of the *Dits et faits memorables*. Gonesse was commissioned to complete this project by Jaquemin Courau, treasurer of Jean duke of Berry, and he finished the task on 28 September 1401.[68] The completed work was presented to Berry as a New Year's gift on 1 January 1402.[69] This translation was a great success, surviving in some two hundred manuscripts, and was used for example by Christine de Pizan between 1404 and 1407 for her *Livre du corps de policie*.[70]

The *Dits et faits memorables* was also the key source used by Boucicaut's biographer, directly cited twenty-eight times by the anonymous author. This new translation of Valerius Maximus was relatively unknown at the time that the biography of Boucicaut was written; only five surviving manuscripts of the complete text of the *Dits et faits memorables* were produced by 1410, and none has any obvious connection with Genoa.[71] So there is a reasonable circumstantial case

65 G. Di Stefano, *Multa mentiere poetae: le débat sur la poésie de Boccace à Nicolas de Gonesse* (Montreal, 1989).

66 Valerius Maximus, *Memorable Doings and Sayings*, ed. and trans. D.R. Shackleton Bailey, 2 volumes (Cambridge, MA, 2000), together with *Translations médiévales. Cinq siècles de traductions en français au moyen âge (XIe–XVe siècles). Étude et répertoire*, ed. Claudio Galderisi, 2 volumes (Turnhout, 2011), II, pp. 253–5.

67 A. Luttrell, 'Jean and Simon de Hesdin: Hospitallers, Theologians, Classicists', *The Hospitallers in Cyprus, Rhodes, Greece and the West, 1291–1440* (London, 1978), chapter 18, and A. Valentini, 'Entre traduction et commentaire érudit: Simon de Hesdin translateur de Valère Maxime', *La traduction vers le moyen français*, ed. C. Galderisi and C. Pignarelli (Turnhout, 2007), pp. 355–67.

68 G. Di Stefano, 'Richerche su Nicolas de Gonesse, traduttore di Valerio Massimo', *Studi francesi*, 26 (1965), pp. 201–21, and C. Charras, 'La traduction de Valère-Maxime par Nicolas de Gonesse', PhD dissertation, McGill University (Montreal, 1982).

69 BNF MS fr. 282 and L. Delisle, *Recherches sur la librairie de Charles V*, 2 volumes (Paris, 1907), II, p. 256 (no. 206).

70 D.M. Schullian, 'A Revised List of Manuscripts of Valerius Maximus', *Miscellanea Augusto Campana: Medioevo e Umanesimo*, ed. R. Avesani, G. Billanovich, M. Ferrari and G. Pozzi, 2 volumes (Padua, 1981), II, pp. 695–728, and Galderisi, ed., *Translations médiévales*, II, pp. 253–5. For Christine de Pizan, see note 11 above.

71 G. Croenen, M. Rouse and R. Rouse, 'Pierre de Liffol and the Manuscripts of Froissart's *Chronicles*', *Viator*, 33 (2002), pp. 261–93.

for assuming that without Gonesse, the biography of Boucicaut could not have included material from the *Dits et faits memorables*.

Nevertheless, the case for attributing the authorship of the biography of Boucicaut to Nicolas de Gonesse is not watertight.[72] The modern editor of Christine de Pizan's life of Charles V, Suzanne Solente, dismissed the notion that Christine de Pizan was the author of the biography of Boucicaut in part because *The Book of the Deeds* did not match the style of her prose, but that argument is even more true in the case of Gonesse.[73] The biographer demonstrated just a fraction of Gonesse's learning. On occasion the anonymous author did showcase Latin-influenced style, such as when he used the scholastic formula 'pro et contra', or invoked the art of *disputatio* in his discussion of knightly love.[74] But these examples are rare and in general the biographer also lacked the lexical richness and debt to Latin that one might expect of a learned scholar like Gonesse. Moreover, in his translation of and commentary on Valerius Maximus, Gonesse had been able to cite over seventy different Latin writers ranging from Plutarch to Petrarch.[75] Superficially the biographer of Boucicaut might appear to have approached this standard, with a total of seventy-two references and usages of learned sources. But on closer examination, 70 per cent of these learned references actually came from the translation and commentary upon Valerius Maximus by Hesdin and Gonesse. Moreover, Gonesse had consistently shown a particular fascination for Giovanni Boccaccio throughout his career, but that author was only cited on one occasion in *The Book of the Deeds*, and in that case the reference had been taken directly from Gonesse's commentary on Valerius Maximus.[76] The remaining learned citations in the biography of Boucicaut that cannot be traced back to the translation of Valerius Maximus were available in other works that had also been recently translated into or written in French, including Aristotle's *Nicomachean Ethics*, Augustine's *De civitatis dei*, Jean Golein's *Livre de l'information des princes*, Jacobus de Voragine's *Légende dorée* and the *Roman de la Rose*.[77] In short, rather than think that the author of *The Book of the Deeds* was Nicolas de Gonesse himself, it is far more likely that the biographer used Gonesse's translation of Valerius Maximus. This would certainly help to explain why the author of *The Book of the Deeds* twice referred to the 'translateur' of Valerius Maximus when citing passages written by Simon de Hesdin, without naming him.[78]

72 D. Lalande, 'Nicolas de Gonesse est-il l'auteur du *Livre des fais du Mareschal Bouciquaut*?', *Miscellania Mediaevalia: Mélanges offerts à Philippe Ménard*, ed. J.-C. Faucon, A. Labbé and D. Quéruel, 2 volumes (Paris, 1998), II, pp. 827–37.

73 Christine de Pisan, *Le livre des fais et bonnes meurs du sage roy Charles V*, ed. S. Solente, 2 volumes (Paris, 1936–40), I, p. xxx, and also see *Livre des fais*, pp. lvi and lxiv–lxv.

74 See pp. 32 and 99 below.

75 G. Di Stefano, 'Nicolas de Gonesse et la culture italienne', *Cahiers de l'Association internationale des études françaises,* 23 (1971), pp. 27–54, here p. 31.

76 See pp. 198–9 below.

77 Lalande suggests that the author may have also used *florilegia*, compilations of excerpts.

78 *Livre des fais*, p. lvi.

It is important to remember that the biography of Boucicaut was a very different kind of book from the highly learned and scholarly works for which Gonesse was famous. The *Dits et faits memorables*, for example, had presented translations of sequences of short anecdotes and tales written by Valerius Maximus, together with a learned commentary that interpreted the content by reference to other classical, theological and historical writings. In contrast the biography of Boucicaut offered an original, sustained narrative of a soldier and his involvement in warfare and politics. That core was certainly dressed up by the addition of intellectual passages offering more learned commentary, clustered above all in the introduction and the final book. The learned material, borrowed above all from the translation of Valerius Maximus's *Facta et dicta memorabilia*, created a frame for the narrative that was unusual compared with other chivalric biographies, and indeed unique in the case of the fourth book that explicitly stepped back from the story to highlight the particular qualities of the governor of Genoa. Nevertheless, the learning on show served as packaging for the real heart of the biography, that is to say the narrative of the career of Jean II Le Meingre.

It may therefore be more useful to imagine Gonesse as an advisor and a member of the small circle around the marshal that reportedly commissioned the biography, rather than being himself the sole author of the text.[79] Moreover the writer also relied upon others within that group, particularly those with first-hand experience of Boucicaut's actions. The biographer recognised the dangers of relying solely upon his own memory,[80] and also admitted that he had not personally witnessed many of the events in question, most notably the Nicopolis expedition of 1396.[81] Therefore he needed to draw upon the eyewitness accounts of others, and attributed specific anecdotes and stories to the testimony of soldiers who had served Boucicaut,[82] and others to eyewitnesses whose roles in the action were not identified.[83]

In addition the biographer quoted documents that provided important details, and also added a veneer of authenticity to the story. For example, his report on the Order of the Enterprise of the White Lady of the Green Shield was supplemented by the letter of foundation that set out in painstaking detail the ethos and rules of the short-lived knightly order.[84] More controversial was the biographer's account of the expedition that culminated in the naval battle at Modone on 17 October 1403, and so the author of *The Book of the Deeds* included Boucicaut's letter of defiance to the doge of Venice and to the Venetian admiral Carlo Zeno, carefully recording the

79 See p. 24 below. Gonesse was one of the envoys that Boucicaut sent on a crucial mission to Paris in March 1410 to secure additional funding.
80 See p. 187 below.
81 See pp. 65 and 68 below.
82 See pp. 24, 65 and 187 below.
83 See pp. 68, 198, 201, 202 and 206 below.
84 See pp. 92–4 below.

marshal's version of events.[85] Similarly, *The Book of the Deeds* recorded two unusual documents relating to the missions of Boucicaut's envoys to the king of Cyprus[86] and to Paolo Orsini.[87]

In short, the author reported upon things that could only have been known to Boucicaut and a very small circle. The author was almost certainly one of that group, but there is no automatic reason to assume that he was a cleric or learned scholar, especially given the availability of Gonesse and his translation of Valerius Maximus to spruce up the core narrative. The biographer of Boucicaut praised the eloquence of the marshal, declaring 'there is no skill that cannot be acquired by someone who shows assiduity, provided that he is sufficiently intelligent – or indeed gifted'.[88] Other late medieval French chivalric texts were certainly written by laymen, from Geoffroi de Charny, Philippe de Mézières and Christine de Pizan to Antoine de La Sale and Jean de Bueil, not to mention Englishmen like Sir Thomas Gray and Thomas Malory. La Sale makes for a particularly interesting comparison with the author of the biography of Boucicaut, because his work showcased a similar knowledge of learned authors and sources, thanks in particular to his effective use of French intermediaries such as Hesdin's and Gonesse's translation of Valerius Maximus.[89]

One obvious candidate for the authorship of *The Book of the Deeds* might be Jean d'Ony, who was named eighteen times in the text, and had taken part in the failed diplomatic missions to the king of Cyprus in 1407 and to Paolo Orsini in 1408 that received such extensive discussion in the biography.[90] In the nineteenth century, Delaville Le Roulx did speculate that the author might have been a soldier such as Jean d'Ony, but that suggestion has been abandoned in recent times as experts have focused upon Nicolas de Gonesse and the clerics around Boucicaut. But it is intriguing that the level of detail offered by the biographer significantly increased after 1400, when Jean d'Ony joined the entourage of Boucicaut. Moreover, the biographer dedicated a significant portion of the narrative after part II, chapter 11 to accounts of the diplomatic manoeuvres of Boucicaut, which were so core to the defence of his actions as governor of Genoa. In that regard, there were obvious reasons for having one of the marshal's diplomats write the account. Finally, the biography included documents that rarely survive from medieval diplomatic missions, including an extremely detailed and first-hand account of the tricky negotiations by Jean d'Ony and Bourc de Larca with Paolo Orsini in Rome in 1408, and Cyprus

85 See pp. 138–44 below.
86 See pp. 168–72 below.
87 See pp. 178–9 below.
88 See p. 202.
89 See note 17 above, together with M. Lecourt, 'Antoine de La Sale et Simon de Hesdin: une restitution littéraire', *Mélanges offerts à M. Emile Châtelain* (Paris, 1910), pp. 341–53, and id., 'Une source d'Antoine de La Sale: Simon de Hesdin', *Romania*, 76 (1955), pp. 39–83.
90 J. Delaville Le Roulx, *La France en Orient au XIVe siècle: expéditions du Maréchal Boucicaut*, 2 volumes (Paris, 1886), I, pp. 212–13.

the previous year by Jean de Vienne and Brother Jean d'Ony. This report offered an extremely detailed account of a particular set of negotiations that was actually rather marginal in the wider context of Boucicaut's diplomacy, and did not serve an obvious significant function within the larger narrative; this was not one of the most controversial 'failures' of Boucicaut. So it might therefore be the case that the author chose to include the report of the mission simply because he himself was so familiar with it.

Ultimately there is insufficient evidence to be certain about the identity of the author of the biography of Boucicaut, or indeed to be certain that the book was the product of just one individual rather than a collaboration. Nevertheless, it is important to recognise the strong possibility that the leading voice or voices were not clerical, but rather lay, more firmly anchoring the biography of Boucicaut within the burgeoning corpus of chivalric writings by laymen who formed part of the aristocratic culture described in such works.

Note to this translation

The *Livre des fais du bon messire Jehan le Maingre, dit Bouciquaut, mareschal de France et gouverneur de Gennes* – the title is supplied in the *incipit* and in the rubric to the first chapter – has been edited a number of times (see Bibliograhpy), most recently and admirably by Denis Lalande; it is this latter edition that is translated, in full, here.

The author is unknown (see pp. 13–18), but he is visibly a product of the courts: he writes in what is known as the *style curial* (curial prose),[91] the standard narrative prose style of the French late Middle Ages, with its complex sentence construction and extensive sub-clauses and synonyms. Our translation preserves this style – though we have simplified or broken up some of the more baroque sentences; the author can be brisk and clear when he describes a battle or a tournament, but he slips into that very different, convoluted syntax and Latinate vocabulary as soon as he steps back into history or moralising (as, for instance, in the first chapter of his *Livre*, pp. 23–4), and that mode of writing is integral to his ambitions as a writer able to stand back from the hurly-burly of events to take a scholarly view of life and fortune, knighthood and learning. As translators, we have tried to steer a tactful course between occasional archaism and more modern idioms; we use modern equivalents where possible, modern proper names where we could identify them (although we also give the original Middle French in square brackets) – and of course we preserve technical terms for things like arms and armour, or shipping, and use something in English to resemble the author's more high-flown style for documents and dispatches, or philosophical-historical musings, or moralistic set-pieces. Where there are doubts

91 See for instance J. Rasmussen, *La prose narrative française du XVe siècle, étude esthétique et stylistique* (Copenhagen, 1958). Curial style was also current in English in the same period: see for instance J.D. Burnley, 'Curial Prose in England', *Speculum*, 61:3 (1986), pp. 593-614.

as to the correct meaning of a particular term, we indicate this in the footnotes; in particular the notes also serve to give the details of places, people and events that make the story comprehensible to the modern reader, and an index of proper names, at the end of the volume, indicates the footnotes which give those details. So that the reader can easily cross-check our translation with the original French text, we give the page numbers of Lalande's edition in square brackets. We hope that this translation will encourage English-speaking readers to enjoy a colourful, sympathetic figure who was central to the chivalric world of the later Middle Ages.

The Book Of The Deeds of My Good Lord Jean Le Meingre, Known as Boucicaut

[6] I: Here begins the book of the deeds of my good lord Jean Le Meingre, known as Boucicaut, marshal of France and governor of Genoa.

God has ordained two things in this world to act, as it were, as pillars to uphold those divine and human ordinances that govern humankind and permit them to live in peace and according to the dictates of reason, and that promote and nurture the human mind in wisdom and virtue while precluding ignorance; those pillars moreover defend and uphold and increase personal and public good; indeed without them, the world would be a place of confusion and disorder. The two pillars bring us great benefit and great reward – and we should therefore prize them, honour them, uphold them, praise them and revere them; they are, indisputably, Knighthood and Learning. [7] It is right that I should connect the two, for any country or kingdom or empire in which one or the other was lacking would scarcely last for long: if Learning were to be lost, so too would be law, and without law, man would revert to beast; if Knighthood were to be lost, any realm would very soon be destroyed by greedy and fearless enemies. Now God, praise be, has given us those two means of defence; in what follows, we shall concentrate further on one in particular, that is Knighthood, in the person of a valiant and noble knight, thank God still living, having reached a good age in good health, good spirits and noble estate: I speak of our lord Jean Le Meingre, known as Boucicaut, marshal of France and governor of Genoa [Jannes]. This book will be composed and completed in his honour and in tribute to his good deeds: [8] it will recount his righteousness, the nobility of his conduct, his generosity and benevolence, as well as his courage and valour in person as in deed, in all of which virtues he grows better day by day.

And since all life is by nature short, it is fitting and appropriate that the deeds of the valiant should be commemorated in perpetuity, in order that they be not forgotten after their deaths: in other words, it is proper that they be registered in books. And this explains why people say of many of those most valiant who are dead, but whose names and deeds have been recorded in books, that they are not dead but living: that is, that their virtues are still alive in this world and will remain so (precisely because they are recorded in the books that still bear witness to them), and will remain so until the end of the world. It is, moreover, right that the names and lives [9] of the virtuous be faithfully recorded so that those who might wish to emulate them can follow their authentic deeds, and thus attain the reward, the good reputation, due to those who deserve it. But to return to my previous remarks: Learning, I believe, should be held in as great esteem as Knighthood. How after all would we humans – who can know of the past only through report – learn of the virtues of good men if Learning could not guarantee the record? Letters and writing are fundamental to Learning, and that is how we are informed of a past which we cannot witness with our own eyes. And that is why Cato tells us to 'read books':[1] no-one, of any estate and rank, can learn anything without letters and books. And this is why, in my opinion, we should revere Learning and those who have transmitted it to us, who have made it possible for us to know so many admirable things that we cannot ourselves witness, and who preserve the memory of the dead [10] whose lives merited that they be recorded.

II: Here we explain how it came about that the present book was written.

In order to ensure that all who see or read this book are aware of the circumstances in which this book was initiated and completed, I should state that it was set in train by a number of renowned knights and gallant noblemen who themselves pursue noble and honourable deeds, and who knew the good and valiant marshal who is our subject, and knew of his ancestors – there are still many who are in that position. They had also been companions of his in all manner of knightly gatherings, and having seen his fortitude and courage under all sorts of conditions that might afflict the valiant, they came to believe that the name and deeds of so dauntless a knight should not be forgotten but rather recorded for distant posterity so that others might follow his example. Having come to this conclusion, they sought out someone fitting and worthy, and commissioned and contracted him to undertake it. The person appointed, thanks to his own reputation and the authority of those who gave the commission, [11] accordingly promised with God's help to accomplish the task to the best of his ability, abiding by their reports of Boucicaut's deeds, and adding nothing of his own invention. It is thus that I undertook the commission, promising to follow faithfully the testimony of those who wish to remain anonymous; they hope thus to avoid any spiteful tongue's saying that they are simply flattering the subject.

III: Here we describe Marshal Boucicaut's parentage, his birth and his childhood.

As from this point, we enter on our true subject – that is the valiant Boucicaut; by God's grace we shall complete the book with the praise he merits, and without flattery. The marshal was the son of the noble and valiant lord Jean Le Meingre, also known as Boucicaut,[2] who was renowned as a fearless and experienced knight and

1 This is a reference to Dionysius Cato, fourth-century author of the *Distichs of Cato*, a collection of moral proverbs very well known in the Middle Ages.

2 Jean I Le Meingre (d.1368) was probably the first to be called 'Boucicaut', a nickname that derived from the words 'boce' and 'bosse', and that referred to a fishing basket. See D. Lalande, 'La naissance d'un sobriquet: Boucicaut', *Revue des langues romanes*, 85 (1981), pp. 115–23.

one who pursued arms for the whole of his life; like the brave of old, he took no pains to acquire wealth, and was interested only in winning honour. For his valour and bravery, during the great wars in France and under the reign of the chivalrous King Jean, [12] he too was made marshal of France.[3] He served King Jean in all his wars – as many still living can bear witness – and to such effect that still today he is referred to as the valiant Marshal Boucicaut. And as evidence, briefly, of his unrelenting pursuit of arms over any other advantage, we shall put on record the words he would use to his family and the friends who would often reproach him for not using his favour with the king to accumulate lands and estates for his children. 'I have', he would say, 'preserved intact and unsold the lands I inherited from my father, and I have no wish to acquire more. If my sons are worthy and valiant, they will possess enough; if they are not, it would be an embarrassment for them to inherit more.' We could say much more about the life and deeds of this noble man – but we need to return to our true subject: [13] we say simply that he was a worthy father to his valiant son, and as the common saying goes, 'good issue comes from good stock'. His wife, and the mother of the hero of our book, was Dame Fleurie de Linières, who was virtuous, beautiful, wise and noble, and led an irreproachable life.[4]

The subject of this book was born in Touraine, in the city of Tours, and at his baptism was given the name Jean. As the eldest son, he was much loved and cherished by his parents, and he was brought up with the warmth and affection due to a child of such parentage. But his noble father survived the birth of his son by only two years; his death was a blow to the kingdom of France and to his noble wife who wept bitter tears, and more especially to his children. But our hero was handsome and sweet-natured, and a pleasure to raise, and thus a great comfort to his mother, for the older he grew, the more courteous and handsome he became. He was a fine-looking lad, amiable, affable and jovial; a little on the swarthy side, and with a high-coloured complexion which suited him; he was friendly, cheerful and courteous [14] in all his childhood deeds. And when he was a little older, his wise mother sent him to school, and he continued to go throughout his childhood. As the saying goes, 'What comes from nature can't be taken away', and indeed, even in childhood, as everyone can see every day, the temperament of the man can plainly be seen. And ancient history bears this out: in the case of Cyrus, for instance, who thought himself to be the son of the shepherd who had brought him up; he was actually of royal blood and the grandson of Astyages, king of Persia.[5] Astyages had ordered the boy to be killed

---

3 King Jean II (1350–64) named Jean I Le Meingre marshal of France on 21 October 1356, following the death of the previous marshal, Jean de Clermont, on the battlefield at Poitiers on 19 September 1356.

4 Fleurie de Linières was the daughter of Godemart I de Linières, head of one of the oldest noble familes in Berry. She died shortly after 25 March 1406, and so the use of the past tense suggests that the biography was probably started after that date.

5 Cyrus II of Persia (c.560/559–530 BC) was the founder of the Persian empire. Christine de Pizan had also recounted the story of the dream of King Astyages in *Le livre de la mutacion de*

at birth for fear that he, Cyrus, would overthrow him; that was how his wise men interpreted a terrible dream that he had had. But the king's command was entirely disobeyed; a shepherd found the baby in the forest, hanging by his swaddling clothes from a branch. The shepherd's wife brought the boy up as her own, but once he was grown, Nature – always the prankster – could no longer hide [15] the gifts she had given him: noble blood and royal birth: he was a fine-looking young man, upright in bearing, aristocratic in manner. His demeanour, his expression and the wisdom of his speech marked him out for who he was – something that shows the marvels performed by inner being and by Nature. So naturally patrician was his behaviour that the other shepherds did him reverence and made him their king; they were in awe of him, and when they were out in the fields, they gathered around him and he sat as judge in their disputes and settled them; thus Nature presaged what he was to become, for he became king of Persia and Assyria and of the Medes [Mede], and conquered Babylon the Great.

Much the same was true of Romulus the founder of Rome and Remus his brother, who from their earliest childhood would gather their fellow children and engage in mock battles: when they were grown men, they continued to do so until they had conquered great lands.[6]

Paris, Priam's son, was also mistaken for a shepherd when he was a child, and indeed thought himself the son of a shepherd, but his nobility of bearing and appearance, his crown of flowers and his golden bow, [16] as well as his beauty, were clues to the fact that his particular tastes and preferences were for love rather than for battle.[7] And we could cite many other noble men whose characters were heralded by their childhood preferences.

IV: Further on Boucicaut's childhood.

As our remarks here have suggested, Boucicaut, whose fine and admirable deeds we hope to record in the book that follows, showed from childhood his good and honourable character and disposition: even his childhood games were such as to show every sign of Knighthood, and indeed Nature early presaged in him the high office for which God and Good Fortune destined him. For he would gather together the children of his own age and go and take up station, for instance on a little hill. He would have allies like his brother Geoffroy – who in good time also became, and indeed remains, a very valorous and daring knight, [17] bold and courageous, fine-looking of face and figure, and now promoted governor of the Dauphiné, or like his

fortune, ed. S. Solente, 4 volumes (Paris, 1959–66), II, pp. 191–7 (vv. 9231–436), completed in 1403.

6 Romulus and Remus were the legendary founders of Rome.

7 Paris was the legendary son of Priam, king of Troy. His seizure of Helen queen of Sparta was the trigger for the Trojan War.

half-brother Mauvinet, son of his mother, who was also, throughout his life, a most valiant knight.[8] The three of them, along with the troop of children, would band together to hold the hill against the challenge of other children – or alternatively, on other occasions, they would choose to be the attackers and put the other children to flight. Sometimes again the two bands of children would square up to each other as if in battle; Boucicaut would fashion his own troop's caps into helmets, and then lead them along riding astride sticks, with weapons made of bark, to besiege some other spot. He loved to take part in games like this, or in Prisoners' Base,[9] or in wrestling,[10] or in jumping, or in casting a spear or a stone or something of that sort. But in whatever game he played, he was always the winner, and he assumed the role of judge and arbiter in the childhood games; at such times his manner would be lordly, and he would stand tall, his hand on his hip – a stance that truly became him – and watch the other children closely to adjudicate on their actions. On such occasions he would neither chatter nor laugh, though not because of pride or conceit: he was always pleasant, good-natured and kind, courteous to the other children, modest, obedient to his tutor and to everyone in authority, but [18] determined that no-one should belittle him: that he would never accept. That he should show such self-possession when a child made it evident from a very young age that he would be possessed of great and superior character. His steadfastness was demonstrated once when his tutor gave him a beating, another child having complained that Boucicaut had struck him for challenging something he had said. Boucicaut did not cry; he simply rested his cheek on his hand as if he was thinking. His tutor saw that he was not crying – unlike other children who burst into tears when they are beaten – and said sharply: 'Look at him! What an arrogant little lordling! He won't even condescend to cry!' The child replied: 'When I'm a lord, you won't dare to beat me – and I'm not crying, because if I did, everyone would know that you'd beaten me.'

When he had grown up a little, our wise King Charles,[11] then on the throne, was conscious of the great service that Boucicaut's father, Marshal Boucicaut, had in his lifetime rendered to the former king, King Jean, and indeed to Charles himself in the wars against the English; he hoped that the son would be as valiant, and

8 Geoffroy, brother of Jean II Le Meingre, was born in either 1367 or 1368 and died in 1429. He served as governor of the Dauphiné from 1 April 1399 to 21 April 1407, which would suggest that this section was written before he lost that office. After their father died in 1368, their mother Fleurie de Linières married Maurice Mauvinet (d.1375), the father of Boucicaut's half-brother Mauvinet, who died before 1409.

9 In the original, the author says 'jouer aux barres'; in his *Thresor de la langue françoyse tant ancienne que moderne* (1606), Jean Nicot describes the *jeu des barres* as a mock battle between two groups, the aim being to accumulate prisoners. The English equivalent is called 'Bars', or more commonly today 'Prisoners' Base'; see Joseph Strutt, *Sports and Pastimes of the People of England* (London, 1903), pp. 67–8.

10 The author calls this a game of 'croq madame'; see *DMF*, 'sorte de jeu, probablement le croc-en-jambe' – literally 'leg-hook', hence 'wrestling'.

11 King Charles V reigned from 1364 to 1380.

acknowledged that he should reward the boy for his late father's service. He ordered that young Boucicaut be attached to the court of his own eldest son, the dauphin of Vienne, who is now himself king, and this was done.[12] So he was brought up along with the dauphin until the age of about twelve. And while he was at court, [19] he behaved most graciously, and made himself much liked by the dauphin himself and by all the other well-born children and young people who were also being trained there; indeed the older great lords also liked him very much; he became known for the excellent good manners and sagacity that all noble children destined for high office should acquire.

V: Here we tell of the first time Boucicaut bore arms.

Boucicaut, as we have implied, had reached the age of twelve, and although that is still very young to start to bear arms, he pestered and complained that he wanted to be armed and go to war – unlike the general run of children who prefer at that age simply to play. And very soon, in spite of the fact that some of the court laughed at him saying 'God, call that a man-at-arms!', he was so persistent that he came to the attention of the duke of Bourbon;[13] the latter was delighted when he heard what the boy had been saying, and at his fervent desire to go to war; he was impressed by his dauntlessness at so young an age, and was convinced that if he lived, he would be a man of valour – something that Bourbon found very pleasing. [20] Boucicaut's character struck the duke as so pleasing that he requested that the king allow him to take the boy to Normandy with him in his army, to lay siege to the castles and fortresses belonging to the then king of Navarre with whom King Charles was in dispute.[14] The king granted the duke's request, partly out of amusement, partly to comply with the boy's demands; he granted the boy a good escort – and Boucicaut was given arms and a fitting entourage. And when Boucicaut found himself equipped just as he had demanded, he was needless to say delighted; and he found full armour not a burden – as he might have done – but a joy: he paraded around like a lady in a new outfit, and showed such pleasure that everyone who saw him was just as pleased as he was. This was how young Boucicaut enrolled in the army led by the duke of Burgundy, brother of King Charles, in whose company there were also the duke

12 King Charles VI of France (1380–1422) was dauphin of Viennois from 1368 to 1386, when his first son Charles was born and assumed the title for a few months until his death, at which point Charles VI resumed the title until 1392.

13 Louis II, duke of Bourbon inherited the title in 1356 and held it until his death in 1410. Bourbon was himself the subject of a chivalric biography written by Jean Cabaret d'Orville, *La chronique du bon duc Loys de Bourbon*, ed. A.M. Chazaud (Paris, 1876).

14 Between April and June 1378, Philippe le Hardi duke of Burgundy (d.1404) led a military expedition against the territories in Normandy held by Charles II, king of Navarre and count of Evreux (d.1387), after Navarre had been caught secretly negotiating with the English.

of Bourbon, the constable of France Bertrand du Guesclin, along with many other captains and a great force of men-at-arms who stormed many castles and fortresses:[15] these were Breteuil, Beaumont, Regnéville-sur-Mer [Reguierville], Gavray, Saint-Guillaume-de-Mortain – which left Navarre with [21] Cherbourg alone; after that, they returned to France. But the boy behaved with such grace and fortitude on this expedition that no-one ever heard him complain of the weight of his armour, or of any other hardship that he had to suffer during the sieges; rather, he remained so good-humoured that it was obvious from his conduct that the pursuit of arms came naturally to him. But on his return to court, his good humour soon turned sour; he had thought himself a proven man-at-arms but was shocked to find that courtiers would say to him: 'Now then, young man, not so much the man-at-arms! Back to the schoolroom!' So he was sent back shamefaced to school with the dauphin, in spite of his protests. But as you have heard, this was the first military expedition on which he went armed: a remarkably early start, and in a career he was to pursue untiringly.

VI: Here we explain how even at a young age, Boucicaut was determined to follow arms, and how he began to take part in expeditions.

In this way, and willy-nilly, the young Boucicaut was kept at court with the dauphin, [22] so much so that he found it more and more frustrating. So he started to pester everyone to be allowed to leave and bear arms – which he ardently wished, since he thought himself strong and hardy enough to exchange heavy blows with lance and sword, and to carry the weight of arms. He complained so vociferously about it that the king heard how determined he was, and how he had said that if no-one was prepared to give him arms he would simply go and serve whatever nobleman would give him horses and armour, because he simply did not wish to remain at court. The king was delighted to see such determination at so young an age, and such resolve to achieve chivalric renown, and was sure that he would take after his chivalrous father; and although the king delayed giving him what he wanted because he was so young, nevertheless Boucicaut acquired such a reputation and was so insistent that, in the end, it was agreed he should be armed. So the king had everything he needed supplied to him, and furnished him with excellent horses; he also allowed him first-rate attendants and a generous allowance, and sent him so equipped to the company of the duke of Bourbon who greeted him enthusiastically; Bourbon, in concert with the duke of Burgundy, was about to join battle with the English under the duke of Buckingham [Bouquigan], who was harrying the kingdom of France.[16] [23] And the

15 Bertrand du Guesclin (d.1380) was appointed constable of France by Charles V in 1370.

16 Thomas of Woodstock, 1st earl of Buckingham and subsequently duke of Gloucester (d.1397), led an expedition from Calais to Brittany in the summer of 1380, before returning to England

two French dukes and their companies inflicted frequent damage on Buckingham, so much so that in the end he retreated back to England having made little progress in France. On this expedition, the young Boucicaut began to show evidence of his courage and daring, for in skirmishes and encounters with the enemy he threw himself into battle with such abandon that there was no-one more intrepid, to such an extent that everyone was amazed that someone so young could be so courageous. He would have been prepared to do even more, but his attendants prevented him from indulging in even more dangerous enterprises. The duke of Bourbon himself, who was very fond of the boy because of his friendship with his valiant father, became more and more fond of him because of the signs he showed of the valiant knight he would become; from that time on he was pleased to find the boy in his company. After this expedition, Bourbon and Burgundy returned to Paris, and Boucicaut with them. He was warmly received by the king and his son the dauphin, who had heard how he had proved his bravery and his determination.[17] [24]

VII: Here we tell of the physical exercises Boucicaut undertook in order to become hardened to arms.

And this was not all that the noble young Boucicaut did. He declared that he would no longer be detained at court, and that henceforth he would be master of his own fate; he saw himself as already a grown man, who needed to perform as others did. So very soon he left Paris and went to Guyenne with the Marshal Louis de Sancerre who was about to lay siege to the castle of Montguyon [Monguison] – and now we shall recount how Boucicaut conducted himself on that expedition.[18]

So unwavering was he in the pursuit of arms that no hardship was too great; privations that would have seemed intolerable to others gave him great pleasure, for even in periods of respite, he could not take it easy. So instead, he would train himself to leap fully armed onto his horse's back, [25] or on other occasions he would go for long runs on foot, to increase his strength and resistance, or he would train for hours with a battle-axe or a hammer to harden himself to armour and to exercise his arms and hands, so that he could easily raise his arms when fully armed. Doing such exercises gave him a physique so strong that there was no other gentleman in his time who was so proficient – for he could do a somersault fully armed but for his bascinet,[19] and he could dance equipped in a coat of mail.

---

the following year.

17 King Charles V died on 16 September 1380, just as Buckingham was laying siege to Nantes in Brittany.

18 Louis de Sancerre (d.1403) was appointed as a marshal of France in 1369.

19 Bascinet: a helmet originally open-faced, but by 1400 or so having a visor and being extended to cover the throat and neck.

Item: he could leap fully armed onto his courser, without putting his foot in a stirrup.

Item: he could leap up from the ground onto the shoulders of a tall man mounted on a large horse, simply by grabbing the man's sleeve in one hand.

Item: by placing one hand on the saddlebow of a great courser and the other between its ears, he could vault between his arms over the horse, holding its mane.

Item: if two plaster walls, the height of a tower, stood an arm's width apart, he could climb up them using just feet and hands, no other aid, and without falling.

Item: fully armed in a coat of mail, he could climb right to the top of the underside of a scaling ladder leaning against a wall, simply swinging from rung to rung by his two hands [26] – or without the coat of mail, by one hand only.

These things are absolutely true – and indeed he trained his body so hard in so many other exercises that it would be difficult to find his like. And when he was at home, he would never tire of competing with the other squires in throwing a lance and other warlike exercises. And this was how he behaved during the whole expedition, and he felt he could never be too prompt to take part in any skirmish. And when the army was besieging Montguyon [Monguison], he was a part of every attack that took place, and he would hurry to be among the first to take part in any enterprise appropriate to a man of breeding. He would risk danger in a way that astonished everyone, and because of his bravery and courage, and his deeds, Marshal Sancerre became very fond of him, and said to his own followers: 'If that boy lives, he will be remarkable man.' And in the end, Montguyon fell, and a number of other castles and fortresses were rendered by agreement – after which the army returned to France. [27]

VIII: Here we talk of love, showing how men of good breeding must love in order to achieve valour.

By now Boucicaut had reached the age at which Love, by nature, demands fealty and due payment from all men of noble courage. And of course it would not have been right for him to be exempt, or to escape those bonds; after all, they do not prevent a keen and chivalrous young man from pursuing the noble exercise of arms – and indeed such bonds are what inspire young hearts, and encourage the desire for honourable knightly pursuits. Ah! How many there are who would never amount to anything, were it not that the hope of acquiring their ladies' grace gives them the courage to risk hazardous enterprises and thus win renown! What danger or hardship will a loving heart not dare to undertake? None, certainly! Love removes fear, undoes the memory of hardship, and makes any labour undertaken for the sake of the loved one a pleasure. And for proof that this is so, [28] one need only read the tales of dead heroes: Lancelot, Tristan, and many others whom Love made valiant and renowned. And indeed we have only to look at some heroes of our own lifetime, in France and elsewhere: those like Othon de Grandson or the good constable of Sancerre, or many others to name whom would take too long:[20] men who in Love's service have grown to perfection in valour. Oh, what a noble thing is Love – provided that one understands how to control it – although some wrongly condemn it. After all, if misfortune befalls those who do not control it, that is scarcely the fault of Love since in herself she is good.[21]

And because some might say that to prove Love is good requires more than the general statements I have given so far, I shall briefly outline the terms in which we can call Love good. Without going into too complex questions, I believe that the heart set on love should base its search on three things. The first is that a man should seek out love in order to be more worthy in his behaviour: to live more contented, to have a heart more courageous and intrepid; to exert himself in the acquisition of all virtues. [29] The second is that he should seek out an object for his affections who is refined, virtuous, inspiringly generous and prudent – for if he loves unwisely, he will become unwise; if the object of his affections is ill-bred and low-born, he will become uncouth and vice-ridden; Love is so constituted that she ensures that the heart of any lover will espouse the qualities of the beloved. It is much better therefore that since to love is to aspire, the lover choose as the focus of his love – be she beautiful or ugly, tall or short – someone who possesses wisdom, grace and virtue. The third thing is that a heart intending love should keep constantly at the forefront of his mind honour, so that even on pain of death he will do nothing to dishonour himself or his loved one. And as long as the heart intent on love keeps these things paramount – that is, that love should give him a more contented life, that it should enhance his virtues, that it should inspire him to nobler thoughts, that it should bring him into contact with better and more worthy circles, and that it should arouse him always to honour, then he will find in Love such benefits that throughout his life he will be more admirable.

There are some, however, who will no doubt say: 'True enough, but I might fall in love with someone who appears generous and well-bred – and then find that they are none of these things; [30] and then it will be too late, I shall already have invested my affections too far.' To which I would answer that to have become inextricably involved with such a person is to have failed to find the good love that I am describing – love that is inspirational rather than injurious; that the more the lover involves himself in such a love, the more he will be damaged; that to forsake such a lover is not wrong – that indeed not to forsake such a lover is madness. And let me explain why, in pursuing love, you may so often find such harshness and such harm. It can only be because you are seeking love not for inspiration or for virtue,

20 Othon de Grandson (d.1397) was a famous Savoyard knight who fought for the English during the Hundred Years War and took part in the crusading expedition to Prussia of Henry Bolingboke (in 1392–3). Grandson was also a famous poet, and friend of both Geoffrey Chaucer and Christine de Pizan.

21 'Amour' in medieval French is feminine – hence 'she'.

but rather for bodily gratification you may hope for. Such indulgence or delight is always brief and short-lived, so that anything based on it is ephemeral – whereas what is based on virtue is lasting, and will bring true good and true joy. But too few of those who love follow these rules, and that is why those who pursue bodily pleasure will find love painful. The fault is their own, not that of Love, because their misfortunes are self-inflicted. There are similarities, for instance, with wine: it is good in itself, [31] it gives pleasure and comfort and sustenance, and can give rise to good things; but if the drinker is reckless and drinks harmfully and to excess, he makes himself ridiculous and even brutish; but this is not the fault of the wine, but rather of the drinker himself. So in summary: I believe that a love that is based rather on bodily pleasure than on virtue and worth cannot last, and that such a love will cause misery and bitterness, even destruction. This is a topic suitable for refined discussion, and one that could raise the subtlest of questions – but for the moment I shall be silent on it and return to my main purpose, that is the life of the subject of this present memoir.

IX: Here we explain how love, and the desire to be loved, fostered Boucicaut's courage and his will to be valiant and chivalrous.

Boucicaut, as a well-bred young man of the sort we have described, and as is natural in a young man of his age when a noble heart is inclined towards Love, began to feel those urges [32] that result from the arrows that the archer Fair Gaze[22] sends into the gentle of spirit. And he became increasingly merry, and good-humoured, and lyrical, and gracious, more than ever before; and he began to compose ballades, roundels, virelais,[23] lays and laments, all devoted to love, in which skills Love rapidly made him past master – as we can judge from the *Livre des Cent Ballades* which he and the seneschal of Eu composed while on crusade;[24] moreover he became more eager than before to acquire robes, horses, armour and all sorts of finery. He had indeed, inspired by Love, picked out a lady who was beautiful, courteous and worthy of his love, and who turned his thoughts more and more towards knighthood.[25] He therefore chose

22 'Doux Regard', servant of the God of Love in the allegorical *Roman de la Rose* (trans. Charles Dahlberg, Princeton, 1971).

23 A virelay was originally a song form, though by 1400 or so largely divorced from music; it has three stanzas, each ending with a refrain that sets the rhyme scheme.

24 *Le livre des cent ballades*, ed. G. Raynaud (Paris, 1905), was a collaborative collection of verses purporting to be a dialogue between a knight and a lady, apparently composed during a crusading expedition in 1388–9 by Boucicaut and three others: Jean de Saint-Pierre (d.1396), seneschal of the count of Eu; Philippe d'Artois count of Eu (d.1397); and Jean de Crésecque (d.1396).

25 Note that Boucicaut did not marry Antoinette de Turenne until 1393.

a device and a motto appropriate to his state, and had them emblazoned on all his garments – but he kept his love a secret, determined to serve his lady covertly and with such spirit, in deeds of arms, that he would be able to win her love. Accordingly, he spent as much time as possible in her presence, although ensuring that gossip did not attach to her. And when, occasionally, he found himself at dancing or at an entertainment where she was, he made sure his gallantry and courtesy, his behaviour and his ability to sing and dance and laugh and converse were unmatched [33]; he would sing songs and roundels whose words he himself had composed, and he would say them covertly, but so pointedly that his lady understood him; his roundels and his songs would lament the way in which he was tormented by his love for his lady. But he was careful not to express himself openly – so different from today's seducers who have done nothing to deserve love, but who demand love from their ladies without a by-your-leave, while indulging, expertly, in tricks and deceptions. This was not the way of young Boucicaut, who on the contrary, in her presence and in that of other ladies, behaved with the docility and courtesy of an innocent girl: he made himself be of service to all, to revere all, for the sake of his chosen one. His mode of speech to his lady was gracious, courteous, even timid; he hid his innermost thoughts from all, and knew instinctively how to govern his glance and his manner so that no-one would guess what was in his heart. It was with modesty and diffidence that he served Love and his lady, convinced that he had done nothing as yet to fit him to ask the love of a lady of such worth; he was merely determined so to comport himself that she would of her own accord come to love him and have pity on him, and to that end he desired that his manners, his temperament, his appearance, [34] should all be enhanced for love of her.

At that time King Charles VI, our present monarch, was quite newly crowned,[26] and in France there were more feast days and jousts and dances than there had been for many years, thanks to a young king whose youth and strength and authority naturally inclined him to enjoyment and recreation. Accordingly, at that time the king organised frequent and regular entertainments in Paris and beyond, to which princesses and ladies and damsels of the highest rank were bidden – and unsurprisingly, there came many who were blithe and beautiful, and richly adorned. At such events the young knights and squires would outdo each other to be ever more affable and agreeable and appealing. There would be jousts, on the grand scale, open to all, and those of noble blood would compete to show their valour for the sake of the ladies. In such company young Boucicaut would appear, likeable, richly equipped, well mounted and well attended, and when he met his lady's glance, [35] he would spur his horse with such vigour that he would unhorse many in his advance; and he conducted himself so impressively that everyone was astonished, for at that time he was still very young. Thus he was much talked about, and the ladies and other spectators watched him with pleasure. Why need I continue? As you have

26 King Charles VI was crowned at Reims on 4 November 1380.

heard, Love inspired Boucicaut to an ardent wish to be valiant, and thenceforward he would be by no means last in seeking out honourable deeds to prove himself. All such thoughts and desires Love inspired in Boucicaut's disposition, and as we shall see in what follows, in our description of his knighthood and his later deeds.

X: Here we shall hear how Boucicaut was dubbed knight, and of his expeditions to Flanders.

I am determined that all those who hear or read the present book should fully understand that no knight or nobleman – of the sort with which this book is concerned – can gain a reputation for valour [36] in the wider world, or serve as example to those who wish to pursue honour and knighthood, without great exertion and the continual exercise of arms and noble deeds. For this reason, in the present book, I shall insist on the ways in which Boucicaut spent his life in the diligent and determined pursuit of arms and in gallant deeds, and I shall recount all the deeds and the expeditions in which he took part, from his earliest youth until today, so as to show how he avoided idleness and foolishness.

But so that you understand what was at stake, I should explain that around that time, the Flemings rebelled against their lord the count of Flanders, and indeed expelled him from his lands, for which reason the count approached the king of France, [37] Charles VI, our present king, as his sovereign to request aid and assistance against the rebels, and to subdue the cities of Flanders and the surrounding country.[27] And acting as a sovereign should for his vassal, when so required and requested, and at the instigation of Philippe duke of Burgundy, his uncle (whose wife was Margaret daughter of the count of Flanders), the king not only sent assistance but actually went in person attended by his uncles and those of the blood royal, with a great host of his nobility, and of knights and men-at-arms.[28]

Boucicaut, still very young, took part in the expedition, and in spite of his youth was dubbed knight by the good duke of Bourbon, the king's uncle, who was devoted to the young knight who was serving in his company. And at that point, impertinently, the Flemings mustered to give battle against their rightful lord the king of France, and against their natural lord the count of Flanders, and it befell them as befits all subjects who rebel against their lords, for on the plain of Roosebeke [Rosebech], in the very presence of the young king, [38] 60,000 Flemings were defeated and killed.[29] And in the course of the battle, the newly

27 The Flemings rose against Louis de Mâle, count of Flanders (d.1384). Led by Philip van Artevelde (d.1382), they expelled the count after the battle of Beverhoutsveld (3 May 1382).

28 Marguerite de Dampierre (d.1405) married Philippe duke of Burgundy in 1369. Following the death of her father Louis de Mâle in 1384, she and her husband inherited Flanders, as well as counties of Artois, Burgundy, Nevers and Rethel.

29 The battle of Roosebeke took place on 27 November 1382.

knighted Boucicaut, with characteristic bravery, determined to measure himself hand-to-hand against a tall, sturdy Fleming; he attempted to fell him with his two-handed battle-axe. The Fleming saw that Boucicaut was relatively small, and took it that he was no more than a child; contemptuously, he struck the haft of Boucicaut's axe so brutally that the weapon fell from his hands, and the Fleming sneered: 'There's something for you to suckle, child! The French must be short of decent men if they have to enlist children ...!' Boucicaut, anguished by the loss of his axe, heard the sneer and drew his dagger and slipped under the Fleming's guard; he thrust the dagger below his enemy's breastplate and between his ribs, and the Fleming fell to the ground overcome by pain – nor could he do Boucicaut any further damage. And Boucicaut said, mockingly: 'Is this a game for Flemish children?' And in this engagement the newly knighted hero performed many more valiant and daring deeds, so much so that all those present entertained great hopes of him. [39] And that is how Flanders was made entirely subject to the king of France, who thereafter returned to Paris.

But once the king had left – for they realised that they could not withstand him, and that their forces were insufficient to harm the French – the Flemings, filled with indignation against the French and wishing for revenge, called the English to their aid and invited them into Flanders;[30] when the king heard this, he returned the following year; this would become known as the expedition of Bourbourg, during which the king took Bergues [Bargues] by storm from the English, who took flight. And in this assault, and in other skirmishes, Boucicaut distinguished himself more than others. Thereafter the king took the field in Flanders for three successive years, by which time the Flemings were entirely subjugated and returned to the rule of their natural lord. After the storming of Bergues [Bargues], to guard the frontier, the king left the constable of France, Olivier de Clisson,[31] in Thérouanne, with a sizeable cohort of good men-at-arms, and young Boucicaut, [40] unlike the usual young and untrained men who after battle seek nothing but repose, insisted on remaining in the garrison with the constable.

XI: How Boucicaut made his first expedition to Prussia, and how he returned a second time.

After the king's party had left the northern border, as we have described, my lord Boucicaut had no wish to follow the others to Paris; he desired, he said, to fulfil his promise to go to Prussia, as do all those valiant knights who hope to improve their standing. So he undertook the expedition, and with a sizeable retinue, he took

30 Henry Despenser, bishop of Norwich (d.1406), led an expedition to Flanders from May to June 1383.

31 Olivier de Clisson (d.1407) was constable of France from 1380 to 1392.

himself to Prussia where he made every effort to do damage to the Saracens, and he spent a season there before returning to France.[32]

It was high time indeed that he saw his lady again – and he deserved to; after all, his gracious heart, young, refined and perfect in loyalty as it was, felt all those pangs of love that make loyal lovers so eager to see the object of their affections. But despite his ever-present eagerness, [41] before he dared venture to request the love of his lady, he wanted to win her favour by his good deeds. And he prized her favour so highly that he felt he could not do enough to earn her grace: all his deeds seemed to him a mere trifle against such a reward. But Love – who values those who humbly serve him – will not allow their ladies to be unaware of their worth as faithful lovers; Love whispers in the ladies' ears to ensure that they notice how their lovers pursue valour for their sakes, and thus, very often, Love's labours awaken Courtesy, who in alliance with Good Will ensures that unwittingly the lovers are loved. And all these benefits come to lovers through their exploits and their merits.

I am convinced that it was in this way that my lord Boucicaut – with no ignoble thoughts – was able to attain his ambition, for a lady must be ignoble herself to refuse so loyal an admirer. Which I believe explains why, on his return, Love reserved the most joyous and tender welcome for him from his loving lady. [42]

In this way, Boucicaut returned to France, and spent some time in Paris. At that time, there were negotiations in train over a treaty between France and England, and for that reason the dukes of Berry and Burgundy, the king's uncles, were to go to Boulogne – and Boucicaut, thinking to advance his honour with expeditions and excursions, asked to accompany them to the talks.[33] When he returned to Paris he was dismayed to see so little military activity in France; he determined to put his youth to good service by making a second expedition to Prussia where, he was told, that season was to see a particularly good *Reise*.[34] He stayed a time in the far north, then returned to France. [43]

32 Taking advantage of the Anglo-French truce agreed at Leulinghen in January 1384, Boucicaut responded to the appeal of the Teutonic Order for assistance against the pagan Lithuanians, commonly referred to at the time as Saracens. A.V. Murray, 'The Saracens of the Baltic: Pagan and Christian Lithuanians in the Perception of English and French Crusaders to Late Medieval Prussia', *Journal of Baltic Studies*, 41 (2010), pp. 413–29.

33 The dukes of Berry and Burgundy led the French delegation negotiating with John of Gaunt duke of Lancaster, Buckingham and the English at Boulogne during the summer of 1384. Though they were not able to secure a final peace agreement, they did agree a prolongation of the truce until 1 May 1385.

34 Boucicaut returned to Prussia to take part in a successful military campaign in January 1385. This type of expedition was known as a 'reysen' in Middle High German; this term is commonly found in both Anglo-Norman and Middle French texts from at least as early as the fourteenth century.

XII: How my lord Boucicaut, after his return from Prussia, accompanied the duke of Bourbon to Taillebourg and Verteuil – both of which were taken – and to other castles in Guyenne.

At that time, the English were occupying large parts of the kingdom of France: they were, that is to say, holding a number of towns and castles in Picardy, Guyenne and other regions – even though, thank God, the valour of the French had done much to dislodge them from lands they had previously held. And by now the position of the king of France was constantly improving, thanks to the courage and determination that was shown by men of valour like the good duke of Bourbon whom I mentioned above, and who made a number of sorties against the English from which he emerged with honour. Now, the old proverb says that 'like attracts like' – and accordingly the good duke valued Boucicaut highly for the boldness and courage that he saw in him, and because, more than most young men, he showed every sign of becoming a man of valour – so he liked to keep him close, and enjoyed his company. [44]

Thus in the season after Boucicaut's return from Prussia, it happened that the duke of Bourbon was gathering his forces to go to Guyenne and lay siege before a number of castles held by the English; the duke got together a fine company of men, including some fifteen hundred men-at-arms and a large number of archers.[35] Boucicaut made sure he was one of their number; he would have been bitterly disappointed had he not been; like a fine lady going to the ball, or a bird of prey cast at game, the fine young man delighted in arms. When the duke of Bourbon arrived in Guyenne, he laid siege before the strong castle of Taillebourg, and captured it;[36] he then laid siege to Verteuil which was a particularly well-fortified fortress, and which therefore could mount a good defence.[37] So there an underground mine was dug, to such effect that the wall was breached and the enemy flocked to the defence – and in combat at the breach, Boucicaut was among the foremost, fighting hand-to-hand with lance and sword. He fought most bravely and endured much hardship, but at the last, thanks to his efforts and those of his followers, [45] the castle was taken; Boucicaut achieved much prestige, and was much admired by his good friends.

---

35 As royal lieutenant, the duke of Bourbon mustered an army at Moulins on 1 June 1385 for an expedition into Poitou that lasted until November, primarily targeting routier garrisons. There are three main contemporary accounts of this expedition: the biography of Boucicaut, Cabaret d'Orville's *La chronique du bon duc Loys de Bourbon*, pp. 136–57, and Jean Froissart, *Chroniques*, ed. S. Luce, G. Raynaud, L. Mirot and A. Mirot, 15 volumes (Paris, 1869–1975), XI, pp. 196–253.

36 Taillebourg (Charente-Maritime), around eighty miles north of Bordeaux, was a strategically important town because of its great stone bridge over the river Charente.

37 The castle at Verteuil (Charente), around one hundred miles north-east of Bordeaux, had been granted to the English by the treaty of Brétigny in 1360, and secured by Sir John Chandos on 25 October 1361. The siege led by Bourbon took place towards the very end of the campaign in 1385, and lasted for two months until early October.

After the storming of these two fortresses, the duke of Bourbon took on another stronghold called Montlieu [Maulaoun]; he ordered the assault, and in the end the castle was taken by mine and by siege-ladder, and many a valiant deed was done.[38] Boucicaut was first up a ladder, and fought long and hard, and in spite of the efforts of the defenders who attacked with heavy blows from rocks and swords, he could not be blocked from being first on the rampart; once there, he performed more deeds of valour than anyone else imaginable. Next, the duke of Bourbon headed to another castle called Le Fan [Le Faon], but rumours of the storming of the other castles had reached the defenders, and they were so dismayed by what they heard of the determination and valour of the duke and his army that they dared not wait for the assault and surrendered – as did another castle called Bourg-Charente [Le Bourc Charente].[39]

Now, I have to deal consecutively with concurrent happening at the same time, but I should say that during the siege of Verteuil, news came to the duke and his men that the English were mustering against a fortified church dedicated to Our Lady.[40] Once this was known, a company of knights and squires determined to gain honour and renown [46] by attacking the marauders. Boucicaut, who longed as always to take part in armed expeditions, volunteered to join them; finally, there was a total of some thirty knights and squires, all of high reputation. They elected as leader Aimery de Rochechouart, who knew all the tracks and byways of the country.[41] Then all thirty of these valiant noblemen mounted, fully armed, and made their way along the byways to confront the English who had no inkling that they were on their way, and who numbered some seventy men. The French party fell on the enemy and the battle was fierce and savage; the adversaries were not well matched, for the English had double our numbers, but nevertheless every one of our men acquitted himself so well that in the end the English were defeated and all killed, apart from nine of them who took flight. Next, Aimery de Rochechouart took them off to another enterprise under the walls of a well-fortified castle called Bourdaraud [Le Bourdrun],[42] where their bravery obliged them to do battle three times in a single day; this time, they were driven back, and as their numbers were too small to conquer the castle, they were obliged to retreat. [47]

38 The siege of Montlieu (Charente-Maritime), around forty miles from Bordeaux, was completed by 15 August 1385, when Montlieu was granted to Arnaudon des Bordes by King Charles VI.

39 The castle of Le Fan (Charente) was taken after a siege lasting eleven days.

40 The precise location for this episode is unknown.

41 Aimery de Rochechouart (1340–97), lord of Mortemart, was seneschal of the Limousin from 1383 to 1389.

42 Lalande has suggested that the castle identified as Le Bourdrun in the text may have been Bourdaraud (Charente), located just a few miles from Verteuil.

XIII: How the duke of Bourbon left Boucicaut as his lieutenant on the frontier, and how Boucicaut jousted with my lord Sicart de la Barde.

Boucicaut's valour – growing and increasing by the day – was by now widely known and recognised by all those who had been his companions in arms. As a consequence the duke of Bourbon, when he withdrew from the country after his conquest of the said castles, made the young man his lieutenant on the frontier and beyond; moreover, in spite of his youth, he left him with a sizeable armed contingent, consisting of my lord Le Barrois, my lord of Châteaumorand and my lord Renaud de Roye, along with one hundred and fifty men-at-arms and a hundred crossbowmen.[43] And the duke's confidence was not misplaced, because Boucicaut did not rest on his laurels: despite the winter cold, he went to lay siege to a fortress called Les Granges [La Granche]; after three days of fighting, the fortress fell.[44]

Once again, however, Boucicaut did not spend the winter as others do, hunting rabbits [48] and hares and other game; rather he preferred to spend his time more enjoyably hunting the enemy, often successfully. And rather like hunters who vary their methods – using dogs or bow-and-arrow or spears, or traps or nets or other means – so Boucicaut, like any other valiant commander, used different strategies to surprise the enemy. Intending to assault the castle at Courbier [Corbier], for instance, he laid an ambush along with his brother my lord Mauvinet and with a number of his other companions – no more than twenty-eight knights and squires, all hand-picked – and meanwhile, he ordered a troop of his other men to parade openly in front of the castle.[45] He himself and his picked men went and stationed themselves in ambush as close as possible to the castle, creeping quietly through the woods and the cottages round about. Then the other troop came galloping up to the castle, and when the defenders saw them, they sallied out and put them to flight so that the attackers were drawn out into open ground. At that point the ambush broke cover and galloped towards the castle gate. The castle guard realised what was happening and gave a signal [49] to the captain and his men who had been part of the sally, and they turned and came back – but they were too late to prevent Boucicaut himself on foot fighting with exceptional courage in front of the gate (he had of course been in the vanguard): by the time his companions caught up, he had taken prisoner the captain's main lieutenant, by far the bravest of the defenders. Boucicaut's men reached him before the defenders made it back to the castle, and thereafter he took

43 Boucicaut served alongside Jean des Barres, lord of Neuvy-le-Barrois (c.1340–99), known as Le Barrois, together with Jean de Châteaumorand (1352–1429) and Renaud de Roye (13??–96).

44 This may be Les Granges on the Dordogne.

45 According to Cabaret d'Orville, this enterprise took place at Christmas 1385: *La chronique du bon duc Loys de Bourbon*, pp. 154–5. For Boucicaut's half-brother, Mauvinet, see p. 27 above. Philippa de Mauvinet, Boucicaut's half-sister, was married to Jean des Barres.

the lead in a fierce and brutal battle, at the end of which all the defenders were either killed or taken prisoner, with the exception of five who fled into the keep. At this, Boucicaut took up station with his men in front of the keep and set a siege in good order. Once those in the keep saw what was happening, they dared not wait for the attack so they surrendered to save their own lives; Boucicaut had the castle razed to the ground and returned to quarters, for he needed the rest.

But while Boucicaut and his men were resting and tending to the wounded, he heard that an English knight from Gascony, a certain Sicart de la Barde, had spoken of him insultingly, saying that Boucicaut hadn't the physique to be as valiant [50] as was claimed.[46] Boucicaut was offended, and although the knight was one of the best and most valiant men-at-arms then known, Boucicaut sent him a message saying that he, Boucicaut, knew him to be one of the best and finest knights known, and that he would be most honoured to have to do with him – for which reason he begged the Englishman to do him the honour of taking up arms against him in some chivalric exploit; Sicart should choose and contrive the means, for he, Boucicaut, was still young and very much a novice in armed combat, and much in need of instruction from a tried and tested champion like himself. Sicart considered himself an excellent jouster, so when he heard the invitation, he replied that he would be delighted to exchange a given number of blows with the lance while in the saddle. Once this was agreed, a time and a place were arranged. When the due day arrived, my lord Boucicaut set out early, well mounted and equipped, with his principal followers in attendance, and arrived at the castle of Châlucet [Chaulucet] where my lord Sicart de la Barde was part of the garrison;[47] remarkably, and courageously, my lord Boucicaut had agreed that the combat should take place under the walls of the enemy fortress. There, the two champions embarked on the joust. At the first exchange of blows, my lord Sicart had the better of it, striking Boucicaut's shield so hard that he almost knocked him out of his stirrups; to his chagrin, Boucicaut missed his aim because his horse swerved off-line. [51] The two champions were handed new lances, and spurred at each other; this time, Boucicaut made sure that his aim was good, and he did not miss. He struck his adversary so hard on the visor that the straps tore apart and his bascinet almost fell off; Sicart was so stunned by the force of this glancing blow that had he not been held up, he would have fallen to the ground. The third time they ran against each other, Sicart struck Boucicaut so hard that his lance splintered and the Frenchman was bent backwards; Sicart, on the other hand, was struck so hard that no armour would have sufficed to prevent Boucicaut's lance lodging between his ribs; he was carried to the ground apparently dead. This brought the jousting to an end, without the champions being able to complete the twenty rounds agreed;

46 Nothing is known of Sicart de la Barde beyond this reference.

47 The castle of Châlucet or Chalusset was located six miles south of Limoges and was the base for the routiers led by Pierre de Fontaines, known as Perrot Le Béarnais.

the accident to one of the parties brought the emprise[48] to a conclusion. My lord Boucicaut left the field, to great acclaim, and very soon thereafter, at the command of the king, the duke of Bourbon sent for him and he returned to Paris. [52]

XIV: How my lord Boucicaut fought a joust of war[49] with an english knight called Sir Peter Courtenay, and then with another called Sir Thomas Clifford.

Once winter was over and sweet spring had arrived – spring, when all nature is joyous, and woods and meadows are green, when the little birds sing in the groves and the nightingales pipe at night, when Love sets gentle hearts afire, inspiring memories that torment and thoughts that afflict – in the month of May, then, Boucicaut, so much the fine and gracious and noble knight, found himself at the royal court which was all dances and feasting. He was blithe and carefree, richly dressed and equipped, and more charming than all the other courtiers – indeed, when Love had distributed his largesse and his good cheer, he had not forgotten how deserving was his faithful servant Boucicaut, and it was thus that Love afforded Boucicaut all luxury, with time and space to see his fair lady. But Valour could not abide his dalliance, [53] and turned his pleasure to pain when he had to leave the lady. Fair Hope assured him that on his return he would be warmly welcomed back by his kind mistress who would know that for her sake he had performed deeds whose rumour would have reached her – and so, having tasted the pleasures of her company in the fair season of spring, he resolved, in order to deserve such pleasure, to return to the field of knighthood on the frontiers of Picardy.

It happened, while he was there, that he heard of an English knight called Sir Peter Courtenay who had come over to France and was going about boasting that he had quartered the whole of France without finding a single French knight who had dared to accept his challenge to a joust with sharpened lancehead,[50] although he had made every effort to locate an opponent.[51] When my lord Boucicaut heard of this braggadocio, he was most annoyed – and he immediately sent his herald to say that

48 By emprise is meant a chivalric undertaking formally declared, such as a series of jousts at a particular place or over a particular period of time.

49 The author's expression is 'jousta de fer de glaive' – that is, using a sharpened lancehead – which suggests a joust of war.

50 As used in war – which, as Ralph Moffat points out, would be highly dangerous, and perhaps particularly appropriate in combat between a French and an English champion.

51 Sir Peter Courtenay (d.1405) was a younger son of Hugh de Courtenay, 2nd earl of Devon (1303–77), and became a member of the Order of the Garter in 1388. Froissart and other chroniclers recounted how Courtenay challenged Guy de La Trémoïlle to joust in front of King Charles VI in late 1389, and had then taken part in a combat at Calais against the lord of Clary, his escort from Paris. Froissart implies that Clary had been justified in fighting against a man who had been placed under his protection because of the Englishman's boasts

he wished to silence the English knight's slurs on the reluctance of the knighthood of France to engage him in combat; he himself – young as he was, and inexperienced – would happily accept a challenge to any arms that Peter Courtenay chose. Courtenay thought himself particularly expert in jousting, and sent back word that he wished no other weapon than the lance, and this was rapidly agreed; he was convinced that he was valiant and renowned [54] enough to make short work of Boucicaut. The two knights therefore met on the field – but although I might be tempted to describe the technicalities of each course of arms, I shall simply say briefly that each of their courses was successful, but that Boucicaut was so obviously the more expert that he emerged with great credit and honour.

Accordingly, very soon thereafter, another English knight, Sir Thomas Clifford, sent Boucicaut another challenge to specified arms, and Boucicaut accepted with alacrity.[52] And although, strictly speaking, the custom and laws of arms would dictate that the appellant submit himself to whatever judge the defendant would elect, nevertheless Boucicaut, fearing that he might be prevented from accepting should the news come to the ears of the king or of one of the great lords, or that the judge he might elect might decline the office, consented to accomplish the jousts agreed at Calais, in front of William de Beauchamp who at that time was captain of Calais and uncle to Sir Thomas.[53] When once they came into the lists and began the joust, both, unsurprisingly, behaved valiantly; however, by the end of their course of arms, my lord Boucicaut [55] had unhorsed my lord Thomas, and flung him, and his horse, onto the field. At that Boucicaut dismounted and they took to sword, dagger and axe – and to be brief, Boucicaut performed so well that everyone agreed that he was most valiant, and he emerged with great honour.

Thereafter, in that same year, the king determined that it would be highly beneficial for his own kingdom, and detrimental to his enemies, if he led a sizeable invasion force into England.[54] With that in mind, a great army was gathered, in which Boucicaut was given command of a hundred men-at-arms. But the invasion never materialised, for winter set in before the preparations were complete and the army

---

and his criticism of the French for not daring to fight him. Froissart, *Oeuvres*, XIV, pp. 46–55.

52 Thomas Clifford, 6th Baron Clifford (1362/3–91) was a chamber knight of King Richard II. On 25 June 1386, Clifford received authorisation from the king to travel to France to joust against Boucicaut, and the following year was licensed to perform deeds of arms in the Anglo-Scottish borders. He also jousted at Calais in 1388 and fought against Boucicaut again at Saint-Inglevert (see below, pp. 48–52) in 1390.

53 William Beauchamp, 1st Baron Bergavenny (c.1343–1411) was captain of Calais from 1383 to 1389. His sister Maud (d.1403) was mother to Thomas Clifford.

54 The admiral of France, Jean de Vienne, led an army to Scotland on 22 May 1385, but the plan for the constable, Olivier de Clisson, to lead the main force to Kent in mid-July was delayed because of the need to put down a rebellion in Flanders. Plans to restage the invasion in 1386 also fell apart, because of a shortage of money and because of tensions between Clisson and the duke of Berry.

had to be disbanded; this expedition was known as the voyage of Sluys [L'Escluse],[55] because the king had intended to take to the sea, and indeed reached the coast, only then to return to France. So for that season Boucicaut was unable to set off on his travels, something that greatly pleased the lady who loved him and who had so often suffered heartache because of the dangerous enterprises in which he engaged. [56]

XV: How my lord Boucicaut went into Spain, and how, on his return, the English ally, the lord of Châteauneuf, challenged him to a duel, twenty of his men against twenty of Boucicaut's – but in the end, Châteauneuf withdrew, or lost his nerve.

The following year, the duke of Lancaster led a great army into Spain to lay waste to the country, and having no intention of returning to England immediately, took his wife and children with him. He had allied himself with the king of Portugal with whom he had long-standing alliances.[56] When the king of Spain found himself beset by his enemies, he sent to the king of France to beg him to send reinforcements, which the latter was most willing to do. France sent my lord Guillaume de Naillac and my lord Gaucher de Passac, with a certain number of men-at-arms; soon thereafter he dispatched the duke of Bourbon [57] with a larger force, of which Boucicaut was a part – much larger indeed, for altogether they numbered some two thousand men.[57] Once the English saw the size of the French army and realised they were at a serious disadvantage, they withdrew into Portugal, which meant that the duke, seeing how little was happening, returned to France via the county of Foix.[58] There, Boucicaut once found himself dining in the company of an English group, who noticed that he was being abstemious: they asked if that was to keep himself in training for arms; if,

55 Jean de Vienne had sailed to Scotland from the Flemish town of Sluys, known as L'Écluse in French.

56 John of Gaunt, duke of Lancaster, laid claim to the throne of Castile by right of his wife, Constanza (1354–94), the exiled daughter of the murdered King Pedro I (1334–69). Gaunt was supported by the Portuguese, who opposed the imposition of direct rule from Castile during a brief interregnum and who fought alongside Gaunt in the great victory against the Castilians at Aljubarotta on 14 August 1385. This secured the Portuguese throne for João I (1385–1433), who in turn supported Gaunt in his attempt to wrestle the Castilian throne from Juan I (1358–90) between 1386 and 1389.

57 On 5 February 1387, two royal chamberlains, Guillaume de Naillac and Gaucher de Passac, were sent to Castile by King Charles VI at the head of an army of 2000 men-at-arms. They arrived in May, and the second force led by the duke of Bourbon reached Burgos at the start of July.

58 Bourbon and his men broke their journey at Orthez, the court of the count of Foix, Gaston III (1331–91), in June or July 1387, just over a year before Jean Froissart's famous visit that he described in *Chroniques*, XII.

they said, that was his intention, he would soon find adversaries among the English.[59] Boucicaut replied that indeed his intention was to undertake arms *à outrance*,[60] though only with a companion in arms, Renaud de Roye – but if some of the English were up for combat, he would be delighted to oblige them; they should name a day once he, Boucicaut, had notified Renaud. Moreover, if by any chance they might wish for a more considerable fight, he would undertake to gather however many knights might be needed, from two to twenty. [58] The conversation became so heated that a local lord from the area who was an ally of the English and who was a kinsman of the count of Foix, the lord of Châteauneuf, accepted the challenge, with twenty men loyal to the French crown against twenty English allies; he, Châteauneuf, would lead the English contingent, Boucicaut the French. The enterprise was agreed, and Boucicaut, having undertaken to find a judge, chose to address himself to the duke of Bourbon; messages were sent, and the duke agreed. But either because the English wanted an excuse to cancel the engagement, or because they had thought better of it, the English rejected both Bourbon himself and all Boucicaut's other suggestions. Seeing this, Boucicaut was dismayed, for he realised that the English were backing down; he remained very committed, so in order to avoid their having any other pretext to withdraw, he offered to have the combat fought in the presence of the count of Foix – but the count demurred and refused to countenance the event; this left Boucicaut with considerable honour.

Meanwhile, the duke of Bourbon left the court of Foix, returned to the duchy of Guyenne and laid siege to the town of Brassempouy [Le Bras Saint Paul];[61] during the siege many fine deeds of arms were performed, especially by Boucicaut who distinguished himself, at considerable personal danger – among other things on siege-ladders, [59] for the moat was more than a lance-length deep, with each bank as steep as a wall, and there was a good-sized garrison. Nevertheless, at the fiercest of the fighting, Boucicaut bravely and unhesitatingly jumped into the moat; a number of others followed him and they scrambled up onto a bridge across it; the enemy had in part dismantled it, but it went straight to the town gate, with no draw mechanism. But to do so they were under fire from two watch-towers – and moreover the enemy had sought to defend the gate with a redoubt set a lance-length forward of it, which was also exposed to fire from the towers. The duke of Bourbon lowered a ladder to Boucicaut and his men to allow them to mount the bridge, and Boucicaut made

59 Froissart, *Oeuvres*, XIV, pp. 118–20, recounted a story not reported in the biography of Boucicaut. Whilst serving in Gaunt's expedition to Castile in 1386, Sir John Dabrichecourt (d.1415) had challenged Boucicaut to a formal combat. Dabrichecourt had then travelled via Orthez and Paris on his way to Calais, searching for the French knight, but the combat had never taken place. The two men would finally meet at Saint-Inglevert two years later.

60 That is, until one combatant is killed or captured: see W. McLean, '*Outrance* and *Plaisance*', *Journal of Medieval Military History*, 8 (2010), pp. 155–70.

61 Brassempouy was a small commune fifteen miles north-east of Orthez, held by the lord of Lascar in the name of the English king. Boucicaut's name was not mentioned in the account of this difficult siege in Cabaret d'Orville, *La chronique du bon duc Loys de Bourbon*, pp. 58–60.

himself responsible for raising it, and was first to climb it and reach the redoubt. But in his wake so many pressed upwards, hoping to win honour, that they hampered each other; they could not in any case make use of their lances given how constricted the space was – so when Boucicaut saw the scrimmage, he threw down the ladder so that the crowd trying to climb it would be frustrated. Meanwhile, they were under fire [60] from an indescribable weight of stones thrown from the two towers – and moreover the enemy, hoping to stem the tide, sallied out of the gates and came to fight hand-to-hand with lances and swords, a threat met by Boucicaut and his men. Boucicaut himself performed valiantly against great odds (for the enemy was very numerous), and pushed the besiegers into jumping back into the moat. But Boucicaut was left standing defiant, alone; he fought long and hard, and friends and foes alike were filled with admiration. The battle was so prolonged that even the fiercest lion would have been exhausted; finally, the press of the enemy was so great that they used their lances to prod him into falling back into the moat – and that brought the assault to an end, for it was getting dark. But you will not be surprised to hear that that evening, the duke of Bourbon saluted Boucicaut's bravery. All the knights and squires present were unanimous in his praise; all ranks spoke only of him and of the deeds they had seen him perform, each of them relating some particularly bold pass of arms that they had witnessed. It was universally agreed that Boucicaut had won the honour of the day. [61]

The following day our men were ready to return to the assault, but seeing this, the enemy surrendered – and a number of other castles and towns in the neighbourhood followed suit and turned French.

XVI: How my lord Boucicaut journeyed to Outremer,[62] and found the count of Eu a prisoner.

Having accomplished his mission, the duke of Bourbon returned to Paris; Boucicaut, on the other hand, eager to visit Outremer, took his leave of the duke. He and his companion at arms, my lord Renaud de Roye, journeyed as far as Venice; here they took ship to Constantinople, where they stayed until the end of Lent. At this point they applied to the Sultan Murad, father of Bayezid, who was at that time in Greece near Gallipoli, for a safe conduct: the sultan gave willing consent.[63] They were able therefore to visit the sultan's court, and he welcomed [62] them with great celebration;

62 'Outremer' was a general name given to the Crusader states established after the First Crusade, but by the end of the fourteenth century was a term used more generally to refer to French-speaking regions lying across the Mediterranean.

63 Murad I was the sultan of the Ottoman empire from 1362 to 1389. Under his rule Ottoman power was expanding into the Balkans, with the princes of northern Serbia and Bulgaria as well as the Byzantine emperor, John V Palaeologus (1332–91) forced to pay tribute to him. Murad's son was Bayezid I who ruled from 1389 to 1403.

they promised him their service should he at any point be at war with the Saracens. The sultan thanked them warmly, and they spent three months at his court – but since no war with the Saracens seemed imminent, they bade him goodbye;[64] he had them escorted across Greece and into the kingdom of Boeotia [Boesse] and Bulgaria [Bougrerie], as far as the frontier of his lands. After that they headed for Hungary, where they were warmly and generously received by the king of Hungary. It happened that at that point the king had mustered great forces to further a dispute he had had with the margrave of Moravia – so he was particularly pleased at the arrival of the French knights.[65] They stayed in Hungary for three months, after which they took their leave of the king and separated, my lord Renaud de Roye going to Prussia, while Boucicaut, eager to visit the Holy Land, returned to Venice and took passage there. He reached Jerusalem and there he made a pilgrimage to the Shrine of the Holy Sepulchre; he also journeyed to all the customary Holy Sites, and in the course of the tour, heard that the count of Eu, who had undertaken a similar pilgrimage, had been arrested in Damascus by the sultan of Babylon.[66] At this news [63] Boucicaut, in spite of the fact that his clothes and equipment had already been loaded onto a ship bound for the winter *Reise* to Prussia, set out instead for Damascus; this was all the more admirable in that Boucicaut had only a very slight acquaintance with the count. He undertook the mission therefore out of personal gallantry and out of respect for the king of France to whom the count was distantly related; the count was delighted at his arrival. Boucicaut, it happened, arrived at the very moment that the sultan had sent for the count, with the intention of summoning him to Cairo [Le Kaire]. The sultan had instructed his officials to list, in writing, all those who were part of the count's entourage and his household; some of those arrested with him were simple pilgrims and those he ordered released to go where they pleased. Boucicaut could have taken advantage of this clemency, but like the noble and virtuous knight he was, and out of his own generous freewill, he did not wish to leave the count alone and a prisoner; rather, he had his name added to the list and thus was committed to prison himself. He stayed there freely for some four months, entirely at his own expense, until the sultan finally released the count.[67]

64 They left the court of Murad I in June 1388.

65 Sigismund of Luxembourg was king of Hungary and Croatia from 1387 to 1437, and became Holy Roman Emperor from 1433 to 1437. For the first nine years of his reign as king of Hungary, he was engaged in a struggle to secure his royal authority against his cousin Jobst, margrave of Moravia from 1374 to 1411, amongst others.

66 Philippe d'Artois, count of Eu (1358–97) and constable of France from 1392 until his death, was held by the Sultan Barquq, who ruled the Mamluk empire from 1382 to 1389 and from 1390 to 1399. During this period in the Holy Land, Boucicaut and Eu were two of the authors of the *Cent ballades*. See note 24 above.

67 Boucicaut joined the count of Eu as a prisoner of the Mamluks from January 1389 and they were both released shortly after the intervention of the Venetian consul at Alexandria on 26 March.

And when he and the count had been set free, they returned to Damascus, taking in on their way the monasteries of Saint Paul the Anchorite [Saint Paul des Desers] in Egypt and Saint Catherine on Mount Sinai [Sainte Katherine du mont de Sinaÿ], [64] and finally directly to Jerusalem. There, my lord Boucicaut paid another visit to the Holy Sepulchre and as before, made all the requisite offerings on his own behalf and that of his men; he then repeated the tour of the Holy Sites that he had made previously. When the count and Boucicaut had completed their tour, they headed for Beirut [Barut] where they intended to take ship for the return voyage to France – but they were arrested by the Saracens who held them for a month before they would give them leave to depart. They embarked on their ship and made their way to Cyprus, then from Cyprus to Rhodes, and there they took a galley[68] for Venice, via which they returned to France. As they passed through Burgundy, they found the king at the abbey of Cluny [Cligny], heading south to take formal possession of the Languedoc which he had never visited; the king was delighted to see them, and held a great feast on their arrival.[69] The count of Eu spoke very highly of Boucicaut to the king, explaining the latter's generosity; he had never, he said, met with such selflessness or such kindness. The king was most grateful to Boucicaut for the benevolence he had shown to his cousin, [65] and all those who learnt the truth of it considered that it showed Boucicaut in a most favourable and flattering light, for which he received much praise.

XVII: Of the emprise in which Boucicaut took part between Boulogne and Calais, at a place called Saint-Inglevert [Saint Tyn-Le-Vert]: along with two others, he set up a challenge against all comers over thirty days.

You will remember that my lord Boucicaut in his youth often accompanied the duke of Bourbon on his travels and expeditions; admiring the courage that the young man had shown from the first; Bourbon had appointed him to his household and often had the young man keep him company. It happened, however, that at Cluny the king, impressed by Boucicaut's growing merit, was fonder of him than ever before. He therefore wished to have him attached to his, the king's, own court; when he made the request to the duke of Bourbon, the latter agreed because of the advancement it

68 The galley was the workhorse of the Mediterranean, for trade or warfare: a flat-built single-deck sea-going vessel propelled by sails and oars, with twenty-five to twenty-eight benches for the rowers; see R. Gardiner and J. Morrison, *The Age of the Galley: Mediterranean Oared Vessels Since Pre-Classical Times* (London, 1995), passim. The editors distinguish several different types of galley: see *great galley* (below, part II, note 77), *galee soubtille* (below, part III, note 75), and *galee complie* and *grande galee huissière* (below, part I, note 177).

69 King Charles VI visited the abbey of Cluny from 11 to 13 October 1389.

meant for Boucicaut who was thus appointed permanently to the royal court, and accompanied the king on the journey to the Languedoc.[70] [66]

Love and Valour, as we know, often inspire in the virtuous a wish to perform honourable deeds which enhance their reputations; Boucicaut, accordingly, was inspired to undertake an exploit of the highest and most courtly order, one which no knight in the whole of Christendom had for many years undertaken. His act bears witness to the old proverb, that it is deed not word that makes the man – and it shows how far he was by nature inclined to bravery, for there is no doubt that the man who is naturally drawn to heroism will devote all his time and effort to showing himself deserving of a reputation for dauntlessness; he will never be satisfied simply to rest on his laurels. That this is the case is amply demonstrated by the life-story of my lord Boucicaut, and by his determination to devote his youth to chivalric greatness. Ever restless, feeling that he could never do too much to build his reputation, [67] he had no sooner accomplished one valiant deed than he would devise another. This time, his emprise was as follows: having sought the king's permission, he sent word to princes, knights and squires in a number of kingdoms and Christian regions – England, Spain, Aragon, Germany, Italy – to say that in company with two other knights, Renaud de Roye and the lord of Sempy, he would hold the field of combat for a full thirty days (unless called away by some inescapable duty), between 20 March and 20 April; the field would be between Calais and Boulogne, at a place known as Saint-Inglevert. The three knights would take up station there, and be ready to challenge all comers to the joust, every day except Friday; the challenge would involve five passes at the joust with each comer, and the weapon would be the lance, or the lance with coronel;[71] if the challengers were enemies to France they might request either weapon; [68] if they were allies, the five passes would be at lance with coronel. The challenge was sent out some three months before the due date – deliberately so, since Boucicaut wished those at a distance to have sufficient time, and since he wished to publicise the *entreprise* and attract as many challengers as possible.[72]

As the due date drew near, Boucicaut took leave of the king and he and his companions went to set up camp at Saint-Inglevert.[73] He had his pavilion – which was particularly beautiful and richly appointed – erected in a broad meadow; his two companions did likewise, in a fine array. A little in front of the three pavilions was

70 Boucicaut and Eu joined the king on his journey south to Avignon for the coronation of Louis II duke of Anjou as king of Jerusalem and of Sicily on 1 November 1389.

71 A coronel was a crown-shaped lance-head, with four blunted tines, used for jousts of peace; it gave the lance purchase on the opponent's armour without being too dangerous.

72 The challenge was issued on 20 November 1389.

73 The jousts almost certainly started on 21 March 1390. Saint-Inglevert was barely ten miles west of Calais, held by the English, and so on 9 March, Richard II had granted safe conducts to the three French knights to stage the event there. For the event at Saint-Inglevert, see E. Gaucher, 'Les joutes de Saint-Inglevert: perception et écriture d'un événement historique pendant la guerre de Cent Ans', *Le Moyen Âge*, 102 (1996), pp. 229–43.

a great elm-tree: on each of three of its lower branches, they hung two shields, one signifying war, the other peace – and interestingly, even the shield of war was made entirely of wood, with no component of steel or iron. Beside each set of shields, the champions had set ten lances, five for war, five for peace. Hanging on the elm was a horn, to be blown by anyone requesting a joust; if he was seeking a joust *à outrance*, he was to strike the war shield; if he intended a blunted weapon, he was to strike the peace shield. Each of the champions had had his shields painted with his own arms, so that they could distinguish to which of them the challenge was directed. [69] In addition to the pavilions I have mentioned, Boucicaut had had another large one erected for arming the challengers, and to allow for their rest and recuperation. Once any challenger had struck the appropriate shield, the appropriate defender was to come out fully armed, on his destrier, his lance raised, ready to spur into action; if all three shields were struck at once, then all three defenders would emerge together. As a result, Boucicaut's arrangements were well installed, and he provisioned the site with excellent wines and meats, and with everything else that might be needed: enough to ensure that he could hold table for all comers during the whole event, and all at his own expense. And of course the champions were not alone in the countryside: a fine company of knights and gentlemen accompanied them, along with a household of attendants and servants for each. There was also quite a crowd of heralds, trumpeters, minstrels ... people of all degree. And as you will have heard, [70] the whole installation was complete and in place by the end of thirty days.

When the first day of the emprise dawned, each champion was armed and ready in his pavilion, waiting for the first challenger. Boucicaut was particularly finely equipped: confidently expecting there to be a number of challengers, English as well as of other nationalities, he was determined, in the event of such a challenge, to show himself prepared for combat in any mode. It was at this time that he firt adopted the motto that he maintained throughout his life, 'As you will'; thereafter, he had it painted upon all his shields and emblems.[74]

The English, who have always been hostile to the French, and who have always tried to get the better of them and do them down, heard news of this most honourable emprise.[75] Many of them, and those high-ranking, swore that the event would not happen without their taking part. As a result, on the first day, a number of them, richly equipped and escorted, [71] and among the highest of the English aristocracy, were present: I shall name them in due course.[76]

74 This motto, 'Ce que vous vouldrez', appears in many of the illuminations in the Book of Hours of Marshal Boucicaut (Paris, Musée Jacquemart-André, MS 2).

75 On 18 July 1389, Richard II and Charles VI had agreed a three-year truce suspending the Anglo-French war.

76 Contemporary accounts listed forty-two participants in the combats, including the three French defenders. See Froissart, *Oeuvres*, XIV, pp. 106–51, together with the *Chronique du Religieux de Saint-Denys contenant le règne de Charles VI, de 1380 à 1422*, ed. L.F. Bellaguet, 6 volumes (Paris, 1839–52), I, pp. 672–83.

On this first day, as my lord Boucicaut and his companions were waiting fully armed in their pavilions, Sir John Holland, brother to King Richard [II] of England, appeared with a sizeable escort; he was fully armed on his destrier, with trumpeters sounding before him.[77] So escorted, by a number of notables, he rode ceremoniously round the field of battle, then rode up to the signal horn and blew it loudly, after which his bascinet was laced up; he then went and struck Boucicaut's war shield. At that, you might have seen Boucicaut ride out, straight as a die, on his destrier, his lance upright against his shoulder, his heralds in front, and with a fine retinue; he took up position and halted briefly, then spurred towards the challenger, a doughty warrior who spurred just as hard towards Boucicaut. They duly met, and dealt each other such mighty blows on their shields[78] that both of them were bent backwards, and their lances shattered. The spectators shouted their names; the champions wheeled round, were given new lances, and spurred towards each other again, with similar results. [72] Thus they completed the designated five blows while in the saddle, all with the lance, so valiantly that they could only be admired. At the fourth course, however, as the lances shattered, the momentum of their heavy destriers was such that the horse of the English knight was forced back on its haunches, and would have fallen had it not been supported by bystanders; Boucicaut's horse, by contrast, tottered but did not fall. Once the five courses had been run, the two champions withdrew to their pavilions – but Boucicaut got little respite, for more English knights were demanding jousts; he undertook two more series, thus completing fifteen courses which he did with such success and such bravery that he was universally praised. While Boucicaut himself was engaged in the joust, we must not imagine that his companions stayed idle: they too were challenged to the joust, and responded with such success that they too won universal admiration. I don't know why I should draw out my account by describing every blow exchanged; I shall simply say that during the thirty days that the emprise lasted, Boucicaut's adversaries were first John Holland, [73] and then Lord Derby (now Henry, king of England), who ran ten courses with the lance – because the duke of Lancaster his father wrote to say that he, the duke, wanted to send his son to learn chivalry from Boucicaut, given that he was so valiant on the field, and begged the French champion to run a further five.[79] Thereafter Boucicaut's

77 John Holland (c.1352–1400), earl of Huntingdon and later duke of Exeter, was the half-brother of King Richard II through their mother Joan (d.1385), daughter of Edmund of Woodstock, earl of Kent. While chroniclers like Froissart had lauded Holland's youthful prowess in formal combats, the Englishman was also renowned for his violent temper.

78 The author here uses the term *targe*: this is a round shield, whereas the usual term *escu* indicates a kite-shaped shield.

79 In 1390, Henry Bolingbroke (1367–1413) held the titles of earl of Derby and Northampton, and would subsequently become duke of Hereford in 1397 and then duke of Lancaster upon the death of his father John of Gaunt in 1399.

adversaries were the earl marshal,[80] Lord Beaumont,[81] Lord Thomas Percy,[82] Lord Clifford, Lord Courtenay,[83] and a throng of some six-score knights and squires from England alone, and from other countries – Spain, Germany, etc. – more than forty more, and all of them jousting *à outrance*. And against all of them Boucicaut and his companions fought the requisite courses – except in those cases where the challengers were wounded, for several of the English were carried to the ground, horse and all, and badly hurt: Sir John Holland, among others, was wounded almost to death, and so were a number of others. Boucicaut himself, however, and his true and tested companions, were by God's mercy unhurt.[84] And thus our champion pursued his emprise for the full thirty days. And he emerged with the greatest honour paid by the king and the knighthood of France, and to the highest praise for himself and his companions, [74] who had thereby won eternal honour. When the jousts were over, Boucicaut returned to Paris with his companions and their retinues; here he was received most jubilantly by the king and the whole court, and was deservedly feted and honoured by the ladies.

XVIII: How my lord Boucicaut went for a third time to Prussia, and how he determined to avenge the death of my lord William Douglas.

Not long after Boucicaut returned from his emprise, the duke of Bourbon, with a large army, undertook an expedition to Barbary to fight the Saracens.[85] Boucicaut was overjoyed at the news, assuming that he would be one of the party; but when he asked leave of the king, the latter made it unambiguously clear that permission would not be given. Boucicaut was very much disappointed, so much so that he refused to stay at court, no matter what incentives the king offered; he made strenuous efforts

80 Thomas Mowbray (1366–99), earl of Nottingham and later duke of Norfolk, jousted against both Renaud de Roye and Boucicaut.

81 Henry Beaumont was admiral of England and captain of Calais, and jousted against Boucicaut on 21 March. He was a diplomat for Richard II's marriage negotiations in 1396.

82 Thomas Percy (c.1343–1403) was a knight of the Garter and had served as admiral under Gaunt during his expedition to Castile in 1386–7. Thomas's brother Henry (1341–1408), earl of Northumberland, was one of the two judges at Saint-Inglevert, alongside Lancelot de La Personne (d.1398).

83 For Peter Courtenay and Thomas Clifford, see pp. 42–4 above.

84 According to Froissart, *Oeuvres*, XIV, p. 110, the French and the English spectators agreed that Boucicaut and Holland had jousted well, in large part because neither had been injured. But the *Chronique du Religieux de Saint-Denys*, I, p. 660, claimed that Boucicaut spent nine days in bed because of his wounds.

85 Between July and October 1390, Louis de Bourbon led the Mahdian or Barbary Crusade that temporarily captured Al-Mahdiya, a coastal city in modern Tunisia that was the principal port for the Hafsid dynasty in the fourteenth century.

to get permission to go to Prussia again instead. [75] Once permission was given, he departed immediately, fearing that the king might revoke it.[86] But once he got there, he discovered that there was to be no *Reise* that season – the winter was not cold enough[87] – so he determined to stay in Prussia to be ready for the summer *Reise*. While he was there, after some time, he was joined by his brother Geoffroy, sometimes known as Boucicaut the Younger and who had been with the duke of Bourbon in Barbary for more than eight months. The two brothers were delighted to see each other. And while they were waiting for the summer *Reise*, Boucicaut received a message from the king to say that he intended an expedition himself, and wished to have the young man with him: he was to return immediately, without delay.[88] Boucicaut could not, of course, refuse the summons, even though he was disappointed; he set off immediately, and travelled tirelessly until he reached Flanders. While he was in Brussels, [76] he received a message that the king had been advised by his council to change his plans: [Boucicaut] was to do as he pleased, either coming to Paris or returning to Prussia – and Boucicaut gladly returned to where he had come from.

He had reached Königsberg [Conisbert] on his way back, and there, by chance, he met up with a party of knights who were also heading for the summer *Reise*; while they were in Königsberg, one of their number, a valiant Scottish knight called Sir William Douglas, was treacherously killed by some English.[89] When Boucicaut, who had, incidentally, no acquaintance with Douglas and was therefore acting out of sheer goodness, learned of this dirty deed – one that would naturally be treated with revulsion by all men of good character – he found it so abominable that he swore vengeance; no other knight or squire was ready to take the lead – although Königsberg contained a large number of Scottish knights, all of whom stayed resolutely silent. Boucicaut let it be known to all the English there that if none of them was prepared to say that Douglas had been killed treasonably by some of their number, he himself would deliver a personal challenge, and be prepared to fight the cause of the slain knight. The English refused to take up the challenge, saying that if one of the Scots there present wished to issue a summons, [77] then they would respond; they did not,

86 Boucicaut left France in December 1390, after securing funding for his expedition from Louis, duke of Touraine (1372–1407), who two years later exchanged that duchy for Orléans.

87 The winter *Reise* depended upon temperatures cold enough to freeze rivers and marshes.

88 Charles VI had planned a military expedition in support of the Avignonese Pope Clement VII (1378–94) and his efforts to regain control of Rome from the rival claimant to the papal see, Boniface IX (1389–1404). This expedition was intended to depart from Lyon on 15 March 1391 but was suspended when Charles agreed to meet with King Richard II by 24 June 1392, to discuss an Anglo-French peace treaty.

89 Sir William Douglas, lord of Nithsdale (c.1360–91) was ambushed and killed at some point between June and August 1391, after blaming a group of English crusading knights for the fact that he and his party were prevented from receiving Mass in Königsberg because of their adherence to Pope Clement VII. The situation may have been triggered by the personal animosity between the Scotsman and one of Boucicaut's challengers at Saint-Inglevert, Thomas Clifford, 6th Baron Clifford (1362/3–91).

however, wish to have anything to do with Boucicaut. That was how things stood when Boucicaut went off to Prussia for the summer *Reise*, which was, as it happens, one of the greatest and most honourable for many years, for the grand master of the Teutonic Order had died earlier that year, and his successor raised so large an army that no fewer than 200,000 horse passed into Lithuania [Lectho] where they crushed a large force of Saracens and stormed many of their castles.[90] Boucicaut, seeing the size and magnificence of the Christian forces, and seeing how great was the company of knights and squires and gentlemen from France and elsewhere, was among the first to raise his standard and did deeds so admirable that he was universally praised; at his instigation and that of the grand master, and in the face of the enemy, a great castle was built on an island in Lithuania, in enemy territory; they called it, in French, the Chastel des Chevaliers,[91] and during the build the grand master and Boucicaut himself spent some time on the site to prevent enemy attacks – after which they returned to Prussia. [78]

XIX: How Boucicaut was made Marshal of France.

While Boucicaut was in Prussia, as we have explained, the marshal of Blainville died.[92] As the old *ballade* says, 'If you are loved, you're not forgot, Because you're far away'; the good king of France, who had a great affection for Boucicaut, indeed still has and will have as has been often made clear, this time made his affection very obvious: although many notables, immediately the marshal was dead, vied for the honour of succeeding him, and although Boucicaut himself was absent and had been for more than a year, the noble king remembered the young man and determined that none but Boucicaut should be marshal; the king sent word that he should return to Paris without delay. The king's message reached Boucicaut, as it happened, when he was already on his way back from Prussia. The young man, hearing the news, hastened his return. [79]

When he neared the French border, he heard that the king was in Touraine, and he turned his steps there and found him in the city of Tours;[93] oddly enough, he found the king lodged in the mansion where he himself had been born and where his father had lived during his lifetime. Boucicaut fell to his knees before the king, and humbly paid his respects. When the king saw him, he was naturally delighted;

90 In 1391, Konrad von Wallenrode (c.1330–93) succeeded Konrad Zöllner von Rottenstein as the grand master of the Teutonic Order.

91 This was almost certainly Ritterswerder, built on an island half a mile from the city of Kaunas.

92 Jean IV de Mauquenchy (c.1322–91), lord of Blainville had succeeded his father as marshal of France in 1368. Boucicaut's father, Jean I Le Meingre, had served as marshal from 1356 until his death in 1367.

93 Charles VI arrived in Tours on 12 November 1391, and met with Boucicaut upon the latter's arrival on 23 December.

I do not believe that for many years, any other knight had enjoyed such a reception. The king said: 'We are told that your father lived in this mansion, and is buried in this town; you were born in this very chamber. We intend to appoint you, in the city of your birth, to the post held by your father. To do you full honour, on Christmas day next, after Mass, we shall confer on you the marshal's baton and administer the customary oath.' Boucicaut, still on his knees, thanked the king with all due humility, as was proper. And on Christmas day, my lord Boucicaut rose early and dressed fittingly and opulently; [80] there were present to escort him many knights and squires, and many of his lineage and affinity. When the time came, he joined the king at Mass. Once Mass had been sung, the duke of Bourbon – who was very fond of him, had raised him, and raised him well and affectionately – led him to the king's presence; he was also attended by many other lords and knights. Boucicaut fell to his knees before the king; the king in his turn welcomed him warmly, and invested him with the office of marshal by handing him the baton. There also was the duke of Burgundy, the king's uncle, who desired personally to administer the oath, although normally that duty fell to the chancellor of France there present.[94] There also were present Olivier de Clisson, then constable of France,[95] and my lord Jean de Vienne,[96] then admiral of France, and a great number of barons who all agreed that the office of marshal could not be in better hands. In this way Boucicaut was appointed marshal of France.

And this is the moment to note the great virtues of this knight who might have emerged from the annals of Roman chivalry, for at that time, when certain boys were thought, in their youth, to be more inclined than their peers to the love and pursuit of arms, [81] and to train with such unusual ardour that even in their boyhood they achieved demanding deeds, and improved their skills daily, their elders would take such leanings as signs that the boys would in later life become men of valour. Accordingly, and even at a very young age, the Romans would promote such boys to the ranks of knighthood, and make them dukes, constables, and commanders of very large armies, despite the fact that, normally, no-one would be appointed to such an office below the age, say, of thirty; the Romans, however, would promote such boys beyond what would be allowed for the common run of their peers. Such boys, they believed, would be the more inspired to passionate love of arms by their rapid promotion; an example could be seen, for instance, in the case of Pompey, that most valiant knight, who showed such outstanding promise in boyhood that by the age of twenty-two he was consul of Rome – an office equivalent to our duke or constable.[97]

94 The chancellor of France from 1388 to 1398 was Arnaud de Corbie (1325–1414).

95 Olivier de Clisson (1336–1407) succeeded Jean I Le Meingre as constable of France from 1380 to 1392.

96 Jean de Vienne (1341–96) was appointed admiral of France by Charles V in 1373.

97 Pompey the Great (106–48 BC) was a Roman military and political leader whose success enabled him to advance directly to his first consulship in 70 BC alongside Crassus, without meeting the normal requirements for office. Gonesse had discussed this in his translation and

Boucicaut, I believe, was as a boy very similar to Pompey: [82] he had many years of achievement in boyhood, his virtues grew from day to day, and thus he was deemed worthy of the high office of marshal of France at the age of twenty-five, the age at which the king granted him the office. And truly, his young age was no bar to his living up to the honour conferred on him, for his goodness, his valour and his virtues exceeded any temptation he might feel to succumb to the follies of youth; he was as mature beyond his years at twenty as others might be at fifty, and he persisted in the same admirable ways thereafter, as will become obvious in those of his deeds that we shall describe here.

XX: How Marshal Boucicaut accompanied the king to negotiations at Boulogne, and how the king entrusted him with troops for further expeditions, and how he took the town of Ussac [le roc-du-sac].

When the king had appointed Boucicaut marshal, he returned to Paris with the said marshal. [83] Boucicaut remained at court for the whole of that winter, taking part in games and entertainments with the ladies who were all delighted with his presence, for just as he was apt for arms, so he was agreeable and graceful in occupations pleasing to ladies and damsels, and this made him very popular and very welcome. At that time there was a truce between France and England, so he was able to stay longer at court.[98] The following summer, still during the truce, the king held a parliament in Amiens; with him were his brother the duke of Orléans, his uncles the dukes of Berry, Burgundy and Bourbon, many others of the blood royal, and many more of the nobility, as well as all the captains of France, Clisson the constable, the marshal of Sancerre,[99] Marshal Boucicaut, the admiral of Vienne, and along with them a throng of lords and knights and squires. An English delegation also came to the parliament; it included the duke of Lancaster, and consisted of a party of lords and knights and squires. A peace treaty was discussed, but not finalised.[100]

The king returned to Paris, but soon there arose [84] a dispute between him and the duke of Brittany;[101] in response, the king gathered a sizeable army of men-at-arms, of

commentary upon Valerius Maximus, VIII, c.15.8, in BNF MS fr. 282, fols 342d–343a, which was also the source for Christine de Pizan in *Le livre du corps de policie*, ed. A.J. Kennedy (Paris, 1998), pp. 61–2 (II, c.4).

98 The kings of France and England had agreed a truce at Leulinghen on 18 June 1389.

99 Louis de Sancerre (1341/2–1402) was constable of France from 1397 until his death.

100 The Amiens conference (26 March to 8 April 1392) failed to secure a permanent peace treaty, but did result in an extension of the truce until Michaelmas 1393.

101 Jean IV de Montfort, duke of Brittany (1365–99) had refused to surrender Pierre de Craon (c.1345–c.1409) who had attempted to murder Olivier de Clisson during the night of 13 June 1392.

which he took command in person. In the course of this expedition, the king appointed Boucicaut to an important command, that is, of some six hundred men-at-arms – who were delighted to find themselves under his control; indeed, such was the affection that the noblemen felt for him and the respect in which they held him, that no fewer than four hundred men-at-arms, in addition to the original six hundred, came to submit themselves to his command, and felt honoured to do so; he meanwhile, as a wise commander, understood how to train and command his forces so that every member loved and feared him. In the course of this expedition, the king appointed the marshal to the command of half of Guyenne, and ordered that once the king had completed his enterprise and returned north, Boucicaut should take a company of knights and go into Auvergne to lay siege to a great castle called Ussac which the English had taken during the truce.[102] The king himself went as far as Le Mans, [85] but forbore to go further because of a sickness to which he succumbed.[103] So his own expedition was cut short, but as from Le Mans, Boucicaut assumed command and headed at all speed into Auvergne to set siege before Ussac;[104] he disposed his forces in a way which was greatly admired by all, and which showed that he was already endowed with all the skills needed for his office. The assault was ferocious for several days, for the castle was very well defended, and the siege saw many admirable deeds, but in the end the castle could not hold out, and the defenders surrendered to the marshal; the conduct of the siege was much admired, for the defence had been fierce, and Boucicaut's success had required considerable strategic sense and considerable effort.

XXI: How the marshal went to Guyenne and took a number of fortresses.

The year following the taking of Ussac, news came to the king that the English had taken a town called Domme [Le Dompne] in Auvergne; the king ordered the count of Eu, by then constable, [86] to go into Auvergne along with the marshal to lay siege to the town.[105] The constable and the marshal took leave of court, intending to fulfil the king's commission. When they arrived in Limoges, they found that the marshal of Sancerre was also in the country and had already negotiated the surrender of Domme.[106]

102 On 18 June 1392, Charles VI appointed Boucicaut captain general in Poitou, Berry, Auvergne and all the other lands in the duchy of Guyenne held by the duke of Berry, just before the royal expedition left Paris for Le Mans on 12 July. Boucicaut retained this title until 31 January 1395.

103 On 5 August 1392, Charles VI suffered the first episode of the mental problems that would afflict him throughout the rest of his reign.

104 Ussac is located in the Limousin, two hundred and fifty miles south of Le Mans. The siege was completed by 22 October 1392.

105 Philippe d'Artois, count of Eu (1358–97) was appointed constable of France in 1392.

106 Louis de Sancerre and the seneschal Guichard Dulphe secured the surrender of Domme on 22 May 1393.

They therefore resolved to shame the English into not breaking truces; they summoned all the English captains who commanded castles and fortresses in the Auvergne, and made them swear to uphold all truces; this done, they returned to France.

A year later, however, still during a truce, the English – notorious for breaking their promises – captured two castles, Le Cor and La Roche, on the border between Saintonge and the Angoumois; the castles were being held against the king by a certain Perrot Le Béarnais.[107] The king ordered Boucicaut to take a force of five hundred men-at-arms to lay siege to the castles, [87] but that he should first go to Bordeaux to require the duke of Lancaster to return the castles taken during the truce. The marshal fulfilled the order, went to Bordeaux and duly found the duke of Lancaster who welcomed him warmly and honourably. The marshal conveyed the king's request, pointing out how dishonourable it was for the English to break the truce and betray their solemn oaths; they should accordingly render any castles taken by treachery. The duke of Lancaster replied honourably, saying that the deeds had been done without his consent or his knowledge; he promised full restitution, and full amends such as he, Boucicaut, might impose. Lancaster sent word immediately to Perrot Le Béarnais, saying he should render the castles immediately and make good any damage, otherwise he, Lancaster, would come in person to lay siege to them. The two castles were immediately rendered, and all damage was made good; the marshal stayed all season in that region, and since this was a time of truce, he frequently found himself with the English; they enjoyed talking about deeds of arms and knighthood. At the end of the season he returned to court.[108] [88]

XXII: Here we start to talk about the expedition to Hungary, and how the count of Eu encouraged the marshal to take part.[109]

It was at this point that the expedition to Hungary was mounted; it was so notable an event, and so many people have wanted to hear the full story and the full truth of an event that has been described in such contradictory ways, that I shall give a full and true account, from beginning to end, of the whole affair, and its causes. First, let me say that the count of Eu, close cousin to the king of France, valiant and young as he was and much travelled, had made many honourable expeditions around the world – among them one to Hungary, along with the marshal as we saw above. The king of Hungary had paid him much honour, and shown every sign of friendship and affection. Because of this alliance and affinity, the king of Hungary sent word by a

107 See note 47 above.

108 Boucicaut left Guyenne at the end of August 1394.

109 For Boucicaut's involvement in the Nicopolis Crusade, see N. Housley, 'Le Maréchal Boucicaut à Nicopolis', *Annales de Bourgogne*, 68 (1996), pp. 85–99. It is striking that the biographer makes no reference whatsoever to Boucicaut's membership of the international crusading Order of the Passion. See p. 2n. above.

herald [89] that the Sultan Bayezid was threatening him with some 40,000 Saracens, 10,000 horse and 30,000 foot.[110] He, the king, had resolved to do battle with him. All good Christians and valiant men of good breeding should sacrifice themselves in the service of the Christian faith, and should support each other against the unbelievers; accordingly he asked the count's aid in his endeavours, and begged him to contact Marshal Boucicaut in whose goodness and valour he had great faith; he also asked the count to advertise the expedition to all good knights and squires who might wish to demonstrate their valour and sense of honour; the expedition, he said, was most honourable, and he had need of their help and support.[111]

When the count of Eu heard the news, he immediately notified the marshal who determined to join the expedition; he replied that, God willing, he would definitely take part, and for three reasons: first because he wished more than anything to do battle against the Saracens; second because of the friendly reception he had had from the king of Hungary, and third because his friendship for the count, and his pleasure in his company, made him resolved to take part. The news of the expedition quickly spread everywhere, so much so that the present duke of Burgundy, then count of Nevers, heard tell of it.[112] He was then in the flower of his youth and wanted to follow the path of virtue [90] – that is, the path of honour and knighthood; he considered that he could do no better in life than devote himself from an early age, and at personal risk, to the service of God, and so longed to join the expedition; he therefore pestered his father, the then duke of Burgundy, to give him leave. News of this was carried everywhere in France, and because the truce meant that knights and squires had little chance to fight in wars, many young lords of the blood royal, and many barons and noblemen, wished to take part to avoid idleness and use their time and effort in the pursuit of chivalry;[113] they believed, rightly, that there could be no more honourable expedition than one in the service of God. News about it spread all over France, and knowing the rank and reputation of those who had promised to take part, there was barely a knight or squire in condition to depart who did not wish to join in. I shall demonstrate this by naming those who did so:

First and greatest, there was the count of Nevers, now duke of Burgundy, first cousin to the king of France; then there were my lords Henri and Philippe de Bar, brothers and first cousins to the king;[114] the count of La Marche;[115] the count of Eu,

110 Bayezid I was sultan of the Ottoman Turks from 1389 to 1403.

111 In August 1395, a Hungarian embassy led by János Kanizsai, archbishop of Gran (Esztergom), arrived in Paris to encourage French support for a crusade.

112 Jean of Burgundy (1371–1419), count of Nevers, would become duke of Burgundy in 1405, following the death of his father, Philip the Bold.

113 On 27 May 1394, the truce between the French and the English was extended until Michaelmas 1398.

114 Henri de Bar (1362–97) and Philippe de Bar (1372–96) were the oldest sons of Robert I duke of Bar (1344–1411).

115 Jacques II de Bourbon (1370–1438) inherited the counties of La Marche and Castres from his father Jean I in 1393. From 1415 to 1419, Jacques was king consort of Naples.

constable and cousin to the king.[116] Of the barons, there were the lord of Coucy,[117] [91] marshal Boucicaut, the lord of La Trémoïlle,[118] my lord Jean de Vienne admiral of France,[119] the lord of Heugueville,[120] and many other knights and squires, upwards of one thousand of the very flower of knighthood and nobility in France. We should note here the courage and goodwill that the valiant French have always shown, and still do, in the pursuit of arms, in which service they expend strength, life and riches – for note that although they had rightly made the count of Nevers their leader, everyone was present at his own expense, except of course those who were in attendance on a particular lord or baron. As an example, Marshal Boucicaut, at his own expense, took seventy gentlemen, fifteen of them knights in service to his family – that is, my lord [Jean des Barres, known as] le Barrois, my lords Jean and Godemart de Linières, my lord Robert de Chauvigny, my lord Robert de Milly, my lord Jean d'Egreville, and others amounting to the number given;[121] other lords took equivalent retinues, and the count of Nevers in particular took a large contingent of the gentlemen attached to his father's court and his own. [92]

XXIII: How the count of Nevers, the present duke of Burgundy, resolved on an expedition to Hungary, and how he was made captain of the whole French contingent.

When the count of Nevers and the other barons had made every preparation for the expedition, they took leave of the king, the queen, the other nobility, and their fathers and relatives.[122] I can well imagine the grief, the tears and sobs of the loved ones, and of the mothers and wives, sisters and kinswomen, and not without cause, for the expedition was dangerous, as indeed it transpired; had they foreseen the terrible news that would be brought back to them, their hearts might in some cases have been broken. The departure of the host inspired pity given how many were never to return. But the count of Nevers set out with his fine company, and travelled through Germany and then Austria [93] until he arrived in Hungary.[123] News was brought to the king of Hungary, who was then in the city of Buda [Bonde], of the arrival of the count of

116 See note 105 above.

117 Enguerrand VII, lord of Coucy (1340–97), who did not die at Nicopolis, *pace* p. 68.

118 Guy VI de La Trémoïlle (1346–97), lord of Jonvelle, was the grand chamberlain of Philippe le Hardi duke of Burgundy. Both Guy and his brother Guillaume, marshal of Burgundy from 1392 to 1397, took part in the Nicopolis expedition.

119 See note 96 above.

120 Jean de Hangest, lord of Heugueville (d.1415).

121 Boucicaut was also accompanied by Renaud de Roye and Jean de Sempy.

122 Jean de Nevers took his leave from King Charles VI on 6 April 1396, and the expedition gathered at Montbéliard before the departure on 30 April.

123 The French contingent travelled via Alsace, Bavaria and Vienna before arriving in July at Buda, capital of the kingdom of Hungary.

Nevers with a great company of lords of the fleur-de-lis and of other high-born barons and gentlemen who were coming to his aid. The king was delighted, and, as soon as he could, he came to meet them with a large escort; he himself had already gathered a large contingent of men-at-arms, some foreign, others from Hungary itself. As the king arrived, he greeted the count with great respect, as he did those of the blood royal and the other barons; he welcomed them warmly and honourably. Then he led them to Buda where he did them all honour, and gave them all the comforts he could.

They had not been there long when the king of Hungary, in concert with the French lords who longed for nothing more than battle, issued orders for his own men to gather in good array and as was fitting in such circumstances; a few days later, they took to the field to advance on the Saracens who, they were told, were approaching. And when the army was fully drawn up, the king of Hungary calculated that counting his own troops with both the French and the other foreigners, he had at his command some 100,000 horse.

At the Hungarian border, they came to the Danube [Dunoe] and forded it. Beyond the river was a great walled city called Vidin [Bondius] [94] which had declared for the Turks; our people decided to attack it.[124] In the field before Vidin the count of Nevers was dubbed knight, as were the count of La Marche and many others. The day after the army's arrival, they attacked the city in force, but no sooner had the attack started than out came the emperor of that country,[125] who was Orthodox Greek, and had been forced into submission by the Turks; he had come to surrender the city and the country as a whole to the king of Hungary, and he entrusted to the latter's army the keeping of all the Turks then resident in the city.

XXIV: Of the many towns that the king of Hungary captured from the Turks in alliance with the good knights of France, and how the valiant Marshal Boucicaut performed admirably.

Once the city of Vidin had been taken, as you have heard, the king of Hungary pushed on with his army to another large town called Oryahovo [Raco].[126] [95] Once the count of Eu and Marshal Boucicaut realised that that was the king's destination, they undertook to ensure that they would arrive first. Along with a number of the great lords – my lord Philippe de Bar, the count of La Marche, the lord of Coucy, the seneschal of Eu and others – they rode all night so that they arrived at Oryahovo by

124 Vidin is a Bulgarian port town on the southern bank of the Danube, just over four hundred miles south-east of Budapest.

125 Ivan Stratsimir (1324/5–97) was the emperor (tsar) of Bulgaria from 1356 to 1396. As a result of Ottoman military success in 1388, Stratsimir had become a vassal of Sultan Murad I and then of his son Bayezid I, and had accepted an Ottoman garrison in Vidin.

126 Oryahovo is a port located around seventy-five miles east of Vidin along the river Danube. Boucicaut may have arrived there early in September.

morning. Once the enemy saw their approach, however, they made a sortie in force intending to destroy a bridge across the great moat, which prevented anyone getting near the walls or the defences of the city; so deep was the moat that the only way to get across it was via the bridge. Our men galloped over to prevent the Saracens from destroying the bridge. The Saracens and our men confronted each other, and our men attacked with great vigour and courage; the Saracens were intent on destroying the bridge, so their strategy was to have half their men pursuing the battle while the remainder were sent to break up the bridge. Their strategy was in vain, however, for the valiant marshal, as the promoter of the emprise, requested the count of Eu to allow him to guard the bridge – a difficult task since more and more Saracens were coming up – and permission was granted. The marshal guarded it valiantly, so much so that none of the Saracens could get near it; [96] the marshal himself did great deeds of arms, pushing back the Saracens by sheer force of arms into the town; they sallied out again and again, but each time he returned to the attack with such force that they were driven back again. To cut a long story short: he performed so well that he demonstrated once again his prowess in arms. The count of Eu and the other French barons who were with him were fighting the other contingent of Saracens that we described; they launched such an onslaught that they forced the Saracens to fall back into the town, and killed many of them.

In the course of the day the king of Hungary came up with his army, and set up his dispositions for an attack on the town. Seeing this, Marshal Boucicaut sent some of his men into a nearby wood and commissioned them to make two long siege-ladders. When he saw the press of men hastening to the attack, he said to his own men: 'It would be a source of great shame if other men were to be first over the bridge that we have been guarding. So, my dear friends and companions, let us act so as to acquire honour and renown.' With those words, he took the lead and all his men followed him most eagerly. He took up station close to the wall, and had the ladders brought up. [97] Then he and his men began the attack before anyone else could come up. You would have been amazed by their remarkable feats of arms, for the courage of their leader made all of them lion-hearted, and so eager were they to scale the walls that they almost overloaded the ladders and broke them. There followed a great battle between the attackers who were intent on mounting the walls, and the defenders who defied them vigorously. They exchanged great blows, and many were killed and wounded on both sides. The Saracens on the other hand managed to destroy one of the ladders with the rocks they hurled down; at the head of the other was Hugues de Chevenon bearing the marshal's standard, and he fought fiercely, but the enemy attacked him with such vigour that they tore the standard from his hands and in the end managed to throw down the ladder so that he was badly bruised and hurt, although his fellows ran forward to drag him out of the press. The assault remained remarkably ferocious; by now the rest of the French, and the king of Hungary and his men, had arrived. The battle lasted until nightfall – and if the marshal had been among the first to arrive, he was also the last to leave, having done such feats of arms that day that news of his prowess spread abroad much to his honour; the same was true of his companions who had performed with such valour [98] that no-one could have done more. And although the marshal and his men were so exhausted that they could scarcely do any more, you must not imagine that they retreated for a rest; on the contrary, they stayed by the bridge to guard it against further Saracen attempts to destroy it – and I assure you that no-one was eager to take over the guard of the bridge.

The following day, as our men were preparing another assault, the inhabitants of the town, nearly all Orthodox Christians, realised that although their town was well fortified, they had no chance of defying the attackers for ever; they therefore surrendered to the king of Hungary in exchange for their lives and for their property. The king determined to accept the surrender on those terms in order to avoid further damage to his own army, and also because the defenders were indeed Christian. The marshal was deputed to ensure that they were unharmed; he entered the town with his men and accomplished his duty so well that the defenders were unscathed. The Christians delivered all the Turks to the king of Hungary, who had them all executed.[127]

This done, the king left to lay siege to the very well-fortified town of Nicopolis;[128] during the approach the marshal, asking only to be allowed to inflict damage on the Saracens, was informed by his scouts [99] of the hiding-places where the Saracens, in great numbers, were setting up ambushes in order to attack our men. In response, the marshal, because of his guile and his watchfulness, was able to fall on them before they were aware of his presence, and so several times he and his men inflicted great damage on them, killing large numbers. The count of Eu and the other French barons did the same and showed such prowess that the king of Hungary and all his followers were inspired to greater courage and came to believe that they need fear no-one.

Alas! Had it not been for the malice of Fortune, the Hungarians could have rejoiced in the coming of the noble company of the French. But Fortune so often brings harm to the good and the valiant, and this time she seemed to resent the excellent reputation that the French were acquiring. Ha! How can anyone resist Ill Fortune? When she wishes harm or mischief to anyone, she has no trouble inventing the means. Hercules the Great could not resist when he unknowingly donned the poisoned tunic.[129] [100] Great Hector too complained of Ill Fortune, he who had performed such great deeds of chivalry, when Achilles came up behind him and

127 According to another chronicler, Michel Pintouin, the inhabitants of Oryahovo were massacred without consideration of their religion, though the wealthy did escape by paying ransoms. *Chronique du Religieux de Saint-Denys*, II, p. 494.

128 Sigismund and the army arrived at Nicopolis, a stronghold controlling the lower Danube, on 12 September 1396.

129 Christine de Pizan discussed the misfortune of Hercules in *Le livre de la mutacion de fortune*, III, pp. 19–25 (vv. 13885–4058).

killed him.[130] The very city of Troy had never imagined that it could suffer from Ill Fortune – but it was destroyed.[131] Was not Alexander the Great, who had conquered all the world, slain in a moment by Ill Fortune?[132] Oh Hannibal, great emperor of Carthage, can you too not complain of her cruelty? Was she not playing with you when she raised you to such heights that you had overcome, conquered, subjugated Rome itself, and had no more to fear? And then a moment later, because she had developed a grudge against you, she undermined you in so many ways, and reduced you to such a state that no-one was lower than you; you had lost all, and had no place to lay your head, then, faithlessly, she led you to such despair that you took poison and killed yourself.[133] [101] What can we say of Pompey, most excellent prince of Rome, who having conquered most of the world fell into such disfavour with Fortune that he had to find miserable refuge with King Ptolemy of Egypt, who he thought to be his friend because he had restored him to his throne. But it was Fortune herself who directed Pompey's steps, for Ptolemy, ungrateful and treacherous as he was, had Pompey killed.[134] Oh Fortune, Fortune! Mad is anyone who does not fear your fickle turns, your double face, who has faith in your bounty, who trusts in your beneficence! For in an instant you can nullify the prosperity and success you have accorded your victim. [102]

XXV: Of the fierce battle known as the Battle of Hungary, and which pitted Christians against Turks.

To return to my story: when the king of Hungary and his army arrived before the city of Nicopolis, they set up an impressive camp, and then began to dig two large mines underground: the tunnels reached as far as the city walls, and were wide enough that three men-at-arms would be able to fight side by side. The siege lasted for some fifteen days. As events were going forward, the Turks, I imagine, did not sit idle; they devised great plans for an attack on the king of Hungary, but so covertly that the king never realised what was going on. I don't know if there was treachery among the king's scouts, or if there was some other trouble, but although he had set a good watch to notify him of any movement on the Saracen side, he

130 Pizan, *Le livre de la mutacion de fortune*, III, pp. 104–6 (vv. 16461–530).

131 Pizan, *Le livre de la mutacion de fortune*, III, pp. 152–7 (vv. 17897–8130).

132 Pizan, *Le livre de la mutacion de fortune*, IV, pp. 61–6 (vv. 23073–250).

133 These comments echo the French translation of Valerius Maximus in BNF MS fr. 282, fol. 385a (IX, c.5, ext. 4), as well as Pizan, *Le livre de la mutacion de fortune*, III, pp. 241–3 (vv. 20319–74) and *Livre du corps de policie*, pp. 31–2 (I, c.18).

134 This account of the death of Gnaeus Pompeius Magnus on 29 September 48 BC derived from Simon de Hesdin's commentary on Valerius Maximus, I, c.8.9, in BNF MS fr. 282, fols 65b–66b. The story was also cited by Christine de Pizan in *Le livre de la mutacion de fortune*, IV, p. 27 (vv. 22029–34).

heard nothing until fifteen days [103] after the beginning of the siege, and for that reason he had no suspicions.

On the sixteenth day, however, around dinner time, messengers hurried in to tell the king that Bayezid with his Turks and accompanied by an astonishingly large army was so close that he, the king, would scarcely have time to call his men to arms and to dispose his troops.[135] When the king, in his tent, heard this news, he was dismayed; he sent word throughout the army that they should take up arms and draw up in front of their lodgings. As you can imagine, the news sowed near panic in the crusading army: everyone scrambled into their arms as best they could. The king himself had already taken the field when messengers came to tell the count of Nevers, who was still at table, and the French in general that the Turks were very close, and that the king had taken up station on the field with his troops in battle-order. The count of Nevers and the French were naturally very annoyed that word had not been sent to them sooner – but worse was to come. Having been told the news, the count of Nevers and his men armed themselves, mounted and issued forth; they were very well organised, so they advanced towards the king where they found that the ranks were set up; [104] already the enemy's banners could be seen not far away.

I emphasise that, contrary to some defamatory reports that the French fled in groups of ten, twelve or twenty, completely chaotic, and therefore were killed in droves, this is not true.[136] Those who were present have reported to me – and it is their accounts that I use – that those knights who were most known for their valour and fidelity, those most deserving of credibility, the count of Nevers and all the lords and barons of France, with all their followings, reached the king's side with time to take up battle stations – which they did most correctly. And the count entrusted the banner of Our Lady – which the French commonly display in battle – to Jean de Vienne, admiral of France, as the most valiant and most experienced of those present; the banner was raised, as was right, in the centre of the host. And all equipment and weapons were deployed as appropriate to the circumstances.

The Turks meanwhile were drawing up battle lines and positioning horse and foot in good order; they had devised a cunning plan to trick our men. To start with, a large body of mounted Turks [105] set up in formation in front of their foot; behind the mounted troops, between each rider and those on foot, they set up a barrier of sharpened stakes, the stakes tilted forwards towards our men, and at a height where they would drive into the horses' bellies. This they did at the double – their men

135 The battle of Nicopolis took place on 25 September 1396.

136 Following the disaster at Nicopolis, there were severe criticisms of the lack of discipline, organisation and courage shown by the Christians, for example from Michel Pintouin in the *Chronique du Religieux de Saint-Denys,* II, 492–514, and from Philippe de Mézières in *Une epistre lamentable et consolatoire adressée en 1397 à Philippe le Hardi, duc de Bourgogne, sur la défaite de Nicopolis (1396)*, ed. Philippe Contamine and Jacques Paviot (Paris, 2008). Also see E. Gaucher, 'Deux regards sur une défaite: Nicopolis (d'après la *Chronique de Saint-Denis* et le *Livre des faits de Boucicaut*)', *Cahiers de recherches médiévales,* 1 (1996), pp. 93–104.

had been trained to erect the stakes at speed – and meanwhile our men advanced in serried ranks at the trot, and were nearing the Turkish lines. When the Saracens saw the Christians were close, the Saracen cavalry turned as one, like a single cloud, and moved back behind the foot soldiers who were drawn up in two battle-groups separated by a space large enough so that another battle-group, of horse, fitted between them; among the foot were something like 30,000 archers. When our men came close and were about to engage the enemy, the Saracens loosed flights of arrows so thick and fast that even hailstones or raindrops couldn't have been more concentrated, so that very soon a great number of men and horses lay dead.

The Hungarians, [106] notorious for their reluctance to engage battle and slow to attack an enemy other than by firing arrows from horseback in retreat, saw the engagement commence; they were terrified of the archers and many of them fled – cowards and deserters that they were! But the brave marshal of France Boucicaut, leading from the front and therefore unable to see the cowardice of those behind him who were already running off – something he could never have imagined – was also unable to see the sharpened stakes that the Saracens had treacherously fixed in the ground; brave and undaunted, he rallied his men. 'Fair lords,' he said, 'what are we doing here? Are we going to let ourselves be stuck like pigs and killed without a fight? Let's engage the enemy right now and fearlessly, and at the run; that way, we can escape their fire!' The count of Nevers, along with all the French, agreed and pressed forward to engage the Saracens – but in doing so they dashed themselves against the barrier of stakes which stood so rigid and razor-sharp that they impaled the horses' bellies; many of our men were killed and wounded as they fell from their horses. Our men were very much encumbered, but they struggled through. [107]

But you will not believe the wickedness, the cowardice and the iniquity of the Hungarians – which will not be forgotten for the rest of time. When they saw our men impaled on the stakes, when they realised that this and the hail of arrows were not deterring them from the attack, then just as Our Lord was abandoned by his followers once he was taken prisoner by His enemies, so the Hungarians turned tail and fled; only a single Hungarian, known as the great count of Hungary, stood firm alongside our men,[137] as did other foreigners who had come from all over Europe to take part in the battle. But they were few in the face of overwhelming odds. And yet, do not imagine that they fled or faltered: like the wild boar brought to bay that stands firmer even when death seems close, so our French too stood firm against the hedge of stakes and passed through it, all courage and fortitude. Ah! Noble France! Not only today are your brave champions paragons of courage and defiance in the face of all the nations! Since the beginning of time, all the histories, Roman and others, bear witness to the great deeds of the French; no other nation has shown itself more brave or more belligerent, [108] more loyal, more chivalrous than the French; few are the battles where they have been defeated other than by treachery or by poor leadership.

137 Nikola II Garai Miklós (1367–1433).

I dare to add, moreover, that when the French are left idle for want of war and battle, it is unwillingly: it is because their leaders fail to find them a battle to engage in. Pity it is when men of such valour fail to find leaders their equal, for with good leadership they are capable of wonders!

But to return to my story: the noble French, enraged by the loss of their comrades both to the hail of Saracen fire and to the sharpened stakes, charged so bravely that they terrified the enemy. I need not describe the ferocity of the attack: no wild boar foaming at the mouth, no rabid wolf was ever so savage. More valiant than all, Marshal Boucicaut threw himself into the thick of the fighting; his grief had made him reckless, for truly he fought with astonishing bravery. But if I insisted on describing the specifics of every blow, every thrust, I would be losing the thread of my story, and might be accused of peddling the sort of commonplaces favoured by writers of romance. I shall therefore avoid such language, [109] and say simply what is the simple truth: that Boucicaut fought with such vigour and such endurance, and performed deeds of chivalry so diverse, that those who witnessed his exploits swore that in many a long year they had never seen such chivalry enacted in a single day. So too did the count of Nevers, the leader of the good French, perform with signal chivalry, performing deeds that were a model for his men. The valiant count of Eu, too, was a whole-hearted champion, charging hither and yon through the throng. So too were the noble brothers of Bar, in spite of their youth. The count of La Marche, the youngest of all the combatants, so young he was still beard- and moustache-less, fought with the greatest self-possession. The lord of Coucy too, a seasoned combatant who had spent his life in chivalry, performed with valour, and demonstrated his particular prowess – as was needed, for Saracens armed with the spiked copper maces[138] that they use in battle, and with cudgels, hammered repeatedly on him. But he made them pay dear: so strong was he and so tough that he cut them all to pieces. The chivalrous admiral of France did as much, and the lord of La Trémoïlle, a fine knight, full of valour, made many a Saracen fall to the ground.[139] [110] All these – seasoned warriors, and known for their bravery – rallied by their example the young knights of the fleur-de-lis who fought alongside them, such that they behaved not as children or boys but as hardened knights – and they had need of such bravery, for the press of the enemy grew ever greater. Our other most valiant knights and squires distinguished themselves beyond any of their predecessors – and they were matched by the great count of Hungary and his followers, filled with shame at the flagrant betrayal by the main body of Hungarians. And all the other foreigners also fought valiantly. But alas: to what avail? They were a mere handful against so many thousands! So few were they that they could engage no more than one of the battle-groups we mentioned above, and even then the enemy were three to

138 The spiked mace was not peculiar to the 'Saracens': medieval arms in Europe included a mace with spiked metal head (sometimes known as a morningstar).

139 The author says that La Trémouïlle made many a Saracen 'tirer en sus'; the precise meaning is unclear.

one. And yet, few as our men were, by their valour, vigour and bravery they managed to defeat the first of the Saracen battalions, and killed many of their warriors – and when Bayezid saw this, he was so alarmed by the valour of the French that he and his second battle-group did not dare await an attack from our men but fled at great speed, until it was pointed out to him that there were so few of the French, and those few abandoned by the king of Hungary and his entire force: he was then dismayed that it might be said that his crack troops had been defeated by a mere handful of the Christians. [111] Hearing this, Bayezid rallied his great army, and his reserves who were fresh and rested. And this force fell on our men, who were unsurprisingly damaged and wounded, and exhausted.

When the good marshal saw the attack, when he realised that the Hungarians who were the reserves had turned and fled, when he saw how few were the Christians in comparison to the Saracen hordes, he recognised that nothing could be done against an enemy force so immense, and that defeat had to be imminent. He was beside himself with grief and dismay, and swore that if he was doomed to die, he would make those dogs of Saracens pay dearly. He dug his spurs into his horse and flung himself into the thick of the battle, striking right and left with his sword so heavily that he threw down any he struck. And he pressed forward so valiantly that even the most courageous of the enemy were filled with fear and their ranks parted in front of him – but there were those brave enough to withstand him, and they struck at him repeatedly with spears and swords in spite of his vigorous defence. You should picture him spurring his mighty charger, which was completely armoured, into the very middle of the battle, with such momentum that everyone he encountered was felled. And marvellous to tell, incredible yet true as witnesses tell us, he pressed always forward right through the Saracen lines, [112] then turned and spurred back to his own ranks. Ah God! What a warrior! May God save him! What a tragedy his death would be! But his death will not be yet, for God will spare him! Our men fought until they could fight no more. Ah, pity it was to see so noble a company, so chivalrous, so expert in arms, so tried and tested a force, deprived of all support and help and falling victim to the cruelty of their enemies as if they had been irons on an anvil. For they were surrounded and attacked on all sides, in an onslaught so deadly that they could offer no defence. And no wonder, for there were twenty Saracens to every Christian – and yet our men killed 20,000 of the enemy, until their strength gave out. Ah, what a tragedy! The pity of it! Should not those who abandoned them so treacherously be hanged? May the betrayers be shamed eternally – for had they done their duty and come to the aid of the French and their allies, they could have wiped out Bayezid and his Turks, killed or captured all of them, and that would have been a blessing for all of Christendom. Those dogs of Saracens killed and slaughtered most of the Christians, and among them the lord of Coucy – a great loss, for he was a man of great valour – [113] and also the admiral and many others. But in spite of fierce resistance, the lords of the blood royal and most of the barons and lords and many knights and squires were taken prisoner, among them the marshal who, thinking himself lost and determined to sell his life dearly, laid about him with such force that around him was a ring of the slain and wounded; no-one dared approach him, for fearless as a raging lion, he thrust into the thick of the enemy ranks. The Saracens in capturing him suffered greatly, and many of them died; but in the end he was assailed by so many that he could not but succumb, and he too was led off a prisoner.

XXVI: Of the pitiful martyrdom suffered by the Christians before Bayezid, and how the marshal's life was spared.

The day following this terrible battle was also marked by great sorrow, for Bayezid, enthroned in his pavilion on the battlefield, had brought before him the count of Nevers and all his kinsfolk, and along with them all the French barons and knights and squires who were still living after the slaughter.[140] It was heart-rending to see those noble lords, still so young, and of the noble blood [114] of the royal house of France, brought out bound and to see them stripped to their shirts[141] by those foul, pitiless dogs of Saracens who dragged them brutally before the enemy of the faith sitting in his tent. Bayezid had found out, accurately, from his interpreters that the count of Nevers was the grandson and a cousin of kings of France, that his father was a duke of great power and riches; he had also discovered that the heirs to the children of the duke of Bar,[142] the count of Eu, and the count of La Marche were also of the blood royal, and close kin to the king of France. He was therefore aware that if he kept them all imprisoned, he could extort great ransoms for them; accordingly, he resolved to keep them, and some of the other great lords, alive; he had them sit on the ground before him. Immediately thereafter there began a tragic martyrdom, for Bayezid had dragged before him naked all the noble lords and knights and squires – and just as you see painted on church walls Herod presiding on his throne over the Massacre of the Innocents, so Bayezid had all our faithful Christians beheaded by the scimitars of those curs of Saracens, and all before the very eyes of the count of Nevers.[143] And you can just imagine, as you read this, how grief-stricken Nevers was, he who is so good and kind a lord, and how it pained him [115] to see his good and faithful

140 The Sultan Bayezid ordered the massacre of around three thousand men, most of whom were knights or squires, in part as revenge for the Christians' treatment of Turkish prisoners earlier in their expedition. J. Richard, 'Les prisonniers de Nicopolis', *Annales de Bourgogne*, 68 (1996), pp. 75–83, and K. DeVries, 'The Effect of Killing the Christian Prisoners at the Battle of Nicopolis', *Crusaders, Condottieri and Cannon: Medieval Warfare in Societies Around the Mediterranean*, ed. D.J. Kagay and L.J.A. Villalon (Leiden, 2003), pp. 157–72.

141 The text reads 'en leurs petits pourpoins'; a *pourpoint* is a short tunic worn as an undergarment.

142 Henri de Bar was taken prisoner at Nicopolis, but his brother Philippe de Bar died during the course of the battle.

143 For King Herod's slaughter of the Innocents, see Matthew 2: 16–18.

companions martyred, and his people who had been so remarkably loyal and brave. I believe indeed that his sorrow was such that he would have wished to suffer the same death as they did. And so each in turn was led out to the place of martyrdom, just as once upon a time were the holy martyrs, and once there great swords were used to strike them around the heads, chests and shoulders, and they were cut down pitilessly. And you can imagine how anguished were their faces as they were led along in that woeful procession – for just as lambs are led by the butcher to the slaughterhouse, the Christians were dragged wordlessly to their deaths before the tyrant.[144] And yet despite these terrible and pitiful deaths, we should as good Christians believe that in receiving such a death they were blessed and born in a holy hour – for man can die only once, and they were blessed by God's grace in suffering the most holy and praiseworthy death that a Christian can die, since our faith teaches us that such a death nurtures our Christian faith, and so these dead are conducted to heaven by all the orders of the saints in paradise. [116] Thus there can be no doubt that those who die so, at the will of God, become saints in paradise.

On this piteous procession Boucicaut, marshal of France, was led naked but for his undergarments. But God, wanting to save His servant for future great deeds, and for him to avenge the deaths of this glorious company on the Saracens, and also to fulfil His purpose in other great deeds, ensured that just as Boucicaut was to be struck down, he caught the eye of the count of Nevers. The count was deeply distressed at the death of so valiant a man, and at the memory of his prowess, his loyalty and his valour. And God inspired him to join his two forefingers together in front of Bayezid's gaze, and thus to imply that Boucicaut and he were brothers and that Boucicaut should be spared – and Bayezid grasped the message immediately and ordered him to be shown mercy. And so when all the executions were complete, and when the battlefield was heaped with the bodies of the blessed martyrs – French, but also from many other Christian countries – the accursed Bayezid rose to his feet and ordered that the marshal, having been spared death, [117] be led to a great city in Turkish Anatolia called Bursa [Beurse].[145] His command was carried out, and Boucicaut was held in prison there until the arrival there of Bayezid.

XXVII: How word was brought to France of the terrible defeat of our army, and of the mourning that ensued.

In the aftermath of this terrible defeat, a pitiful outcome awaited the French Christians and all those who had gone to Hungary in the service of the count of Nevers and the other lords, knights and squires: such people as chaplains, clerks, varlets, pages and

144 The author was echoing Isaiah 53: 7 and Acts 8: 32.

145 The captives were sent to Gallipoli and from there to the city of Bursa in north-western Anatolia, now Turkey.

other unarmed followers; the same went for many men of noble blood who emerged living from the battle. They were not a little dismayed to find themselves in such a predicament, with no leader, and in the hands of the Saracens. They were like sheep left wandering among wolves by their shepherds. Those who were able to fled at full speed towards what they hoped would be the safety of the Danube: [118] with no-one in command, they were simply running from one danger to another. They flung themselves into any boat they could find, but soon the boats were so overladen that they came close to sinking and drowning everyone. Others who came too late to scramble into a boat threw off their clothes and started swimming – but most of them were drowned, for the Danube there is too wide and fast-flowing; they did not have breath enough to cross, and uncounted numbers of them died.

Of those who did survive, a few men of noble blood made it back to France and brought the terrible news; they also carried messages from the count of Nevers to his father the duke of Burgundy, and from other lords to their fathers and kinsfolk.[146] Once the news became public, it is impossible to describe the grief all over France:[147] on the part of the duke of Burgundy fearing that no ransom would be large enough to save his son who would therefore be put to death, and on the part of countless other fathers, mothers, wives, and kinsmen and kinswomen learning of the deaths of other lords, knights and squires. A great mourning spread throughout the country: [119] everyone lamented the deaths of the noble knighthood that had been the flower of France. The duke of Burgundy, already grief-stricken by fears for his son, mourned the noble gentlemen of his household who had died in his son's service. The duke of Bar lamented the deaths of his sons – and rightly so, for he was never to see them again. Mothers of the dead and missing were beside themselves with grief, but nothing could compare with the grief of the wives. The countess of Nevers – a most virtuous lady who loved her husband dearly – feared that her heart would break, and yet she could retain no hope of his return.[148] The wise and virtuous lady the countess of Eu, daughter of the duke of Berry, was just as dismayed: nothing could comfort her; whatever consolation was offered, her heart told her that she would never see her husband again – which indeed was true, and when she learned of his death, she thought she would die of sorrow.[149] The good baroness of Coucy wept such

146 On 22 December 1396, Charles VI and the duke of Berry took part in a procession to the priory of Sainte-Catherine du Val-des-Écoliers in Paris, to seek divine help for the count of Nevers and the other prisoners. Bayezid had released Jacques de Heilly to bring the news to the French royal court, and he reported to the king on 24 December.

147 Christine de Pizan examined the grief caused by the tragedy at Nicopolis in the *Dit de Poissy*, probably completed in April 1400. See *The Love Debate Poems of Christine de Pizan*, ed. B.K. Altmann (Gainesville, FL, 1998), pp. 203–74.

148 The wife of Jean, count of Nevers, was Margaret of Bavaria (1363–1423).

149 Marie de Berry (1360–1434) was the widow of Philippe d'Artois count of Eu who died in 1397 while a prisoner of the Ottoman Turks. She suffered further tragedy when their son Charles d'Artois (1394–1472), count of Eu, and her new husband, Jean I (1381–1434) duke of Bourbon, were captured at the battle of Agincourt on 25 October 1415.

bitter tears for the death of her husband that it seemed her heart would break: never thereafter did she consent to remarry, in spite of several offers, and nor did her grief diminish.[150] The daughter of the lord of Coucy, who had lost not only her father but also her husband Lord Henri de Bar, the father of her two fine sons, had every reason for grief – as did so many other ladies and damsels from the kingdom of France, so that it was touching to hear their tears and lamentations;[151] [120] nor is their grief yet at an end, though the deaths were long ago, and I do not believe it can ever be assuaged, for a heart that truly loves does not easily forget.

And all our lords ordered Masses for the dead, and had services said in their chapels for the good lords, knights and squires, and all the Christians, who had perished. The king ordered a solemn Mass at Notre Dame, and he and all his court were present.[152] It inspired pity to hear the bells ring out across all the churches in Paris where Masses were sung and prayers said on behalf of the dead, and all who heard them fell to prayer and to grieving – although it is perhaps we who need the comfort of prayer, rather than those who are, if God wills it, saints in paradise. The duke of Burgundy hastened to send Bayezid messengers with rich gifts; so too did the king of France and the other great lords, begging the sultan to set a ransom quickly and release the prisoners unharmed and unscathed. But because the way was long the messengers did not arrive quickly, to the dismay of those who were waiting. But now I shall leave affairs in France and return to the prisoners themselves. [121]

XXVIII: How the count of Nevers and many other barons were taken as prisoners to Bursa, and of the ransoms that were sent to Bayezid, and of the benevolence of the marshal.

A few days only after this defeat, Bayezid repaired to the town of Bursa and took with him the count of Nevers and the other prisoners. He had them confined under strong guard in a secure fortress. When they had languished there, in considerable hardship, for a number of days, the count of Nevers took counsel with his fellows: they determined that they would send word to Bayezid to ask if he were prepared to ransom them. The deputation was entrusted to the marshal and the lord of La Trémoïlle; they managed to free themselves from the prison and to go and present their message to Bayezid. But their efforts were in vain, for whatever they said, the sultan would not listen. When they returned and explained what had happened, the count of Nevers ordered them to return [122] immediately to Bayezid's presence, and

150 The second wife of Enguerrand VII, lord of Coucy, was Isabelle (d.1423), daughter of Jean I duke of Lorraine. Enguerrand died on 18 February 1397.

151 Marie de Coucy (1366–1405), daughter of Enguerrand VII de Coucy and countess of Soissons, married Henri de Bar in 1384.

152 The funeral service for those who had died was held on 11 January 1397 at Notre Dame and in all the churches of Paris.

beg that they at least should be ransomed in order to gather the sums needed to free himself and his men, for the need was urgent. So the two ambassadors returned to Bayezid and conveyed the count's request – which the sultan accepted quite readily: he had the marshal and La Trémoïlle ransomed and gave them leave to go wherever they wished under safe conduct. When the two of them came back to the count of Nevers and his men, these latter were delighted that they were to be freed and charged them with going to negotiate the collection of the ransom money.

The two of them made immediate preparations and left for Rhodes, but when they arrived there, the lord of La Trémoïlle was immediately stricken by an illness of which he died shortly afterwards – much to the grief of the marshal who had done everything he could to find a cure, and who had taken great care of him; he had him buried with all due ceremony.[153] When this had been done, he commissioned two galleys and went to Mytilene [Methelin], where he spoke to the lord of Mytilene on behalf of the count of Nevers and the other lords, and begged him, against good security, for his financial assistance.[154] [123] The good marshal worked on the lord of Mytilene so conscientiously and with such grace and wisdom that he obtained from him and from other rich merchants of the island a good thirty-six thousand francs, to achieve which he offered himself, generously, as guarantor. When these finances were in place, he hastened back to the count of Nevers and his fellows, who were delighted and much reassured by his return and by the promise of so much needed a sum. The marshal therefore left them and approached Bayezid to pay his own agreed ransom; he was granted permission to leave and could go where he pleased. But you should not imagine that so loyal a knight abandoned the cause of the count of Nevers and his fellows; on the contrary, he went back to their prison with great determination, as if he were still a prisoner, something for which the remaining prisoners were very grateful. The count of Nevers said: 'Ah, marshal! How can you bear to return to this hideous, damnable prison when you could be off living free in France?' To which the marshal replied: 'My lord, heaven forbid that I should leave you in this land; I shall never do so as long as I live. If I left you here in so fearful a prison and fled to France, it would rightly be thought heinous and dishonourable.'

The count of Nevers thanked him warmly, then sent him back to Bayezid to negotiate the terms for their ransom and release, something the marshal did most dutifully, [124] although he found the sultan remarkably harsh and unyielding; he

153 Boucicaut and Guy de La Trémoïlle met in Rhodes with Philibert de Naillac, grand master of the Knights Hospitaller (1396–1421) who had taken part in the Nicopolis expedition. Guy died on 4 May 1397.

154 Francesco II Gattilusio (c.1365–1404) was lord of the island of Lesbos, of which Mytilene was the capital and port. He later pledged 110,000 florins towards the ransom of the prisoners. C. Wright, 'An Investment in Goodwill: Financing the Ransom of the Leaders of the Crusade of Nikopolis', *Viator*, 45 (2014), pp. 261–97, and *The Gattilusio Lordships and the Aegean World 1355–1462* (Leiden, 2014).

seemed unwilling to listen, and could not be brought to co-operate. The marshal went backwards and forwards many times between the sultan and the prisoners, and the discussions continued for a long time, for Bayezid was hesitating as to whether to put all the prisoners to death or to ransom them; he feared that if he let them return to France, they would muster a very large army and return to take revenge, and that that would lead to the destruction of his own lands; Bayezid came to believe therefore that it would be better to put all the prisoners to death. When the wise marshal realised what it was that Bayezid feared, he was much afraid for the lives of the good lords his friends; he exerted himself to go back to the sultan and talk him into an agreement. He coaxed him by saying that if he freed the prisoners, he would be well regarded in France; he would receive generous gifts and considerable wealth. If on the other hand he insisted on keeping them in prison longer than was reasonable, he would have all the princes in Christendom against him, for the love of the king of France, and they would destroy him. The marshal reiterated these warnings so adroitly and to such effect that in the final analysis, Bayezid, fearful of the consequences if he should put the prisoners to death, came to think an agreement necessary. Thereupon he and the marshal negotiated the terms of the ransom, [125] and discussions continued until Bayezid, who had originally demanded one million francs, was persuaded by the marshal's wisdom and diplomacy, in lengthy, inch-by-inch discussions, to accept the offer of one hundred and fifty thousand francs, provided also that the count of Nevers and all those of his lineage would swear on their lives that none of them would again take up arms against him. To this oath the prisoners had to agree, otherwise they were never to be released. And in return for this oath and the surety that it offered, Bayezid agreed to lower the ransom demanded. But in the event, the prisoners were not held to the oath for long, for Bayezid died shortly thereafter.

Once this agreement had been reached, the marshal delayed not a moment; he was very much afraid that Bayezid would change his mind. He first addressed the count of Nevers and explained the terms of the agreement, to which the count and his fellow prisoners acceded, much though they might have wished to avenge themselves on Bayezid – but needs must when there is no alternative. At that they were released from prison and brought before Bayezid to swear the oath and have it certified. The prisoners found much comfort in these events, [126] although the death of the brave count of Eu who died in prison left them saddened and grieving – and rightly so, for he was a man of great valour and goodness.[155] They had him interred with all possible honour, and later had his body transported to France. The lords swore the prescribed oath before Bayezid, and thus circumscribed their possible future actions; the marshal took responsibility for the count because he was so much trusted and honoured for the good sense that the sultan saw in him. Even so, however, the prisoners were obliged to leave important hostages to

155 Philippe d'Artois, count of Eu, died on 16 June 1397 at Mikhalitch in central Anatolia.

guarantee the agreement. The count of Nevers sent the marshal to Constantinople to arrange the finances; he did so as favourably as he could, and once again engaged his own credit.

As these events were transpiring, there arrived envoys from France: they were among others the lord of Châteaumorand and the lord of Vergy, and they brought money and news of friends.[156] They were greeted most joyfully by the prisoners, after which the ten envoys went to Bayezid's court and presented him with rich and beautiful gifts from the king of France and his courtiers, including the finest hawks and falcons imaginable and precious, valuable hawking gloves [127] studded with pearls and precious stones, scarlet cloth, fine linen from Reims, and other things of the sort that Turkey could not supply; the intention was to make Bayezid and his men behave more favourably and with greater courtesy towards the prisoners and their ransoms. The envoys were received most warmly, as was the finance that they were able to provide. The ransoms were paid and the prisoners were given leave to go where they wished.[157] So they left Bayezid's court and went to Mytilene where they were received most honourably by the lord; they rested there for some time, for they had great need of repose.[158]

Once freed from Bayezid's prison, the count of Nevers and the other prisoners left the lord of Mytilene and set sail for France. They journeyed as far as Venice, but on the way there, at Treviso nearby, Lord Henri de Bar fell ill and died.[159] This was a source of great grief to the French and they lamented him very much, for he was a fine upstanding gentleman; they paid every respect to his body. After that they proceeded to Venice, where they were held as hostages;[160] they stayed there, or rather in nearby Treviso, [128] where they sought escape from an epidemic which was raging in Venice, for four months until the money due was sent from France and until they were able to repay a part of what they had been lent. Then they left and arrived in France, where they were greeted most joyfully.[161] And the count of Nevers

156 On 7 or 8 December 1396 the duke of Burgundy had dispatched his chamberlain, Guillaume de L'Aigle, to negotiate with Bayezid, before precise news of the situation was reported by Jacques de Heilly. On 20 January 1397 a second embassy left Paris, led by Jean de Châteaumorand (1352–1429), Jean de Vergy (d.1418) marshal of Burgundy and a Flemish knight named Gilbert de Leuwerghem. The biographer undoubtedly exaggerates the role that Boucicaut played in the negotiations.

157 On 24 June 1397, the French ambassadors agreed that Philippe duke of Burgundy would pay a ransom of 200,000 florins for all of the prisoners of note.

158 Jean de Nevers and his companions stayed at Mytilene on the island of Lesbos from 5 July to 15 August 1397.

159 The Frenchmen arrived in Venice on 10 October 1397 and Henri de Bar died soon afterwards.

160 By the convention agreed on 24 June 1397, the French prisoners had promised to remain as hostages in Venice until Francesco Gattilusio, Gaspard de Pagani and Nicolas Paterio were repaid the money that they had advanced to the Ottoman Turks for the ransom. The hostages remained in Treviso until the end of January 1398.

161 Jean de Nevers made a formal entry into Dijon on 23 February 1398, and on 3 March there was a formal service there in honour of those who had died on the Nicopolis expedition. On

praised the marshal most fulsomely to his father the king, and said that it was only by the latter's wisdom and goodness that his own life and those of his companions had been spared; he laid out the efforts that the marshal had made to have them freed. The king and the great lords were extremely grateful.

XXIX: How after the marshal's return from Hungary the king sent him off to Guyenne with a goodly company of men-at-arms, to confront the count of Périgord who was in revolt against the crown. And how the marshal took the count prisoner and brought him before the king.

After his return from Hungary, the marshal spent the remainder of the season resting: [129] he had great need. It happened that during this time the count of Périgord rebelled against the king of France, and had the English garrison his castles and fortresses, quite without due cause; he began to make war on the king's lands in Guyenne, to set fires, to kill the inhabitants and generally to behave as badly as he might.[162] News of this development came to the king, and he sent the viscount of Meaux and Lord Guillaume de Tignonville, with a sizeable company of men-at-arms, to restore order.[163] When they arrived, the viscount sent word to the count of Périgord that he was to surrender to the king and put an end to his acts of war and his crimes, but the count refused to take any notice, still less to obey. Our people felt that they had insufficient men to force him to do so, so after a while, they returned to Paris without having done anything. And so the winter passed.

When spring came, the king ordered the marshal to make an expedition into Périgord, [130] taking with him 800 men-at-arms and 400 crossbowmen; he would also have command of 200 men-at-arms who were already there as a garrison, and that would give him a force of a thousand men-at-arms; he would be armed with an *arrêt de parlement* that had been promulgated against the count following his refusal to answer for himself before the king.[164] The marshal set off therefore with a sizeable company, and accompanied by the vidame de Laon (now the master of

10 March, the count and his companions were welcomed into Paris.

162 From 1378, the town of Périgueux had repeatedly complained about the actions of Archambaud V (1339–98), count of Périgord and his supporters, and in particular the disruption caused by French and English routiers at Auberoche, Bourdeille and Roussille.

163 Robert VII de Béthune (1352–1408), viscount of Meaux, and Guillaume de Tignonville (d.1414) had led an expedition against the count of Périgord that had laid siege to Montignac in early 1394 rather than in 1396 as this account suggests.

164 On 3 February 1397, the Parlement of Paris had issued an *arrêt* or judgement condemning Archambaud V and his accomplices to banishment and confiscating their property. On 16 May 1398, Boucicaut was charged by Charles VI with the task of enforcing the judgement against the son and heir of the count, Archambaud VI, who lost the title in 1399 and died in 1430.

the king's household), by my lord Guillaume Le Bouteiller, my lord Bonnebaud, Parchion de Nangiac, and a number of other knights banneret and bold knights.[165] As soon as the marshal arrived in Périgord, he sent to the count to say that he should submit to the king's commands and wishes, and should beg pardon for the great wrong that he had done the king; if he agreed to do this, he the marshal would himself seek to reconcile the count with the king, and would ask the king to grant him pardon. But the count took no notice; on the contrary he seized the opportunity to sally out and attack the marshal's forces – but this was to his loss, and he was brutally repulsed back into his fortress; unfortunately, however, my lord Robert de Milly, who was and still is a member of the marshal's household, was wounded in the skirmish. The marshal was incensed by the count of Périgord's disobedience to and defiance of the king, [131] and said that the count would pay dearly for his foolhardiness. He set up a well-organised siege around the castle of Montignac where the count was holed up: it is very well fortified and was felt to be impregnable. The marshal sent for siege engines and artillery from all around, and built others so that he was well prepared; he then had the engines carefully positioned. And to the amazement of the defenders, his machines bombarded the walls of the castle with huge stones and cannonballs so thick and fast that a second missile would be in the air before the first had landed. By this means they breached the walls repeatedly, in many places, so that by the end of the two months that the siege lasted, the walls were no longer secure; the defenders realised that they could not hold out, and that they could not prevent the storming of the castle. They advised the count to surrender; when he could no longer resist he did so, and submitted to the king's will and to the marshal's orders; he also surrendered all his castles and towns to the king, and the marshal, as the king's wise lieutenant, had them well garrisoned.[166] Meanwhile, the marshal sent the count, along with his sisters who had been taken captive with him, to the king who pardoned them [132] once they had begged for his mercy and sworn to be loyal servants of France – although the count was to break his oath, for very soon thereafter he fled to England without leave and never came back.[167] The marshal spent the whole of

165 Boucicaut left Paris at the end of July 1398. He was accompanied by Jean de Montaigu (1349–1409) who became sovereign master of the household of the king in 1401 (an office that was renamed grand master of France after 1413); Guillaume Le Bouteiller was the seneschal of the Limousin, Jean de Bonnebaud was the seneschal of Rouergue, and Parchion de Nangiac was the seneschal of the Auvergne.

166 Archambaud VI and his sister Brunisande surrendered in early October 1398, after a siege that lasted for two months. He handed over Montignac and Auberoche to Boucicaut; his castle at Bourdeille had already been secured by Charles de Savoisy and Guillaume de La Trémoïlle the previous month.

167 Archambaud VI secured letters of remission from the king on 1 February 1399, but on 19 July 1399, the Parlement of Paris condemned the count and his accomplices to perpetual banishment and confiscated his property. Archambaud fled to England where he paid homage

the winter season in Guyenne consolidating the defence of the province, and then returned to court the following summer.

XXX: How the emperor of Constantinople sent to the king of France for help against the Turks, and how the king sent the marshal with a fine army.

During the time when the marshal was in Guyenne as I have explained, the emperor of Constantinople, known as Kayr-Manoli, sent an embassy to the king to beg him for help and reinforcement against the Turks, for he could no longer resist them; he hoped that the king would send help lest he and his noble city fall to the unbelievers.[168] In the same vein, the Genoese [133] and the Venetians – who knew how serious these warnings were – simultaneously sent their own embassies to beg the king to send help to the emperor; they would do the same, that is have each state send eight galleys, quite apart from any sent by Rhodes. Just as the king was agreeing that this was a worthy cause, the marshal returned to court. At that, it was agreed in council that for the good of Christendom and to offer assistance to the emperor, the marshal should be sent, for no more effective leader could be imagined. The king expressed his consent, and assigned to the marshal's expedition four hundred men-at-arms, four hundred infantry and a company of archers. The marshal was delighted to have this command, and he saw to it that by the feast of St John [24 June 1399], he and his men, his ship and all the equipment needed were ready at Aigues-Mortes; he himself arrived there two days later, loaded four ships and two galleys, and set sail. With him were [Philippe] lord of Linières and his son Jean de Linières, the lord of Châteaumorand, the Hermite de La Faye,[169] the lord of Montenay, François d'Aubercicourt, Robert de Braquemont, Jean de Torsay, Louis de Culant, Robert de Milly, Louis de Cervillon, Renaud de Barbazan, Louis de Loigny, and Pierre de Grassay who bore the standard of Our Lady; [134] there was also a sizeable number of good knights and squires of high reputation, whose names I leave aside for reasons of brevity.

---

as count of Périgord to King Henry IV, and so Charles VI granted Périgord in apanage to his own brother, the duke of Orléans, on 23 January 1400.

168 Kayr Manoli was the Greek term for lord Manuel, that is to say Manuel II Palaeologus (1348–1425), emperor of Byzantium from 1391 to 1425. His uncle, Theodore Kantakouzenos, had visited Paris in October 1397, seeking aid against the blockade of Constantinople by the Ottoman Turks and their ally, John VII Palaeologus, son of Manuel's older brother Andronikos IV, who had been removed from the succession for plotting against their father in 1373. In response, Charles VI had promised financial aid by a treaty signed on 24 December 1397.

169 Guillaume de Montrevel (d.1413).

The marshal sailed to the port of Savona [Saonne], and there he mustered all his captains and assigned them appropriate commands and set off again.[170] During the voyage, he heard that five galleys belonging to Ladislaus of Sicily and Hungary were laying siege to a city and castle off Naples called Capri [Crapi] which was in the allegiance of Louis of Anjou, titular king of Naples.[171] When the marshal heard this news, he told his men that he wanted to relieve Louis's castle, and commanded them to prepare. He headed for Capri – but when he arrived he found that the castle had already surrendered.[172] He offered, if they would return to their proper allegiance, to ally himself with them against Ladislaus, but their leader refused like the traitor he was, as evidenced also by his expelling many of the French who were resident there from Capri. The marshal gathered them and took them with him. But that was not all that he did: rather, he engaged Ladislaus's galleys, and put them to flight. [135] As he was proceeding towards Constantinople, he came upon the count of Peraude, an ally of Ladislaus,[173] and gave chase and forced him to beach his ship; the count leapt out of the ship and fled, and thus our men took possession of the ship and all its cargo. Thereafter, the marshal headed for the kingdom of Sicily, and landed at a city called Messina.

XXXI: How the marshal set sail with a goodly company, and how he engaged the Saracens.

The marshal stayed only a short time in Messina; he sailed to the island of Chios [Syon] where he expected, as agreed, to find the eight Venetian galleys that were to be sent to the aid of the emperor of Constantinople – but they were not there, and he was told he would find them at Negroponte.[174] He left Chios in search of them, and on the way visited the lord of Mytilene who was delighted to see him. [136] The lord

170 Savona is a seaport on the coast of north-western Italy, forty miles west of Genoa.

171 Louis II (1377–1417) was duke of Anjou from 1384, and also laid claim to the kingdom of Naples through his father, Louis I (1339–84), the adopted son of Joanna I (1328–82), queen of Naples from 1343 until her death. This Angevin claim to the kingdom of Naples was contested by Joanna's second cousin and previous heir, Charles III of Durazzo (1345–86), who secured the throne upon her death in 1382, and by Charles's son Ladislaus (1377–1414). Following the murder of his father in 1386, Ladislaus claimed to be king of Naples, as well as titular king of Jerusalem, Sicily, Hungary and Croatia, and had resisted Louis II of Anjou since his arrival at Naples in 1390.

172 Louis II of Anjou renounced his claim to the throne of Naples to Ladislaus on 10 July 1399, and the Angevin garrison at nearby Capri surrendered, refusing the assistance of Boucicaut because the captain at Capri was secretly supporting Ladislaus.

173 The identity of the 'count of Peraude' is unknown.

174 The fleet travelled from Messina to the island of Chios, controlled by the Genoese, via the Greek island of Sapienza. Negroponte was a kingdom held by the Venetians on the second-largest Greek island of Euboea, west of Chios across the Aegean.

had, however, notified the Turks of his visit, in order not to break the agreements and pacts that he had with them; the marshal was unmoved, and bade him adieu. And indeed the lord of Mytilene volunteered to accompany the marshal on his expedition. When the marshal arrived in Negroponte, he still did not find the galleys; he decided to wait there a little, and sent word of his arrival to the emperor so that he could muster his army against the Saracens. He appointed the lord of Châteaumorand to the command of one of his existing two galleys, and the lord of Torsay to the other, before sending them off to Constantinople to deliver this message.

In the galley under the command of Châteaumorand, there was among many other valiant men a noble squire from Burgundy whose name was Jean d'Ony; he was master of horse to the duke of Burgundy, and was a man of considerable gifts, courageous and skilled in arms, who had had much experience in a number of different theatres of war. To achieve even greater honour, he had joined the marshal's expedition knowing that the marshal was of such valour and worth that there was no-one better with whom to spend time – and his decision was right, for before returning to France he did many valorous deeds, as I shall describe in what follows. As the two messenger galleys were departing the port of Negroponte, the marshal escorted them until they were within sight of Gallipoli, [137] and he anchored there to offer assistance if it should be needed: this was a measure of his good sense of strategy, and of his devotion to his followers. And indeed the two galleys had much need of his assistance, for the Turks, knowing that the marshal was close, had set up two ambushes with seventeen fully armed galleys: one ambush, with several ships, was within the port of Gallipoli, the other was beyond the town on the route to Constantinople. Now it happened that as soon as our two galleys went past Gallipoli, the Turks sprang the first ambush, of seven galleys, and at the same time, approaching off the bow, the men on our galleys saw the second ambush, this time of another ten galleys – so that they were surrounded by the enemy. They saw no alternative but to return to the marshal, but to do so they had to make a way through the enemy. They soon found themselves in the midst of the enemy fleet which attacked chaotically from all sides. Our men – brave and courageous as they were – fought back vigorously to such effect that they could not be halted, and however hard the Saracens tried to halt them, they continued their course. But they were vastly outnumbered, and eventually the battle came within earshot of the marshal; he made hurried preparations to go to their aid – and indeed they had every need of his assistance [138] for their own resources were exhausted. The Saracens however were so numerous that the marshal's advisers told him that he should leave the galleys to their fate: it would be better for the two galleys to go down rather than risk the marshal's main fleet. But the marshal took this advice badly, and responded that he would rather die himself than let his men perish or die because of his negligence: God forbid that he should live accused of such cowardice! He sailed out as quickly as possible to engage the enemy, looking so determined on combat that when the enemy saw him coming, they abandoned the two galleys and made off at full speed – at such speed in fact that the flagship of the Turkish fleet ran aground so unexpectedly and so violently that many of the crew were killed or injured. In this way the marshal saved his two galleys; that night the Christian fleet anchored in the port of Tenedos [Thenedon], off the Strait and close to great Troy.[175] The following morning the Venetian galleys arrived, as did two galleys from Rhodes and a galiot[176] from Mytilene; soon thereafter there came the whole fleet intending to go to the aid of Constantinople. By everyone's consent and acclamation, the marshal was made commander and leader of the whole force; he made his dispositions and as bearer of the standard of Our Lady he assigned Pierre de Grassay, as the most qualified in arms and the most experienced, and as a most valiant knight. The following day, after Mass, the marshal set out with his company [139], and made haste directly to Constantinople, where the emperor received him and his host with great joy and honour.

XXXII: Of the emperor's joyful reception of the marshal and his company, and how they hastened to attack the Saracens.

The emperor, who had been forewarned of the arrival of the marshal and his fine company, had already made his preparations and assembled his own army so that when reinforcements arrived, he could set off immediately to attack the Saracens. The marshal made no delay once he arrived; no more than four days later he mustered the emperor's forces on a nearby plain for inspection. He found that they consisted of 600 men-at-arms, 600 foot and 1000 archers, not counting the very large [Greek] host and assembly of the emperor. [The marshal] organised them for their departure; he appointed captains and commanders and gave them command of contingents of men according to his estimate of their competence and to the missions that he intended for them. [140] Then the emperor and all his men embarked on the new fleet: there were twenty-one *galees complies* and three *grandes galees huissieres*[177] carrying 120 horses, as well as six galiots and brigantines.[178] The fleet set sail from Constantinople and crossed to Turkey; the army disembarked at a place called the Sound of Aréta [pas de Naretez].[179] They then proceeded some

175 The island of Tenedos in the north-eastern part of the Aegean was a Venetian outpost, although the entire population had been evacuated in 1383 in the aftermath of the War of Chioggia (1381) against Genoa.

176 Galiot: a smaller, lighter-weight galley, with fewer rowing-benches than the galley proper and hence with a smaller crew. Gardiner and Morrison, eds, *The Age of the Galley*, p. 188.

177 A *galee complie* may simply signify a galley that was fully fitted out; a *grande galee huissière* designates a great galley fitted out with a hatch for horse transport. Gardiner and Morrison, eds, *The Age of the Galley*, pp. 115–16, and see Glossary.

178 A brigantine is a small galley with both oars and sails, perhaps with some room for cargo.

179 Aretae was situated six or seven miles north-east of Constantinople, on the Asiatic side of the Bosphorus, in the valley of the Göksu and Küçüksu rivers.

two leagues into Turkish territory, and began to devastate, burn and lay waste the lands all along the seaboard, and wherever they went: there were some very pleasant villages and manors there.[180] They put to the sword every Saracen they encountered, then having completed the raid they withdrew back to Greece. A few days later, they returned to Turkey; this time they made their way a good two leagues into the interior to sack a large village called Izmit [Dyaquis] on the Gulf of Nicomedia; but when they arrived in front of the village, they found a large contingent of local Turks who thought to defend it, and who were drawn up on foot and on horse before it, armed with whatever weapons they could find. Their defiance did them no good, for within a very short time those who had not fled were dead or captured; very few, however, were able to flee before they were put to the sword. In this village there were a number of fine manors and an opulent palace which had belonged to Bayezid; [141] our men set fire to them all and to all the country around, then withdrew to their galleys and spent the night at sea. The following day their intention was to attack the city of Izmit;[181] the Saracens however had anticipated their landing and had gathered in great numbers to defend the port, but to no avail for our men gained harbour in spite of them, and threw them back brutally to capture space to land. Our men then attempted to storm the town and set fire to the gates, but the fire would not take because the gates were reinforced with iron shutters. They brought siege-ladders and raised them against the walls – which were marvellously thick and stout, and so tall that the ladders were more than six metres too short.[182] They failed therefore to storm the walls, but they killed all the Saracens that they came across, and burned the outskirts of the town and the villages in the surrounding country. Then they withdrew to their ships and sailed all night. The following morning they moored as close as possible to a country village called Ak-Séraïl [Le Serail], which stood a good league from the seaboard.[183] All the Saracens from round about had gathered to deny our men access to the town, but to no avail: the French burned it and all the country around, and killed all those that they encountered. But while they were thus occupied, word went around everywhere: large numbers of Saracens had gathered, and as our men [142] were withdrawing in good order to their ships – as was necessary – the Saracens harried them so close that several times the rearguard had to turn and confront them to prevent their disrupting the order of march; on the other hand, the Saracens did not dare a full-frontal attack. Our men, however, preferred not to spend the night on the Turkish shore, so they regained the galleys and returned to Constantinople.

180 A league was the distance that a person could walk in an hour, usually defined as three miles.
181 Nicomedia was about sixty miles east of Constantinople and is today called Izmit. It had been conquered by the Ottoman Turks in 1337.
182 The French text says 'three fathoms' which is just under six metres.
183 Lalande identifies 'Le Serail' as Ak-Séraïl.

XXXIII: Of the towns and castles that the emperor, the marshal and their troops captured from the Saracens.

The emperor and the marshal and their men stayed in Constantinople for about six days, and then left and returned to Turkey where they set off to attack a fine castle on the Black Sea [Mer Majour] called Rive;[184] they arrived at daybreak. But the Saracens, who had been warned of their coming by spies on the seashore who kept them informed of all eventualities, [143] rallied in open country; they did not oppose the Christians' landing, but rather stationed themselves in front of the castle; there were about six or seven thousand Turks. Once they were aware that they had so large a body of men, and in such good order, they added to their forces by enlisting the members of the castle garrison, leaving just enough personnel, among them the bravest and most experienced, to hold the castle for a single day; they assumed that it was so strong and tall that it needed no more than a token garrison. Having done this, the enemy withdrew to a position slightly above the castle, so that once our men were scattered along under the walls, engaged in the assault, they would be able to surprise our forces before they had time to regroup; they expected to be able to accomplish this same manoeuvre six or seven times during the day. But the marshal in his wisdom had foreseen the ploy; accordingly, when his army – the emperor, the knights of Rhodes, the great company of men-at-arms and crossbowmen – had disembarked, he had them drawn up in due order before the castle with the banner of Our Lady in its due place, thus preventing the Turks from thwarting the assault. When all was ready, he ordered a daybreak attack on the castle. [144] But the Saracens had devised another ruse to prevent the attack: on top of the outer walls, and in between them and the inner walls, they had piled up on scaffolds wet straw and bundles of sticks that would give off a thick smoke when set alight. So as soon as they saw that the attack was imminent, they set fire to the scaffolds so that our men would be unable to approach because of the fire and smoke. But the ruse was in vain, for in a short time, in spite of the fires, the marshal and his men were at the foot of the walls. At that point, and in spite of all opposition, they dug two mines so that the walls were breached in two places. There followed fierce fighting, for the Saracens made a brutal defence of the breaches; there ensued valiant feats of arms, and our French proved their own valour mightily. And one man was everywhere as an example to all: I refer to their good captain the marshal who gave unstintingly of himself, no-one more wholeheartedly. Several times during the course of the day, the marshal himself raised a ladder at points where his brave men were fighting hand-to-hand against defenders who flung down such a rain of great stones and rocks against the ladders that it was impossible to prevent their being smashed – and indeed the heavy weight of the men-at-arms, pursuing glory by climbing the rungs, also made the ladders bend. When the marshal, [145] having fought tirelessly and with marvellous valour all day without a moment's rest, saw that his siege-ladders

184 Lalande identifies 'Rive' as Riwa Kalessi or Iriva, which may be Beykoz.

could not breach the enemy's defences, he had a new, heavy ladder swiftly made out of two sail-yards from a galley, and at sunset he had it raised against the walls. He was determined to avoid its being overladen, and so took personal charge. The first to climb it was Guichart de La Jaille, who fought valiantly hand-to-hand with the defenders for some time; in the end, however, there were so many of the latter that he lost his sword, for which reason – nothing to do with lack of courage – he fell back against the next on the ladder, a valiant squire called Hugues de Tholigny, who forced his way first into the castle, closely followed by lord Guichart. Meanwhile, those still fighting in one of the mines also forced their way into the castle: one of the most valiant of these was the good squire called Jean d'Ony whom I mentioned earlier, and who by sheer force and courage, and in the face of a determined enemy, was the first to pierce the defence, followed by my lord Fouques Viguier, then by Renaud de Barbazon and many others. They hurried to the aid of their companions who had climbed the ladder; a very necessary help, for there were still no more than ten or twelve fighting on the walls, and the ladder had now broken [146] under the weight of the many knights who were competing to climb up. In this way they took the castle, which had seemed so strong as to be impregnable. They killed all the Turks who were there, and then, the following day, the marshal had the castle razed to the ground; it had been a real stronghold, for one side was protected by the sea, and the other by a river flowing from Turkey, so that no attack could be made except from one direction. But the other Turks, whose army was there in battle-order, made no move to defend it; they could see that their forces were insufficient, and so they decamped.

And when all this had been done, our own forces left and re-embarked on the galleys to return to Constantinople. They sailed to a fine town called Hieron [Le Girol], which sits at the entrance to the Black Sea;[185] they arrived there at sundown, and spent the night. In the morning, the marshal – whose one desire was to do as much damage to the Turks as possible – had his forces arm themselves and trumpets sound as a signal to disembark and attack the town. The resident Turks had heard two days earlier of the fate of the castle of Rive; when they saw the preparations in train for an attack on the town, they set fires in more than one hundred places, and fled into the high mountains. The fires set to the houses [147] were very soon burning fiercely and consuming the town. The marshal realised what was happening, but did not wish to abandon the town until it was entirely consumed; when the whole town was burned down, he said that the Turks had done most of what he himself had intended, and left. While they were on the return voyage, news came to the emperor that the Turks had landed with a good twenty ships at the straits of Naretae;[186] they were doing great damage to the inhabitants of

185 Lalande says 'Le Girol', now Hiéron.

186 The text gives Naretés, which Lalande identifies with Aretae, on the coast of the Bosphorus north-east of Constantinople.

Constantinople and of the city of Pera [Pere];[187] they had overrun the whole district and were starting to lay waste to it. As soon as this news reached the marshal, he ordered his fleet there. He had intended to land his troops in good order, but the Turks did not dare wait for the attack, so they fled. Our men burned and destroyed the Turkish ships, and then returned to Constantinople.

XXXIV: How the emperor, having with the help of the marshal rid the surrounding country of Saracens, decided to journey to France to ask for help from the king for money and provisions were running low. [148] And how the marshal who escorted him left the defence of Constantinople in the hands of the lord of Châteaumorand in command of a hundred fine experienced men-at-arms, as well as archers.

I see no point in prolonging my account of the marshal's deeds, the castles he stormed, the towns he took and all the other exploits he accomplished during his time in the East; if I detailed them all, I would risk boring my readers. So, to be brief: I can guarantee that during that time he took no rest lasting more than a week; he harried his enemies every single day; he took so many castles, towns and fortresses that the whole country – which had been plagued by Saracens – was emptied of them; he did so many good deeds that it would be impossible to list them. As a result, he was held in the highest affection and esteem by the emperor and his barons, by all the inhabitants of Constantinople and by all true Christians.

He was responsible in addition for other benefits, for the Emperor Manuel II, who is still living today, [149] had been in dispute for eight years with a nephew of his called John VII Palaeologus, and they were at war with each other.[188] The cause for war was John's claim that he ought to have succeeded to the empire, because his own father [Andronikos IV] had been the elder brother of the emperor Manuel [II] who had seized the empire by force; the emperor [Manuel II], meanwhile, was at war for other causes.[189] This war, and the quarrel that caused it, had been at the root of the destruction of Greece – and the two of them were so stubbornly inflexible in their demands that no-one had been able to bring about peace between them. The nephew had allied himself with the Turks, and with their military aid was making war on his uncle. The marshal – believing that this war was prejudicial to Christendom and unworthy of both of them – undertook to make peace between them, and did so

187 Pera is now called Beyoğlu; it is a suburb of Constantinople, on the European side of the Golden Horn.

188 The French text referred to Manuel as 'Karmanoli' and his nephew as 'Calojani'.

189 See note 168 above.

with such diplomacy that he managed to engineer a pact between them; he himself went to a border town called Silivri [Salubrie][190] and brought the nephew back to Constantinople, where his uncle gave him a warm reception.[191] All the Greeks were delighted, and gave thanks to God that He had brought the marshal who had made a holy peace and brought so many other benefits to the country.

The marshal and his men had now been nearly a year in Greece, and of course, [150] as is usual in a war-torn country, provisions were short and expensive; moreover, he no longer had the funds to pay his men-at-arms, nor the means to provision them. For this reason, the marshal had no choice but to leave, although he was very much afraid that the Turks would take advantage of his leaving to attack the Christians. The emperor and his subjects were naturally even more alarmed, so it was determined that the best course of action would be for the emperor himself to accompany the marshal to France to ask help from the king; in return for military help against the infidel, he would offer to cede the sovereignty of the empire and of the city of Constantinople to the king, the emperor being no longer able to defend it against the Turks; if the French king were unwilling or unable to do so, the emperor would appeal to all the other monarchs of Christendom. It was ordered that while the emperor was absent, John his nephew would serve as regent for the emperor in Constantinople until his uncle returned with whatever aid he had managed to secure. John, however, replied that he would not agree unless the marshal were prepared to leave him with a contingent of men-at-arms and archers, for he realised that as soon as the marshal and the emperor left, Bayezid would bring his whole army to lay siege to the city, to starve it out and destroy its defences. The marshal, well aware [151] that all could be lost if no provision was made for defence, left for the protection of the city a hundred men-at-arms, a hundred of his armed foot and a good number of crossbowmen; he appointed as commander the lord of Châteaumorand, left them enough provisions for a year, and handed over to reliable bankers enough money to pay them a monthly wage, also for a whole year. Before he left, in other words, he left everything in good order, so much so that when the Genoese and the Venetians who were there saw the marshal's prudent and honourable arrangements, they agreed between themselves that they would leave eight galleys fully manned, four from Genoa and four from Venice, to help in the defence of the city. The citizens of Constantinople, who had been reduced almost to despair, and who had seen no way out but to flee the Saracens and abandon the great city, were much reassured. All this accomplished, the emperor and the marshal, who had been there for a full year, [152] left Constantinople for France.[192]

190 A port town near Istanbul, on the coast of the Sea of Marmara.

191 Boucicaut travelled to Salembria to meet with John VII Palaeologus on 4 December 1399.

192 They departed from Constantinople on 10 December 1399.

XXXV: How the lord of Châteaumorand fulfilled the charge of defending Constantinople, how it was stricken with famine, and how the famine was relieved.

The lord of Châteaumorand, left in command of Constantinople, fulfilled his duty in the post, worthy as he was in God's sight and a most valiant knight.[193] He should be forever honoured, for he kept guard conscientiously on the city, and especially so when, soon after the emperor's departure, there arose a famine so desperate that, to assuage their bitter hunger, men would rope down the walls of the city and surrender themselves to the Turks. In response, Châteaumorand made every effort to set a good guard so that the citizens would not flee as if defeated by the enemy, nor be tempted to surrender the city to them. [153] He was greatly affected by the disaster, and often charged his men to go out in small bands and take the enemy by surprise so that they could forage among the Turks who were farming rich farmland. He inflicted considerable damage; sometimes he acquired good prisoners and then held them for ransom, some for money, others for provisions. And by these means, thanks be to God, he saw the city well provisioned – and particularly because not a Saracen ship passed that was not detained by the watchful galleys of the Genoese and the Venetians. These measures saved the city from death, famine and the enemy, and left it well stocked; by his vigilance, moreover, he made gains on the Saracens, and for three years saved the city from the Turks. To be brief, he and his small company performed so effectively that those who know the truth of the matter say that it was he who saved the noble and ancient city of Constantinople from defeat and destruction – and this, of course, is pleasing to God and confers great honour on the king of France and the French (who showed themselves highly courageous), and is of great benefit to Christendom. All these blessings arose from the good judgement the marshal showed in making these dispositions; it is impossible to exaggerate the great value that came from the marshal's visit to the country. [154]

XXXVI: How the emperor arrived in France, preceded by the marshal.

The emperor and the marshal sailed from Constantinople to Venice; the emperor determined to stay there a while because of business with the Venetians.[194] The

193 Christine de Pizan also praised Châteaumorand's achievements in Constantinople in her *Livre du debat de deux amans* (probably written between 1400 and 1402), in *The Love Debate Poems*, 124, vv. 1627–30.

194 Boucicaut arrived in Venice on 23 January 1400, though there is no evidence that the emperor arrived with him, perhaps delayed by the need to leave his family in the despotate of Morea under the protection of his brother Theodore I Palaeologus (c.1355–1407).

marshal left him there and preceded him to France to announce his coming and to explain the reasons for it. He made his way to court where the king, who had been eager for his return, greeted him with the greatest delight and honour; he was also welcomed, warmly and deservedly, by all the lords and knights and squires, and indeed by everyone.[195] He then spent some time at court, for he was in need of rest and respite; he had had neither for some time, [155] although he was so level-headed and wise that he had no need of pleasures other than those esteemed by the virtuous. He spent much of his days with lords who questioned him about his exploits, and about the deeds he had performed while he was abroad; he obliged them with stories not of his own deeds, but rather with the deeds of his men to whom he attributed all his successes. This merely increased the respect in which he was held, for Renown perfectly understood the realities of the situation, and knew no limits to his valour.

So the time passed until the emperor arrived in Paris.[196] The king and our lords the dukes, and a large number of nobles, went out of Paris to greet him; they received him with great honour, and rightly, for Manuel is a most worthy prince, virtuous, prudent and wise, and it is most regrettable that he is today in such dire straits. He rested a while in Paris, during which time, and indeed as long as he stayed in France, the king defrayed all his expenses. And when he had recovered from the journey, he explained fully and carefully to the king, in full council, the reasons for his coming to France. He received a positive and gracious response, and was given reason to hope. The king then discussed the matter with his council, on several occasions, before a decision could be taken. [156] In the end, for the sake of Christendom and because any prince should provide aid and relief to any fellow prince especially against unbelievers, the king promised him the help of twelve hundred combatants fully funded for a year, the marshal to be in command; the emperor had specifically requested this last provision, and had spoken most warmly of the marshal to the king and his council, telling them how valiantly he had behaved in the East. The emperor thanked the king warmly for his assistance and then left Paris, where he had now been for some time; he wanted to visit other princes of Christendom to ask them also for their help and assistance, both in terms of money in which he was sadly lacking, and in terms of men who might help him recover those parts of his empire which were now, sadly, in the hands of the enemies of the faith. His first visit was to the Holy Father who promised the remission of sins to anyone who would agree to his request; he then went to England and to other Christian kings, all of whom promised him aid; he spent some three years on this mission.[197] [157]

---

195 The date of Boucicaut's return to Paris is not certain, but may have been February 1400.

196 The emperor arrived in Paris on 3 June 1400.

197 The Avignon pope, Boniface VII (1389–1404), issued an appeal in support of the emperor who also visited the court of King Henry IV of England from December 1400 to February 1401, and then remained in France until 21 November 1402. Yet Manuel II was unsuccessful in securing the aid promised by the French or English crowns.

XXXVII: How the emperor of Constantinople made peace with Bayezid; how Tamerlane brought vengeance upon Bayezid, and of the death of Tamerlane.[198]

While the emperor was abroad and seeking help, as I have described, and while Châteaumorand was in command of Constantinople's defences, it happened by the will of God, Who wishes all evil to be punished, and Who exacts unforeseen vengeance for ill or damage done to His faithful – as He did long ago for the children of Israel whom He left for long years in slavery to King Pharaoh, finally taking a cruel revenge on Pharaoh, as the Bible tells us,[199] and freeing His people from their bondage; it happened, then, that God resolved to avenge those good Christian souls who, as we saw, had been killed and cruelly slaughtered before Bayezid; He made a great prince of Tartary, named Tamerlane, His instrument to exact vengeance. Tamerlane was so audacious that he resolved, with the help of Fortune, to conquer the whole world – but he failed in his ambition, [158] for as the old proverb says, 'Man proposes, God disposes'. Nevertheless he was indefatigable in arms: for thirty years he never slept in a town but rather out in the field, accompanied by an astonishingly large army. His grasp of supply in the field was acute, for he brought with him all the provisions which would be needed by the army, along with a wonderfully inventive cattle-train in which each beast, however small – even goats or sheep – also acted as a pack-animal. I am tempted to amaze my readers by describing his miraculous military accomplishments, the great rivers he crossed, the sheer hardihood of his troops, but I must not allow myself to be diverted from my story – although I believe that our Christians, who prefer to live in comfort, would do well to follow his example if they wish to be great conquerors: he carried out the conquest of the whole land of Egypt, and the destruction of the city of Damascus, the subjugation of Syria [Surie] and the surrounding lands, then proceeded to invade Turkey and wage war on Bayezid.[200] He was thus so occupied elsewhere that he left the Christians in peace. The Tartars under Tamerlane began to lay waste to Bayezid's lands, to pillage and destroy them, [159] and Bayezid in turn was obliged to raise an army to defend himself. At which the Christians to the rear of Bayezid, namely Châteaumorand and his company, began to harry his army from the rear – they were no helpful neighbours, and indeed they often did him very significant damage. The war between the Turks and the Tartars continued for some time, with Bayezid defeated in a number of battles and losing a large number of men dead or taken prisoner, and seeing many of his fortresses, towns and cities captured and razed to the ground; in the end, his forces were so depleted

198 Tamerlane (d.1405), identified as Tamburlaine by the French author, was the founder of the Timurid dynasty in central Asia, known in the Middle Ages as Tartary.

199 Exodus 1–15.

200 In 1399, Tamerlane started a new war with the Ottoman empire and the Mamluk sultanate of Egypt, attacking Anatolia, Armenia, Georgia and Syria.

that he could no longer withstand Tamerlane; in a final battle, he was defeated and his men were put to flight or taken prisoner; he himself was captured and taken to prison, where he died a miserable death.[201] So died the dominion of Bayezid, who had done such harm to Christendom; so were avenged the count of Nevers and the nobility of France, not to mention the emperor of Constantinople whom he had dethroned.[202] But of course had Tamerlane lived, he would have been no better friend to the Christians than was Bayezid; he would never have been satisfied with his existing conquests. But God, Who directs all things, did not wish His Christian peoples to be subjugated by the enemies of the faith – and so sent Bayezid to the death which is the end of all. [160]

XXXVIII: Here I explain how the marshal took pity on a group of ladies and damsels who complained that wrongs were done to them with no-one to take their part, and how for that reason he founded the Order of *La Dame Blanche à l'Écu Vert*, under whose statutes he and twelve others bearing the device committed themselves to the defence of the ladies.

I return now to my main subject – that is, praise of the inexpressible generosity of the marshal towards the emperor while the latter was in France at the royal court.[203] While the marshal was resident in Paris, a number of complaints were made to the king by ladies and damsels (some of whom were widowed), [161] to the effect that they were being harassed by certain powerful men who were using their influence and authority to disinherit them of their lands, possessions and reputations, and indeed had actually, in some cases, succeeded. By this means these ladies were being greatly wronged, and yet there was not a knight, not a squire, not a gentleman, no-one at all to take up their defence or to argue the justice of their causes and disputes. They had come before the king, as before the fount of all justice, to beg him to furnish them with reasonable and appropriate compensation.

201 Bayezid was captured at the battle of Ankara on 28 July 1402, and died on 9 March 1403 while in captivity.

202 Manuel II's predecessor John V Palaeologus (d.1391) supposedly died because of his humiliation at being forced to undo the repairs to the Golden Gate in Constantinople by Bayezid I, who was holding John's son Manuel as a hostage.

203 The Order of the Enterprise of the Green Shield of the White Lady was founded on 11 April 1400, before the arrival of the emperor in Paris. Boulton has described this as a votive rather than a fraternal order because the members took a vow to perform specific actions and the society simply dissolved once those actions were completed. D'A.J.D. Boulton, *The Knights of the Crown: The Monarchical Orders in Later Medieval Europe, 1325–1520* (Woodbridge, 1987), pp. xix–xx.

The marshal, on a number of occasions when he was in the king's presence, heard the piteous appeals and entreaties put forward by several different ladies, and he was much moved; he used all his powers of persuasion to plead their cause to the king and in council; perceiving the righteousness of their cause, he pleaded it as charitably as one might expect of someone who was and is everything that is noble. He thought to himself that it was a shameful thing that in a kingdom like France, home to the flower of knighthood and nobility, there should be no recourse for a lady or a damsel of honour having good cause for complaint, [162] and that such a lady should not find, among so many knights and squires, a champion to defend her rights; this meant that the corrupt and the cowardly felt no compunction in abusing ladies, who are, by nature, weaker, and who could offer no defence. Moreover, he thought to himself that it was a great pity, a great sin and dishonour to men in general that there should be ladies who had reason to complain of treatment from men who, had they been as reasonable as they ought to have been, should by nature and from duty have defended and safeguarded them, with every fibre of their being, from any threat. Since on the other hand there were evidently men who did not defend ladies, he himself resolved to put heart and soul, and funds, into upholding the justice of their causes in the face of those who exploited or harmed them, on any occasion when his help might be requested.

Such were the thoughts of the good marshal. And when he had fully pondered these developments, then out of his nobility of soul and of his generosity, he determined to institute an outstanding order of knighthood in defence of those wronged, and which would confer all honour on any knight; he proceeded to explain his proposal and the reason for it to some of his closest companions and friends, [163] all of whom found it most praiseworthy and begged to become companions and brothers of an order which seemed to them just, fair, honourable and chivalrous; he accepted their offers most willingly. That made a total of thirteen knights, each of whom was to bear on an armlet, as evidence of the vows that he had sworn, a shield of gold enamelled in green, emblazoned with a lady in white.[204] The marshal determined that, as a guarantee of authenticity, there should be a document signed and sealed by all thirteen knights, setting out the covenants that each of them had sworn to in entering the order; once this was done, the document should be promulgated all over France so that ladies and damsels were aware of it and knew to whom they could appeal in the event of mistreatment. I shall not summarise the covenants, for they can be consulted in full in the very letter that I have certified and copied here in full. The marshal, incidentally, did not wish to be the first-named of the knights in the letters, [164] because Charles d'Albret, the king's own first cousin, had chosen to be

204 Christine de Pizan praised the members of this order in four of her *Autres ballades* (II, III, IV and XII), in *Les oeuvres poétiques de Christine de Pisan*, ed. M. Roy, 3 volumes (Paris, 1886–96), I, pp. 208–12 and 220–1.

one of the order, and the marshal did not wish his own name to precede Charles's – which is why both of them are named together, as can be seen.[205]

XXXIX: The contents of the *Lettres d'Armes* according to which the thirteen knights undertook to defend, to the best of their ability, the rights of any lady of noble blood who might submit an appeal to them.

'To all ladies and damsels of good and noble birth, and to all lords, knights and squires, greetings. Be it known as relating to the thirteen knights-companion bearing as their device the *escu vert a la dame blanche*:

First, whereas all knights are duty bound to guard and defend the honour, the estate, the possessions, the repute and the good name of all ladies and damsels of noble blood, and whereas the thirteen are resolved to this duty, they invite and pray any such lady, should she find herself reduced or harmed in any of the following particulars, [165] and should she so wish, to call upon or summon one of the said company, jointly or severally as the severity of the crime would dictate; the knights, in return, will jointly or severally engage their aid to the said lady or damsel, and vow to set their bodies to defend the justice of their causes, guard them and protect them against any other lord or knight or squire, in brief to do all that a knight can or may do in arms and in combat, as many as all thirteen being available for help; they vow to respond jointly or severally within a short space of days to any appeal from a lady or damsel, and with all due haste. And should it be – God forbid! – that one of the thirteen so entreated has business so pressing that it can by no means be delayed, that one will be required to designate one of his companions who will ensure that the request conveyed be duly accomplished and completed.

Item, should any lord, knight or squire of noble blood and irreproachable character wish to issue a challenge to the members of the Order, or has made or makes a vow to carry out and accomplish any deeds of arms, [166] then provided such a challenge or vow is honourable and fitting, and given that the oath-taker will be eager to fulfil the terms of his vow, then those of the Order, in order to do everything to fulfil their oaths or facilitate the relief of the ladies, will by God's grace, jointly or severally, according as to the nature of the challenge issued, stand ready to accomplish the feat of arms so prescribed. And in order duly to complete the deed, within forty days or fewer of the request made and the nature of the arms defined, they will undertake to do all in their

205 Charles d'Albret (d.1415) was constable of France from 1402 to 1411 and from 1413 until his death at Agincourt in 1415. He and Boucicaut were also members of the *Cour amoureuse* founded on 14 February 1401 as a venue for the performance of poetry in praise of women. See C. Bozzolo and H. Loyau, *La cour amoureuse, dite de Charles VI*, 2 volumes (Paris, 1982–92), I, pp. 42 and 128.

power to find an appropriate judge; such a judge once identified, and a date set by the said judge, they will undertake to be ready to take the field for the attainment of the said act within no more than thirty days. And should it be that those of the Order can find no such judge, then the challenger(s) or the oath-taker(s) are bound themselves to seek out such a judge as may be appropriate and sufficient; those of the Order will be ready to take the field no more than thirty days after they are notified of the identity of the judge appointed. And should it be necessary for safe conduct or guarantees to be arranged for the combatants, then those appointing the judge will undertake to procure such safe conduct or guarantee as circumstances will dictate.

Item, should it be that more than one contestant [167] in turn issue a vow or challenge to any knight of the Order, then this knight will undertake to meet the challenge of him who first issued it; that done in due form, and if God ensures that he be unscathed, he will then proceed to meet in turn the next challenger.

Item, in the event that one or more of the said knights named above fears being unable to fulfil what is requested of him, he or they shall nominate one or more of the other knights, as appropriate, to answer the challenge or perform the said deed.

Item, should it occur that on some occasion as many as all those knights named above be required to fulfil together some particular deed of arms, of whatever kind, and should it then be the case that one or more of them be absent, or detained by some other reasonable duty which would prevent their presence at the said enterprise, those remaining, once warned that their companion(s) cannot be present, should be obliged to do all that they can to recruit replacements such that the said deed may be performed. Should it moreover be the case that no such companion(s} can be recruited in the way described, those duly present, of whatever number, are bound [168] to accomplish everything as above.

Item, should it happen that one or more ladies or damsels request the aid of one, of all or of some of the said knights, and should it then happen that subsequent to that request from the ladies and damsels, some knight or squire or group of knights and squires then also approach the same ten knights to challenge them to a deed of arms of the sort we have just described, then those of the said lords, knights or squires challenged to respond to the request for a deed of arms will first, rightly, ensure the safety of the lady or damsel concerned; only after that will they accomplish the deed of arms as requested by the challenging group. Should it, alternatively, happen that when a knight or a squire from the group of ten be engaged in meeting a challenge to a deed of arms from one or more of the knights mentioned above, and while meeting the challenge also be solicited for help by a lady or a damsel, then such a knight or squire may designate such a proxy as he pleases to respond to the lady's request, and thereafter, once the initial deed of arms is completed, and if with God's help he remains unscathed, he may return to offer any aid that the lady or damsel will still require.

Item, should one or all of the said knights named above have been nominated to fulfil an oath or a request by taking part in a deed of arms, and should he or they

[169] receive an additional challenge to take arms *à outrance* against one or more other lords, knights or squires, one of those challenged, or some, or all may leave the first challenge to take up the second.

Item, if one or more of the said knights or squires should commit themselves to a combat *à outrance,* as described, against these thirteen knights or against one or more of them, in order to fulfil a vow or a challenge, willingly or unwillingly, and should it be that those defeated become prisoners of the victor(s), then before the combat, a sum of money should be agreed by both sides and by the judge before whom the combat is to take place; the defeated party/ies will then remain prisoner(s) detained by the said judge until he is able to pay and disburse the sums agreed to the knight or knights that will have inflicted the defeat; once the moneys have been remitted, the knight imprisoned will be free to leave.

Item, should it be that one or more knights be killed in the combat *à outrance*, or die of his wounds, then he should be quit of any moneys due. [170]

Item, should one or more of the aforementioned thirteen knights, during the emprise as described, die in combat or be in a state where he can no longer bear arms, the remaining knights shall recruit further companions to ensure that the due number of members of the Order is maintained.

Item, the aforementioned knights swear to do everything they can to fulfil the statutes detailed and inscribed above, with God's help and the help of Our Lady, for the space of five years as counted from the date of signature of the present document, and promise to wear the insignia for the full five years. And to ensure that all ladies and others that hear of these endeavours recognise and believe that the knights concerned are firmly resolved to fulfil their vows, the knights thereto have set their seals as emblazoned with their arms and have signed their names, this Palm Sunday 11 April, in the year of Our Lord 1400.[206]

Lord Charles d'Albret, Lord Boucicaut marshal of France, his brother [Geoffroy Le Meingre] Boucicaut, François d'Aubercicourt, Jean de Linières, [Jean de] Chambrillac, [Bernard de] Castelbajac, [Raoul de] Gaucourt, [Jean de] Châteaumorand, [Jean] Betas, [Jean de] Bonnebaud, [Guillaume de] Colleville, [Jean de] Torsay.' [171]

At this I draw to a close the first part of this book, and embark on the second part, following in due chronological order the deeds of Boucicaut marshal of France; I hereby leave the matters covered thus far, and address new matters which will, with God's help, bring me back to my main subject. May God – Who endorses praise for the good – give me grace to fulfil these new matters, and to give due honour to my subject who is most worthy of all praise.

Here ends the first part of this book.

206 The date was given in the document as 11 April 1399 because in the old style the calendar year started and ended at Easter which in 1400 fell on 18 April.

[176] I: Here begins the second part of this present book, which will speak of the wisdom and prudence of Marshal Boucicaut, and of his principal gallant deeds from his governorship of Genoa until his return from Syria. First, we shall speak of the [177] ancient custom of the Guelphs and Ghibellines that holds sway in Italy.

It is universally known, and notoriously so, that the country of Italy has long been riven by an old and diabolical custom inspired, as many Italians believe, by the devil himself as a punishment sent by Our Lord for the many and horrible sins that beset certain of their countrymen and certain regions of the country; after all, as Holy Scripture tells us, sometimes the many are punished for the sins of the few.[1] This perverse custom, the origin and true beginning, and the first cause of which no-one can explain, although some claim to do so, is so deep-rooted and entrenched that every town, and indeed the country as a whole, is poisoned and corrupted by it. [178] This accursed affliction leads to a universal destruction through a spilling of blood that has gone on between them for so long that no-one can remember a time of peace. And this plague is such that chiefly in the many notable cities, which could be as fine and prosperous as any in the world were they at peace, the citizens are at mortal enmity one with another, neighbour with neighbour, divided into two groups, one called the Guelphs, the other the Ghibellines; the different factions do not invade each other's territory, do not claim sovereignty over each other, but simply say: 'You are of the Guelph clan, I am of the Ghibelline; our ancestors hated each other, and so shall we.'[2] For this reason alone, day by day, the factions kill and maim each other like dogs, the sons following the fathers. And so, from generation to generation, the curse continues, nor can any justice bring healing, for those who uphold this custom would absolutely refuse that in such a case justice be invoked. Such deadly hatred means that, as one side or the other is in the ascendant, [179] the different cities come under new control – and this explains the advent in Italy of a succession of new tyrants, elected with no rhyme or reason simply by the fickle voices of the people. For the common practice among the Italians is that when one party is the stronger and triumphs over the other, those who are on the winning side cry out: 'Long live so-and-so, long live so-and-so, and death to so-and-so!' And then they elect one of

1 Romans 5: 18.

2 The Guelphs and the Ghibellines were factions competing within Italian cities from the twelfth to the fifteenth centuries; their rivalry was originally based upon their support for the pope and the Holy Roman Emperor respectively. Christine de Pizan also reflected on the rivalry of the Guelphs and Ghibellines, in the *Livre de la mutacion de fortune*, II, pp. 14–18 (vv. 4605–732).

their own party, and kill the former leader if he doesn't take flight. And then, when this latter defeated party returns to power in its turn, they do exactly the same to their adversaries, and the rage of the people – from which God defend us! – destroys everything once again. In this way, across the whole country, city destroys city, castle castle, neighbour neighbour – worse and worse then ever it was. And it is sad to see such destruction in one of the world's best, richest and most fertile of countries. The result is often – and indeed we have seen it happen – that when one side has been so roundly defeated that it sees no prospect of vengeance or retaliation, it seeks rulership from places abroad; [180] when this is accorded, it pledges unconditional submission in the hope of support and backing. And what is the result? The citizens of Italy are so faithless and inconstant that for the least incentive – or simply because they are bored by the new regime – they will very soon turn against any ruler and against any of his officials and harry and harass them, rebel against them, if possible kill the ruler and his representatives, and take to the streets and elect another in his place. Given all this, and given that such ways are the norm in that country, it seems to me absolute madness, however ardently the Italian citizens promise loyalty and submission, for anyone to assume rule there, no matter how high-born or how powerful, unless he can be sure he has the advantage in terms of military strength in men-at-arms or weapons in general. For any ruler can be certain that his subjects will rebel when they are able; no-one can rely on them; and if the ruler isn't wary, he'll be wasting his efforts and will soon be disappointed. And to return to our story: because of these divisions between them, it has become common that the unhappy citizens of Italy call on a ruler from abroad to take charge. But let my readers take note of how poisoned a chalice this is: was even Egypt devastated by a plague so extraordinary?[3]

[181] II: Here we speak of the city of Genoa, and of its sad state before the marshal became governor.

Now, to return to the events to which my previous remarks were a prelude, and which will be the subject of the next section of my history: in the Italy riven, as I have described, by fire and flame and murder, the city of Genoa, rich, noble, ancient, founded long ago by Janus, a scion of the royal house of Troy, was a victim of just such a plague.[4] So torn apart was the city that there remained scarcely a man of virtue, scarcely anyone of standing or who pursued an honourable life. For we should remember that in spite of the appalling custom I have described, there are in Italy valiant gentlemen and upright and honest citizens who wish only for good and who

---

3 Exodus 7: 14 to 12: 36.

4 The Roman god Janus was usually identified as the founder of Genoa, but some chroniclers also claimed that Genoa had been established by a Trojan prince. C.E. Benes, *Urban Legends: Civic Identity and the Classical Past in Northern Italy, 1250–1350* (University Park, PA, 2011), pp. 63–87.

lament horrors of this sort: they are indeed numerous, and they would wish if they could to improve things. But the arrogance and pride and lack of discipline that has now infected the common people – who lack all judgement – leave little room for the wise and the good to exercise their good sense. Thus all that was left in the city were the dregs of society, thieves and blackguards, [182] and as a result the power of Genoa was entirely destroyed. But God moves in mysterious ways to bring relief, either from pity, or perhaps in answer to the prayers of some good man – or yet again, perhaps God, for the sake of Christendom, does not wish to see the destruction of so noble a city, or yet again, perhaps, He wishes to reward the city for those times when it made war on the enemies of His faith; whatever the case, God wished to save the city from the burning fires, and restore it to life and health.

III: Here we describe how the city of Genoa ceded itself to the rule of France.

In about the year of Our Lord 1397, following the ancient customs relating to the government of the city and its surrounding region – that is, that by statute the ruler should be elected from among the wise and sage citizens – there was elected a doge [183] who seemed to them fit and capable of installing good government. This doge was Antoniotto Adorno – and although he was a scion of the people and not noble by blood, he was wise enough to govern Genoa well and wisely and justly.[5] But as I have already said, it is impossible to keep the common people of Italy under control, for in their arrogance and their desire for power they can be subdued only by sheer force: they rebelled against their doge and drove him from the city. Later, however, having via different alliances been recalled to power, he was wise enough to recognise the turbulent nature of the citizens who were, he realised, fomenting discord and rebellion against him. He saw that in so divided a city he would soon be unable to hold power, and could do so only if he could call on great forces. For the good of the city, he hit upon a cunning plan; using gifts and promises and honeyed words, he persuaded the most influential of the nobles – who by rights should have been at the head of the city but who with a few brave exceptions had been driven out by the mob – to agree unanimously that they should cede themselves to the king of France. He even managed to secure the agreement of the most influential of the common people. When he had managed to negotiate this agreement, [184] he sent word hastily to France.[6] The king and his counsellors agreed that this was not an offer they should reject; rather it should be seized so as to acquire a jewel so desirable as the city of

5 Antoniotto Adorno served as doge on five occasions, in 1378, 1383, 1385–90, 1391–2 and from 1394 to 1396.

6 In November 1394, Adorno called for French intervention in Genoa and signed a treaty with King Charles VI on 25 October 1396.

Genoa which would greatly enhance his power on land and on sea. He sent a French knight with a fine company to receive the homage of the city and to govern it in the name of the king.[7] But this knight soon became unpopular and had to leave, after which a number of other French knights were sent, including even the count of Saint-Pol. Some of these delegates, however, tried to make themselves popular by treating the citizenry with too great leniency and familiarity; spent too much time socially with them, and danced with their ladies – and this is no way to govern the citizens of Genoa; as a result, each of the French governors had in turn to leave. [185]

IV: How virtue alone should govern advancement.

As a way of introducing the events that we wish to describe, we might perhaps provide a short prologue devoted to instances of knightly valour and their definition. What, we may ask, should be the causes of man's advancement? Having considered this question deeply, having studied the writings of the ancients, having weighed up events, I believe that the cause should be virtue, and virtue alone. On this, judging from their writings, Aristotle is agreed, as is Seneca, as are all the other wise men of the past.[8] [186] But how then are we to judge the virtue of a particular man? In all truth, just as pure gold or pure silver can be seen only when they are refined in the furnace, so the virtues of a man can be judged only in the furnace of great and weighty affairs of state in which he can demonstrate his wisdom by bringing them to a wise conclusion, by showing fortitude in the face of ill luck, by preparing for all eventualities, by bearing the burdens of office, by unsparingly undertaking great enterprises, by managing them with care and wisdom – and by showing fortitude in everything. All these virtues might well pass unnoticed if a man is not put to the test in the ways we have described. But when such a man, one so tempered by events, is elected or raised to such an office, [187] he does so deservedly. And that virtues of this sort should be sole cause of promotion and elevation is demonstrated for instance, as Valerius Maximus tells us, by the case of Scipio, the valiant knight later to be known as Africanus:[9] he was on active service with the main Roman army stationed in Spain,

7 François de Sassenage, governor of Asti, received the homage of the Genoese on 27 November 1396 in the name of King Charles VI. Adorno became governor until 30 December 1396, when he was replaced by Waleran III de Luxembourg (1355–1415), count of Ligny and of Saint-Pol, who entered the city on 18 March 1397.

8 Aristotle, *Nicomachean Ethics*, trans. Roger Crisp (Cambridge, 2004), pp. 68–72 (IV, c.4) and Nicole Oresme, *Le livre de ethiques d'Aristote. Published from the Text of MS 2902, Bibliothèque Royale de Belgique with a Critical Introduction and Notes*, ed. A.D. Menut (New York, 1940), pp. 235–6; Seneca, *Moral Essays, Volume III: De beneficiis*, trans. J.W. Basore (Cambridge, MA, 1935), pp. 176–8 (III, c.28).

9 Scipio Africanus (236–183 BC) was elected proconsul to lead the Roman army into Spain in 210 BC. The source for this discussion is Nicolas de Gonesse's translation and commentary upon Valerius Maximus, VIII, c.15.1, in BNF MS fr. 282, fols 340a–341a.

engaged in the conquest of lands overseas (as was then the Roman ambition), when his legions sent word to the senate and consuls of the city that he, Scipio, should be made governor of Spain: all the captains of the army, they said, were unanimous in this request, although Scipio was at the time very young for such a position. But as Valerius shows, youth should not be a bar to honour if it is deserved: on the contrary, in such a virtuous young man, attention should be paid not to age, but precisely to virtue. For the captains of Scipio's army had witnessed his military acumen and his sheer courage and fortitude, and had such faith in him that they considered him a most worthy ruler and leader – and they were not mistaken, for their request was granted, and they were led by Scipio with such valour that they were triumphant in all their enterprises. [188]

V: How thanks to his virtue and valour the marshal was elected and installed as governor of Genoa.

I have now demonstrated how a man should be elevated to high office for his virtue alone, as was the valiant knight Scipio Africanus; now I return to my subject to point out that this was the case when the Genoese – who were not of his lineage or his nationality or his affinity (by contrast with the case of Scipio) – sent to the king of France to request that Marshal Boucicaut be named governor of their city, in spite of his being very young for such a responsibility.[10] For the Genoese, who operate often overseas, had witnessed him in operation in a number of his voyages, now in the company of the count of Eu (close kin to the king of France), now in the crusade to Hungary, now in action in Constantinople, now elsewhere as the first part of this book has shown. The Genoese had carefully considered the virtues of the marshal, his sagacity, his righteousness, [189] his chivalry, his personal bravery and his hardihood, and their considered judgement was that he was worthy in every respect to undertake great responsibilities. They had not arrived at this conclusion hastily; on the contrary, they had weighed up his qualities after long deliberation and by common consent, and so sent envoys to the king to ask that he be given the governorship of Genoa, and that he be sent forthwith to their city; they had elected him unanimously, and awaited the king's consent. The king considered their request at length, for although their petition was framed justly and in due form, it was no small thing for the kingdom of France to divest itself of the presence of a marshal who embodied so many virtues; the debate on the subject attracted many views both for and against. But in the end, since the kingdom was not at that time engaged in war, and since it would be right to take measures to prevent the ruin of the city and region of Genoa, now sick and beset by famine and at a very low ebb: a city moreover which had ceded itself to the

10 Colart de Calleville, governor of Genoa, was forced to flee the city on 12 January 1400 and Boucicaut was appointed as his replacement by Charles VI on 23 March 1401.

crown of France in search of help for its miseries, it was agreed that the marshal would indeed be so delegated. At which point the king duly committed to the wise and good Marshal Boucicaut the governorship of the city of Genoa [190] and of all the region over which it holds sway, made him his lieutenant to represent his person, and granted him, as his representative, jurisdiction and authority in all matters, and responsibility for all edicts, ordinances and commands; this the king confirmed by letters patent, signed and sealed in the presence of his council.

VI: How the marshal went to Genoa, and how he was received.

Now that the king had assigned him the commission as governor of Genoa, as we have seen, the marshal made rapid preparations for his departure. Wise as he was in all things, he recognised that along with the wisdom and sagacity necessary to govern the Italians, if he was to restore the decline and devastation that had overtaken the city he would also need military might to counter the challenges and hostilities that are the result of Genoese rivalries. For that reason, with the king's support, he recruited a force of men-at-arms as numerous as his foresight thought necessary. When everything for the expedition south was ready, he took leave of the king and the other lords. He set out with a substantial escort, heading direct to Genoa [191] via the city of Milan, which is just two days short of Genoa.[11] There he halted for a few days, waiting for his company of men-at-arms. While he was there, the notables and dignitaries of Genoa came to greet him; they showed him due deference, and made a show of their delight at his coming. Some of them, of course, were probably simulating delight, since they could see that they were no longer in the ascendant; others however were genuinely pleased, hoping that he might restore a lasting peace to the city and restore its prosperity. The marshal received them all benevolently. His aim now – and indeed what he had wished, secretly, for some time – was to discover which of them could be trusted as worthy citizens who were content to accept the rule of the king of France, and who would be delighted to see peace and justice restored, and by contrast which of them were seditious and liable to cause trouble, and hostile to the rule of the king. He found reliable informants and was thus able to ascertain that some of the most prominent and well-born among them had hoped to snatch the city for their own rule; they would foment enmities and treasons, and this was true of one of them in particular, to whom we shall return below. Once he had determined the truth as to the good citizens and the bad, he never forgot it – something they were to learn when the time came. [192]

He then left Milan for Genoa, and along his route there came to greet him noblemen, citizens and men of the people, celebrating his coming whatever some might have been thinking; all of them, upright citizens or not, left the city to show

11 Boucicaut arrived in Italy on 14 August 1401 and visited Gian Galeazzo Visconti (1351–1402), duke of Milan since 1395, en route to Genoa. Visconti's daughter Valentina (1371–1408) was married to Louis duke of Orléans.

him due respect. He entered the city on All Saints' Eve 1401, and was greeted with joy.[12] A fine company made up of men-at-arms but also of citizens escorted him to the palace, a fine building that had been luxuriously prepared for his arrival, with everything appropriate to his position. I suspect that there were those among them who, when they saw his formidable aspect and the company he had brought, were distinctly alarmed, knowing their own guilt. But those who were blameless were much reassured, sensing that a champion had arrived to defend them against the traitors and against renewed calamities. Once he was installed, he issued a proclamation that all citizens, of whatever rank, were to lay down their arms and deposit them at the palace; they might have knives only to slice their bread; no-one should dare to have arms of any sort in his house, and anyone who disobeyed would be executed. They could not but obey, though in many cases reluctantly – at which point the Genoese understood that they were now under the rule of a new master. [193] Then you might have seen crowds of them hurrying to deposit arms and armour at the palace: they had possessed quantities of them, often fine and costly. The governor had the arms safely stored and well guarded. Moreover, he forbade them – also on pain of death – from possessing knives or daggers, and from gathering in churches or elsewhere.

VII: How the marshal addressed wise words to the Genoese.

The very next day, all the notables and dignitaries of Genoa gathered in council with the marshal. He addressed them very wisely, and told them in calm and measured words that the king his master had sent him there at their request; he thanked them for their confidence and the trust they had placed in him, and explained that he had been sent to offer some remedy for the devastation to which they had been reduced by the ill will of those among them who persecuted those of good will; his role would be to punish the evildoers, to keep the peace for upright citizens and ensure justice for all. To accomplish this he had need of military means, [194] and he promised to give all his energies, unsparingly, to their cause, as a matter of honour to himself and the king. In which enterprise he begged them to be true and loyal subjects to the king of France, as they had promised; in return, they could be certain that with God's help he would defend them to the best of his ability against their enemies, he would uphold justice, he would ensure they could live in peace and equity – and he would endeavour to maintain the public good. But should it be that he detected or suspected that they were hostile, or that any of them were hatching treasons or plots against the king's majesty or against himself, then they should understand, beyond any doubt, that he would exact punishments on even the most mighty that would deter anyone. If, however, they showed themselves loyal and worthy subjects, they

12 Boucicaut arrived in Genoa on 31 October 1401, but refused to swear an oath to respect the constitution of the city-state, as required of any French governor by article 14 of the treaty of 25 October 1396.

need have nothing to fear from him, in spite of his appointment as their governor and lord; they should not imagine that he intended his regime to be arrogant or cruel, arbitrary or wayward. That was, he repeated, not his intention; rather he wished to live with them peaceably as a friend of Genoa, to heed their loyal advice without which he would make no decisions, and to do nothing that would adversely affect the policies and governance of the city.

The governor spoke wisely to them in these agreeable and well-judged terms, because of which, and because of his stately and cordial manner, [195] they esteemed and respected his sagacity and expressed themselves content. They thanked him profusely, and offered, heart and soul, their faithful and loyal obedience to the king their lord and to him as vicar, lieutenant and governor. After these opening remarks, they spoke of many things – notably, he was given the names of all the worst of the conspirators and traitors, those who had most often fomented rebellion. Many had come to Milan to offer their respects to him; chief among those was a certain Battista Boccanegra, who in actual fact had conspired to murder all the contingent of French sent by the king, in order to seize possession of Genoa.[13] Knowing this, the governor ordered Boccanegra and some of his most prominent followers to be seized; the order was immediately fulfilled when, much to Boccanegra's dismay, he saw himself made prisoner by the governor in the name of the king; he had imagined that no-one would dare to lay hands on him because of the power he could exert. In the event, however, this did him no good, for the wise governor, perfectly well aware of the hatred and envy felt for each other by members of Italian families, was determined that in response to any accusation, he would ensure that justice was informed by full and proper information, and this he did with the greatest diligence. He had the prisoners carefully questioned, and once he had heard the reports of the questioning and their own confessions, [196] they were found guilty. For their crimes, and so that any others tempted to treason might take warning, this Battista and two other members of his following were publicly beheaded.[14] The inhabitants of the town, who had thought their execution impossible because of their rank and because they had such influence in the town, were so daunted that they were afraid to transgress, even if they were in the governor's entourage. They became much afraid of his justice, having seen that he was determined to spare no malefactor, no matter what his position; indeed he had one of his own following beheaded for having allowed a prisoner entrusted to his guard to escape.[15] After this he began to dispense fair justice to everyone and to punish wrongdoers according to their deserts, however

13 Battista Boccanegra (c.1359–1401) was the son of the first doge of Genoa, Simone Boccanegra. He was briefly elected captain of the king during a popular uprising in Genoa in January 1400, holding power until 20 March: S.A. Epstein, *Genoa and the Genoese, 958–1528* (Chapel Hill, NC, 2001), pp. 256–8.

14 Boccanegra was arrested on 2 November 1401 for acting without the authority of King Charles VI, and beheaded four days later.

15 Battista Franchi had been elected captain for the king after Boccanegra but deposed on 22 September 1401, shortly before Boucicaut's arrival. Like Boccanegra, Franchi was arrested on

great or lowly they were. He had those who had betrayed or rebelled against the French crown publicly beheaded, thieves and crooks hanged, heretics and recusants burned, limbs amputated as appropriate to the crime, [197] traitors and rebels exiled, some temporarily, others for life depending on the offence. On the other hand he showed compassion and mercy to the poor and ignorant when they were in want. That way, he behaved like the good shepherd who separates out the scraggy sheep from the healthy, so that its disease does not infect the rest of the flock, or like a good doctor who cuts out decayed flesh lest it contaminate the sound.[16] He also showed no favour to anyone, whatever bribe he might be offered, whatever the affiliation of the accused, whatever faction he might belong to.

Thus the noble governor, with his determination to pursue justice and fairness, might have seemed a product of the school of knighthood existing formerly in Rome and as described by Valerius, who said that Romans universally and strictly followed the rules of virtue – the discipline of knighthood, he insists – to such an extent that they would spare no-one, relative or friend, not even someone closest to them, if they deserved punishment for breaking these rules. Valerius gives the example of a certain valiant prince of Rome, Paulus Rupilius (Rustilius), [198] who punished his very own son for transgressing against certain edicts that were enjoined on all, on pain of punishment.[17] Ah, that was true virtue! Ah, there was a man worthy of praise! Holy Scripture equates true justice with divine virtue, as Solomon said: 'He who does not stint on justice brings peace and prosperity';[18] that is to say that where true justice reigns, there we find peace and happiness. Thereafter, the governor in his wisdom and goodness was feared for the rigorous justice he dispensed to all, far and near, high- or low-born: all feared falling into wrongdoing.

From that time wise old men and men of noble birth, who had been driven out of the city for fear of the robbers and thugs who lived off thieving, and who frequently murdered each other, began to return to live in the city. They were drawn to the governor and celebrated his beneficent rule; he in his turn welcomed them with open arms; the guilty, by contrast, took to their heels and mustered outside the city. But the wise governor had them pursued over hill and dale and tracked like wolves through the forests, until they were finally cornered by force or by guile; [199] he then had their leaders executed, as an example to all.

---

2 November on charges that he had acted without royal authority, but Franchi escaped on his way to the scaffold.

16 These were commonplace metaphors in contemporary discourse about kingship, used for example by Philippe de Mézières, *Le songe du vieux pèlerin*, ed. J. Blanchard, 2 volumes (Geneva, 2015), I, pp. 22–3 (prologue) and by Christine de Pizan in *Le livre de l'advision Cristine*, ed. C.M. Reno and L. Dulac (Paris, 2001), 22 (I, c.11) and *Livre du corps de policie*, pp. 13–15 (I, c.9).

17 The story of Paulus Rupilius was presented by Simon de Hesdin in his translation and commentary upon Valerius Maximus, II, c.7.3, in BNF MS fr. 282 fos 108b–c. Both Hesdin and the biographer presented the individual's name as Paulus Rustilius.

18 This quotation echoes Proverbs 21: 21 and 29: 4.

VIII: Here we tell of the wise edicts and ordinances that the marshal established in Genoa.

Next the wise governor issued his own edicts and ordinances. He ordered that a suitably large company of captains and men-at-arms be stationed day and night on the city's fine main square that extends in front of the palace, to guard the palace itself and the city. After that he made enquiries to discover which were the wisest and worthiest among the city's jurists; he commissioned them to be in charge of justice, and instructed them to administer the law without fear or favour, for rich and poor alike, such that he would never have to hear a murmur of complaint or a hint of corruption. Indeed if he were to detect that any jurist had favoured one party or the other in a particular case, they should know that he would inflict a punishment that would be an example to all. Moreover, in order to prevent trickery of any sort, he decreed that he himself would hear complaints about any judge. By now he had determined who would constitute his council, and had picked out the wisest and most appropriate of the elders of the city; he used them as councillors in the establishment of his own regime, relying on their knowledge of the ancient statutes and customs. [200]

Item: he had it proclaimed throughout the city that on pain of death, no-one should be so bold as to attack another citizen or provoke fights around the divisions between Guelphs and Ghibellines; everyone was to return to his business or trade and to live in peace with his neighbours; if anyone felt harmed or damaged, he should appeal forthwith to the judiciary, and if justice failed him, he should come to the marshal himself and there true justice would be done. At this the worthy merchants and men of goodwill, who had had to trade in secret for fear of being robbed by highwaymen or thieves, were delighted and glad to buy and sell and export openly, on land or on sea. And the financiers and money-changers, who for so long had kept their currencies concealed and their transactions under wraps – because if they traded openly they risked being robbed – started to reopen their changing-houses and to hold and display their stocks of coins openly and freely, as is right, with no fear of robbery or theft; jewellers could exhibit their precious gems in the marketplace, or in the elegant homes, built of fine marble, that they owned around the city. Everywhere shops [201] reopened selling all sorts of merchandise, and the shopkeepers were displaying treasures that they had kept concealed for many a year. And craftsmen – many of whom had turned to robbery – now returned to their crafts, and thus everyone was able to go back to his own trade. The good governor, by his good sense and firm principles, had thus restored order and justice, and returned the city to tranquillity [201].[19]

19 In addition, Boucicaut founded the celebrated Bank of Saint George (Ufficio di San Giorgio) at the Palazzo San Giorgio in 1407; this played a central role in Genoese history until its dissolution in 1805. Epstein, *Genoa and the Genoese*, pp. 228–70.

IX: How the wise marshal ordered two strong castles to be built, one guarding the harbour, the other the rest of the city, and how he set about restoring everything that was damaged or in ruins.

Once these prudent ordinances were in place, the wise governor, as we have said, recognised that a public show of force was indispensable in governing peoples of that country, and that this was even more urgent in the case of the rebellious factions among the Genoese – although he had no intention of extorting money from them, or doing them harm, or imposing tyrannical laws on them, or unduly oppressing them; [202] rather, it was to discourage them from the sort of temptation towards rebellion which they had harboured for so many years. At that point he summoned skilful, well-trained workmen and master masons, and had them build two fine strong castles, the first overlooking the harbour, the Darsena [La Darse], where ships and galleys dock: this one is a fine stronghold, with two great towers. The intention was to provide security for shipping against enemies or any other threat that might materialise. The works went well, and the castle was built according to the brief established by the wise governor: it was strong and handsome, as can be seen today. Once it was completed, the wise governor had it equipped with artillery and other weaponry and everything else necessary, and garrisoned with good men-at-arms. In this way he made his rule secure: ships could come and go freely, whatever the circumstances, and he himself could ensure that any such comings and goings were done at his discretion. The other castle he had built on the main square of the city: it is known as the Castelletto [Chastellet], and it is so well fortified that it can be defended by a small force against any attacker: there is a passageway between this and the castle on the harbour or Darsena, in the event of an attack.[20] He also had two further castles built outside the city, one in Chiavari [Chaury], the other in La Spezia [Lespesse]. [203]

In addition, he ensured that all the castles and fortresses outside the bounds of the city but which were in its sovereignty – there were many of them, very fine and important, but which had been seized by individual Genoese strongmen – were rendered and returned to the authority of the city; he did so by sending envoys to demand, on pain of death, that the occupiers surrender the castles without delay, and he was obeyed without question.[21]

Item: he sent experienced envoys by sea on official visits to all Genoese colonies and territories to ascertain their circumstances and the regime they were under; Genoese held significant lands in the Levant, on the Black Sea and in other parts

20 Boucicaut did not build the Castelletto ('small castle'), but merely restored it.

21 Monaco had been seized from Genoa by the Grimaldi family in 1297, but was taken back from Louis de Grimaldi (d.1402), lord of Monaco from 1395 until 1402. Also, the castle at Aquila d'Arroscia in Liguria was recaptured from the Carretto family.

such as Caffa [Capha], in Asia Minor.[22] In Greece, they controlled the city of Pera, a fine city near Constantinople.

Item: they controlled the island of Chios, the source of mastic, off the west coast of Turkey.[23] In Cyprus, they controlled the fine city of Famagusta. Around Azof [Tane],[24] [204] off the Black Sea and beyond Caffa and fourteen hundred miles north-west of Constantinople, the Genoese held substantial lands and many fortresses, not to mention the islands, many of them well peopled and prosperous; there were also under Genoese authority other lands, too many to list. Around this time, incidentally, a populous island near Genoa called the island of Elba [Erbe] declared war on the city; the governor sent a well-armed expeditionary force of four galleys, which took control of the island.

X: Here we explain how, after he had restored the city of Genoa to prosperity, he brought his wife there, and how she was received.

When all this had been accomplished, prosperity began to return to Genoa; its noble and rich inhabitants felt able once more to display their wealth fully and in public: costly robes and clothes for the men, rich dresses, head-dresses and jewellery for their noble ladies – velvets, gold, silks, pearls, expensive gems in the Genoese fashion; [205] at the same time they could dare to live contentedly, confident in a new peace, under the aegis of the wise governor. They felt able moreover to return to maritime trade, sending goods overseas in greater quantity than they had previously dared, and to trade profitably in all domains – all of which returned them to their previous settled prosperity. When the wise governor saw all this, he decided it was time to send for his much-loved and virtuous and fair and wise wife Madame Antoinette de Turenne, who, like him, was languishing in the absence of her husband, for they were profoundly in love and had led a most happy and virtuous life together, although, for this time, they had been obliged to live apart. The governor therefore sent back to his own domains an escort of well-known knights and men of honour to attend her fittingly and suitably. When he heard that she was within a day's journey of Genoa, he set off with a fine retinue made up of knights and noblemen of his own company,

22 On 23 May 1402, Boucicaut dispatched five inspectors, known as the 'sindicatores', to review each of the Genoese colonies. The Genoese port of Caffa in Crimea, on the Black Sea coast, is now known as Feodosia.

23 Chios is situated in the Aegean, four miles off the Anatolian coast. It came under Genoese control in 1261 and was known above all for the production of mastic, a resin known as 'Arabic gum'.

24 Azof, known as La Tana when it was a Venetian and Genoese colony in the thirteenth and fourteenth centuries, is a town on the mouth of the river Don, where it flows into the Sea of Azov.

and also of the most important dignitaries from the city. Thus as she neared Genoa, she was welcomed by Genoese in their richest attire, for they all dressed in different liveries, from the wealthiest in their velvets and other finery, to the artisans, or craftsmen as we might say – until it seemed that the whole city had ridden out to pay their respects and give her a joyful reception. Thus she made her solemn entry into the city in rich array – in dress and in trappings – and attended by ladies, damsels, knights, squires, well-born burgesses, upstanding citizens of Genoa, [206] and was joyfully received by her husband and others who were waiting at the palace; her arrival was celebrated with jubilation.[25] And her coming instituted a sense of elation in Genoa, for her virtue, her honour, her courtesy and her sagacity strengthened the pleasure that the citizens took in the presence of their good governor; they were delighted to find in his spouse the wisdom, the compassion, the grace and the humility they had welcomed in him. The ladies of Genoa paid her official visits, and promised her their unquestioning service and obedience – and as a lady of good breeding she received them most graciously, and showed them such generosity that all were loud in her praise.

XI: How news came to the marshal that the king of Cyprus had laid siege to Famagusta, a Genoese city, and how in its defence he mustered a great army from Genoa.

The good marshal had been in Genoa for about a year, [207] busy returning it to prosperity as we have described, when news came to him that the king of Cyprus had laid siege to Famagusta, a fine city still standing today in Cyprus. The city had been under the sovereignty of Genoa, as we have said, for many years (and is so today), since the Genoese had conquered it in the course of a war against the king of Cyprus who had succeeded good King Peter II of Lusignan; it was the present king of Cyprus who had attacked Famagusta in the hope of recovering the city if possible.[26] The chivalrous governor was determined that under his rule Genoa should lose none of its dominions or colonies; on the contrary, his wish was to extend the Genoese territories and spheres of influence for which he was responsible; when he heard the news, he swore immediate action, and that the situation would soon be put to rights. So he had an army mustered immediately, with the intention of leading it in his own person. However, with his habitual thoroughness – he did not wish to act without

25 Antoinette de Turenne arrived in Genoa on 5 July 1402.

26 The Genoese had seized the port of Famagusta on the east coast of Cyprus in 1373. They had forced Peter II of Lusignan, king of Cyprus (1369–82) to accept their ownership by a treaty dated 21 October 1374, and this was confirmed on 19 February 1383 by his uncle and successor, Jacques I de Lusignan, king of Cyprus (1382–98). The next ruler, Janus I, king of Cyprus (1398–1432), attempted to recapture Famagusta from the Genoese in 1403, after having spent the first eighteen years of his life, from 1372 to 1392, in Genoa as a hostage.

due thought and wise consideration [208] – he decided that he should follow due process: he would therefore, before launching an attack, send to the king of Cyprus to exhort him to lift the siege and to desist from doing any damage to a city subject to the king of France; he requested, with great warmth, that the king do so out of love and duty to the king of France; otherwise, he was to be sure that war would be declared, and that he would be provoking an enemy able to do him great harm. Once this had been agreed in council, the embassy was entrusted to a wise knight who had behind him a lifetime of valour in arms: a man of scrupulous character and the soul of discretion, the Hermite de La Faye.[27] The marshal had a galley prepared for him, and the ambassador – God be with him – embarked.

Item: the marshal did not intend any act of war against the king of Cyprus until he had heard his response to the embassy, but his courage and chivalry were such that he preferred as he always had to take part in the deeds of arms which are the mark of honour for a knight; he considered therefore that he should confront the enemies of the faith. Accordingly, he planned a two-pronged expedition: first against the king of Cyprus if the latter failed to see reason, and then against the unbelievers. [209] So he had his fleet prepared and equipped with everything necessary for war. He promulgated ordinances as to the government of Genoa in his absence, and assigned as his deputy a fine, wise knight, the lord of La Vieuville, and made sure that he was left with a fine body of men-at-arms.[28] When all these preparations had been made, the marshal set sail on 3 April in the year 1403, in a fleet of eight galleys laden with good men-at-arms, crossbowmen and all the equipment necessary for war. Soon he was well out to sea, with a following wind, and heading straight for Rhodes.

XII: How the Genoese and the Venetians were entrenched in a long-term feud.

I shall continue my account of the marshal's expedition to Cyprus and neighbouring countries, and of his principal adventures and deeds on that expedition, but first I need to leave that aside and turn to another matter; the digression will, I hope, bring me back to the marshal's life-story. [210]

It is a truth universally acknowledged, and has been for many years, that when, as often happens, two principalities similarly or equally powerful are neighbours, they will never be friends. This can be attributed to the sin of pride, which inspires a mutual envy, and the wish for each to compete with the other, to outdo them in reputation

27 Guillaume de Montrevel (d.1413), known as the Hermite de La Faye, embarked on 24 March 1403. He was a royal chamberlain and later councillor, governor of the Dauphiné from 1398 to 1399, and one of the most important companions of Louis II duke of Bourbon, for whom Montrevel served as an executor.

28 Pierre de La Vieuville (d.1421) had been a chamberlain of the duke of Orléans and had previously served in Italy between 1394 and 1396.

and fortune. For these reasons the Genoese and the Venetians have never been at all friendly, and as a result there has been an endless succession of war and aggression between them, and their enmity has turned to mortal hatred, not unusual in such a case. In the wake of a great war, and even if peace has been negotiated, memories of resentment will naturally persist when lands remain ravaged and devastated, when there are still visible signs of killings and burnings and buildings ruined and destroyed. Such things remain only too obvious to the children of those directly affected, and continue to signify the harms and injuries that their enemies inflicted on their forebears – and such things, constantly visible, will scarcely inspire love between those whom war has hurt or damaged. Now it is the case that there have been so many occasions in Greece and elsewhere – disputes or attacks [211] – over lands or castles or sovereignty, and there are so many points where Genoese and Venetian lands border on each other that there have been many wars between the two powers, wars so vicious that one side or the other has been close to destroyed. At which point efforts at goodwill have resulted in peace being declared – but the participants cannot forget their hatred and resentment, which has now become deeply engrained on each side. Now when someone filled with hatred sees his enemy thrown down, either by himself or by someone else, his hatred is appeased and he thinks no more of it – but if by some stroke of luck the object of his hatred recovers his power and prosperity, then hatred and envy revive redoubled. That is just how it is with the Venetians and the Genoese; true enough, after many a deadly war, they have declared peace, but their deep-rooted resentment has not been appeased. For some considerable time, this has had no ill effects: the Genoese were for many years so consumed by their own internecine struggles that no-one could feel envious – one cannot be envious of misfortune – and thus Venetian resentment remained dormant. But God and good fortune conspired, via the good offices of the king of France, to provide the Genoese with a wise governor [212] who was like the man the Romans called a second Romulus – Romulus was the first founder of Rome – because he revived the empire after a great defeat and destruction and restored Rome itself, long left desolate.[29] Similarly, the Genoese could legitimately call their wise governor, restoring their fortunes, a second Janus after their founder – and now the Venetians, seeing the renewed and growing prosperity of their enemies under their good governor, felt their former envy and enmity revive; their resentment became such that they were ready to do anything to disrupt the new prosperity of Genoa. They saw that prosperity as potentially harmful to them: if it continued and grew, the Genoese, they felt, would soon surpass them in power, in strength and in reputation, and they feared that, in such a case, the Genoese would return to old disputes to the detriment of the Venetians. In those circumstances, they would very much have wished, if possible, to damage the man they considered to be the leader and figurehead of Genoese

29 Marcus Furius Camillus (c.446–365 BC) was given the title of 'Second Founder of Rome' for having saved the city from the Gauls in 390 BC. See pp. 207–8 below.

prosperity, the wise governor; if, they felt, they could manage that, they would have little to fear. [213] But to achieve such damage, they would need to act by cunning and underhand means, such that no-one would realise until too late what they were plotting. So they kept their machinations secret until the opportunity presented itself. So when they heard that the marshal had put to sea for an expedition in foreign parts – as I described earlier – they realised that the opportunity had come for them to put their schemes into action. So without revealing their intentions, they hastily armed thirteen galleys, manning them with good men-at-arms and crossbowmen and whatever weapons might be required for naval warfare. When all was ready, they swiftly put to sea and sailed in pursuit of the marshal.

And thus, to come back to my story, the marshal was scarcely south of the kingdom of Calabria when he was told about the Venetian forces – although no-one understood what they were intending. The marshal, thoughtful as ever, pondered their appearance, and even wondered if it was intended to do him harm. But finally, unwilling like all those of goodwill to suspect that anyone would wish to damage him, he allowed his suspicions to be allayed; after all, he had been at peace with the Venetians for some time, and had done nothing to disrupt relations between Genoa and Venice. So he concluded that the Venetian fleet was not intended to do him harm, and he discounted it and continued on his route. When he was around twenty miles from Modone,[30] a Venetian city, [214] he received news that the thirteen Venetian galleys were at anchor there, and once again he wondered what enterprise could have caused the Venetians to gather so large a force. He anchored off an island nearby and in order to discover the Venetian intention, he sent a galley to Porto Longo [Portogon] carrying Mountjoy Herald, a wise and worthy person and very shrewd, instructing him to find out, if possible, what the Venetians were intending;[31] Mountjoy returned to say that after careful enquiries, he could only confirm the presence of the thirteen galleys, but that no-one on land was able to tell him what the Venetians were planning. The marshal became very suspicious of their intentions; he could conceive of no legitimate reason for the Venetians to have mustered so large a force. But he was undaunted, even though his own force was smaller in men and in ships; he determined that if the Venetian force was indeed intending to attack him, he would duly accept the challenge, and he agreed this with his council. On the other hand, because still he could not be sure that the Venetian manoeuvres were directed at him, he forbade all his own men from making a first move; he did not wish to provoke action, nor that the Venetians should be able to accuse him of aggression; he urged them however, [215] if the Venetians did attack, to respond valiantly. The following morning, the marshal made sure his galleys and his men were in battle-order, ready to fight if required: he set his crossbowmen ready to fire, and ordered

30 Modone was the Venetian name for Methoni in Messena, in the south-western part of the Peloponnese. From 1125 to 1500, it was a Venetian stronghold and an important trade centre.

31 The identification of 'Portogon', a harbour near to Modone, is unclear, but it may well have been Porto Longo.

his men-at-arms to make a show of strength to deter any attacks. Thus arrayed, the marshal and his eight galleys made sail to Modone. When he neared the harbour, he sent a galley forward to scout out the situation. When the Venetians saw the galley coming, they welcomed it joyfully, and showed every sign of delight at the coming of the marshal. They drew anchor and came out to escort him into harbour, and the captain of their fleet, a certain Carlo Zeno, exchanged jubilant greetings with the marshal so that they all seemed fast friends.[32] They all sailed into Modone harbour together, with the marshal's suspicions entirely laid to rest.

XIII: How the marshal assisted the emperor of Constantinople to return to his realm.

When the marshal arrived in Modone, he found messengers from Manuel II, emperor of Constantinople [216] waiting for him; they were begging him, for the love of God and for the honour of knighthood and nobility, not to sail further before they had the opportunity for talks; the emperor was in the [despotate of] Morea, some twenty miles inland, and if the marshal were willing to wait a little, the emperor would come to join him.[33] The marshal gave the messengers a fitting welcome, and graciously agreed to their proposal. He appointed two envoys to receive the emperor: the lord of Châteaumorand with his company, and the Genoese lord Giovanni Centurione d'Oltramarino with a galley; he himself would wait for him at a port called Basilipotamo [Basselimpotano].[34] When the marshal was told that the emperor was near, he naturally went to meet him and his wife and children, and did them great honour. The emperor asked if he would be so kind, for the sake of God and Christendom, as to ensure his safe passage to Constantinople. The marshal replied that he would do so most willingly, and would happily offer him any other help. To provide the escort, he ordered a fleet of four galleys under the good Châteaumorand. The emperor then left, and the marshal escorted him as far as Cape Maleas [Cap Saint-Angel].[35] At that point, [217] messengers arrived from the Venetians; they had heard that the marshal had designated four galleys to take the emperor to Constantinople, and were minded, if he considered it useful, to send

32 Carlo Zeno (1333–1418) was a Venetian admiral who had saved Venice from the Genoese at the battle of Chioggia on 1 January 1380.

33 Manuel II had visited Genoa from 22 January to 10 February 1403, where Boucíciaut had promised to escort the emperor back to Constantinople, following the defeat of Bayezid I by Tamerlane at the battle of Ankara on 20 July 1402 that had ended the immediate Ottoman threat.

34 Giovanni Centurione d'Oltramarino was a Genoese admiral who had famously commanded the fleet that carried the duke of Bourbon to the siege of Mahdia in 1390. Basilipotamo was also known as Eurotas, and was the principal river of Laconia or Lacedaemonia.

35 By 'Cap Saint-Angel', here, the French author refers to Cape Meleas at the south-east tip of the Peloponnese.

another four in order to ensure his safety on the voyage. The marshal responded that this would be an excellent move, and one that would do honour to the Most Serene Republic of Venice and to the commander of the galleys.[36] At this point the emperor bade farewell to the marshal, and headed straight for Constantinople. Meanwhile the marshal set sail, with his four remaining galleys, to Rhodes, and those Venetians who had remained, with nine galleys, accompanied him every step of the way, as far as the island of Nicosia.[37] At that point the marshal, ever mindful of what would be of benefit to the cause of Christendom and of the true faith, and wishing therefore to inflict confusion and damage on the Saracens, devised a cunning – and promising – plan: if the captain of the Venetian galleys would concur, and if together they could mount an attack on the infidels, they were a sufficient force to inflict considerable damage and loss. He sent an eloquent and persuasive envoy to propose the plan to the captain of the galleys, and to explain that if, please God, he was able to negotiate peace with the king of Cyprus, his wish and intention was to inflict destruction on the enemies of the faith on any possible occasion; [218] this seemed to him a fine and laudable ambition; if the captain would agree to ally himself, he, the captain, would take a share in the credit and honour that would accrue; he was confident that with God's help, such an enterprise would be a fine and honourable success. The captain responded, by the envoy, that he sent his heartfelt thanks to the governor for the honour he was doing him; when he reached Rhodes, which he expected to do within two or three days, he promised to send a reply that the governor would find pleasing.

XIV: How the marshal arrived in Rhodes and was welcomed by the grand master of Rhodes, who requested that he proceed to Cyprus to negotiate peace.

The marshal was by this time nearing Rhodes, and when the grand master, Philibert de Naillac, heard of his approach, he took a great company of knights and citizens to greet him; they did so joyously and with great honour.[38] The grand master escorted him to the Order's fine castle which dominates the town; he had had it set in good order against the marshal's coming. [219] There they dined together and discussed many enterprises and the latest news. Afterwards, [Carlo Zeno], the captain of the Venetian galleys, sent messengers to the marshal to say that although he had encouraged the captain to make common cause in an assault on the Saracens, he had had no authorisation from the Serene Republic of Venice, and without that he

36 The commander of the Venetian vessels was Leonardo Mocenigo.

37 The author talks of the 'isle de Nicocie', for which Lalande suggests Nicosia, the largest city on the island of Cyprus. But this is over 250 miles to the east of Rhodes, and so unlikely to have been the place that Boucicaut broke his journey.

38 Boucicaut arrived at Rhodes at the start of June 1403 and met with Philibert de Naillac, grand master of the Knights Hospitaller (1396–1421).

could not engage in any new enterprise; he would therefore have to call a halt to his participation in the enterprise, and begged the marshal's forgiveness. Thereafter he refused all communication with the marshal.

Now, when Châteaumorand, as we explained, had left the fleet to escort the emperor, the marshal had ordered him, as a way of swelling his forces, to bring back all the galleys and galiots belonging to Genoa or to its allies that he could find. This commission he fulfilled conscientiously, with the result that he gathered several vessels: a galley and a small galley from Pera [Paire], a galley and a galiot from Ainos [Ayne],[39] a galley and a galiot from Mytilene, and two galleys from Chios [Syon]. Châteaumorand led all these vessels back to Rhodes to the marshal, who was awaiting the response of the king of Cyprus to whom, as we explained, the Hermite de La Faye had been sent in embassy. Soon thereafter the Hermite arrived, and reported that whatever arguments he had put forward, he had found the king in no mind to agree peace. When the marshal heard this, [220] he said that in the face of the king's refusal to see reason and admit his culpability, he had no option but to declare war. At this point he had his fleet made ready, and embarked with all his horses and his men. The grand master of Rhodes was dismayed, foreseeing the ills that would ensue from the war between the king of Cyprus and the Genoese that was now inevitable; he begged the marshal for a boon, which the latter willingly granted: he entreated the marshal not to invade Cyprus before he, the master, had been to treat with the king of Cyprus. [221] To this the marshal agreed; the master embarked on his own galley; the Hermite re-embarked on his, and ordered the galley from Mytilene to accompany them.[40] And thus all three galleys set off to parley with the king of Cyprus.

XV: How the marshal proceeded to Turkey and to a great city called Candelore [l'Escandelour].

When, as we have explained, the grand master of Rhodes had left for Cyprus, the good marshal was reluctant to kick his heels waiting for a treaty to be signed; on the contrary, he decided to employ his men in an attack on the Saracens. He took council with the local knights and with the Genoese to decide where it would be best to launch a *Reise* against the enemies of the faith. They told him that his best option would be a fine town and citadel in Turkey called Candelore; even better, this

39 Enez is a town on the bank of the river Hebrus and was known in the late Middle Ages as Ainos in Greek or Aenus in Latin; it was held by the Gattilusi, a Genoese family that ruled much of the northern Aegean.

40 Guillaume de Montrevel, the Hermite de La Faye, departed Rhodes with Philibert de Naillac by 14 June 1403, in order to meet with Janus I, king of Cyprus.

town was on his route to Cyprus.[41] He had his galleys made ready without delay, and embarked with his fine company [222] of picked men-at-arms, all of them of good pedigree and eager to win renown by matching themselves with the infidel. They set off from Rhodes in fine array, and as they put out to sea, they came across a large Saracen ship; they attacked and captured it, and the capture was very profitable. A few days later, at noon on a Sunday, the fleet arrived before Candelore.[42] The marshal examined the town closely: it sits on the coast, with a great tower to guard the harbour, and then spreads upwards to the summit of a hill topped by a fine castle that keeps watch over the two districts of the town proper. At the foot of the hill, there is a flat plain spreading from the sea, with good pasture-land and properties and gardens. At this point the men-at-arms sallied out of the ships in battle-order, just as the wise marshal had instructed. And when they were all on land and drawn up on the plain, the marshal dubbed a number of new knights; I remember some, though not all, of the names: Louis des Barres [son of Jean des Barres]; [Hugues Cholet], the son of [Gilles Cholet], lord of La Choletière and who was nephew to the marshal; the lord of Châteauneuf in Provence;[43] my lord Menaut Chassagnes;[44] my lord Louis de Montigian who was to die on the field there,[45] and a great quantity of others. Many other valiant knights and squires [223] raised their banners there, all determined to acquit themselves well. There were about eight hundred of them, all well trained and experienced, all elite warriors, all valiant and with good reputations in arms, and there may well have been as many as three thousand combatants altogether, all longing to perform brave deeds in the service of their Christian faith and to enhance their reputations. Among them there moved the most valiant marshal, bravely mustering them and encouraging them to behave with the utmost valour – for he was confident, in his faith in God, in Our Lady and in Saint George, that they would emerge from the day with honour. Ah, what a pleasure it was to see this fine company, bristling with such famous banners: the banners of Our Lady, of the marshal himself, of the lord of Châteaumorand, of the lord of Châteaubrun – also known as Guillaume de Naillac – of the lord of Châteauneuf, of the lord of Puyos, and of so many others whose names I do not know!

41 Candelore was the name used by Italian traders in the thirteenth and fourteenth centuries for the city of Alanya on the southern coast of Turkey, north-west of Cyprus.

42 24 June 1403.

43 The identity of this lord is unclear.

44 Unknown.

45 Unknown.

XVI: How the marshal made a well-planned attack on Candelore.

The marshal split his troops into three parts: [224] one under the valiant lord of Châteaumorand to take up position towards the seaboard, and his own marshal, my lord Louis de Culant, with a hundred men-at-arms, a hundred crossbowmen and a hundred foot, to guard a ravine through which reinforcements might come to reinforce the town; he and his own men, with the lord of Châteaubrun, would attack by the city gates. When all the troop dispositions were in place – around mid-afternoon – he had the trumpets ring out so that the sound echoed everywhere.[46] Then the attack began from all quarters, with the defenders displaying great vigour; the battle lasted until there were great numbers of dead and wounded on both sides. Châteaumorand found himself up against a stalwart defence on the seaboard, for the tower that guarded the harbour was well manned by archers and crossbowmen and men-at-arms who defended it with a hail of missiles. But had you been there, you might have seen our men, undeterred, use grappling irons and ladders to mount the walls, competing and vying to see who would be first on the rampart – but their ladders were too short, so they were unable to make the progress they would have wished.

For his part, Louis de Culant, who had, as we said, been ordered to guard the ravine, [225] did not battle in vain, for he fought with such energy, under the marshal's standard and with the goodly company of men at his disposal, that although the struggle was fierce, he held the ravine against the enemy; his efforts were highly praiseworthy, for, on an earlier occasion, the good king of Cyprus had tried in vain to do the same. It was moreover valuable that they held the ravine, for by this means they could starve out the town if a siege were to become necessary. The overall assault – conducted with great bravery – continued until nightfall.

The following day the marshal's men returned to the fray and launched two fierce assaults; this time again the defence was strong, but the valiant Châteaumorand and his men fought with such ferocity that they took the lower part of the town despite the efforts of the defenders in the tower. In that sector they found merchant warehouses – they call them 'magazines' – full of all sorts of goods, for this is very much a trading city. They carried off all that they could, and then set fire to all the ships in the harbour – four light galleys,[47] two galleys, a galiot and two *naves*[48] – and burnt them to the waterline. [226]

---

46 The attack started on 25 June 1403.

47 The author uses the term *fuste*, meaning a small, fast galley designed for combat. Gardiner and Morrison, eds, *The Age of the Galley*, p. 249.

48 A *nave* was a sailing-ship – that is to say, a ship not equipped with oars. They were usually broader and deeper than a galley, and would be used largely for the transport of cargo.

XVII: Of the skirmishes fought daily by the marshal's forces against the Saracens, and how they defeated them and put them to flight.

At this same time, the lord of Candelore was away at war with one of his brothers, and he had deployed his forces some five days distant. But when he was told of the coming of our men, the ruler returned with his forces, intending to give battle. But once he saw the valour and determination of the gallant marshal and his chivalric company, he was daunted and lost all will to lift the siege; he therefore encamped half a mile to the rear of our men, and initiated a counter-siege, and whenever he saw an opportunity he would come and engage combat. This was not, however, a game that they could win! They were invariably fearlessly received: our men engaged them in fierce skirmishes, and on every occasion the Saracens left hide and hair, and were repelled. The marshal was most eager to offer pitched battle, but the Saracens would flee and lie low in the thickly planted gardens near the city walls; he wanted if he could to tempt them out and catch them in the open, [227] to achieve which he devised a cunning plan. He ordered that, one night, eighty horses would be led out of one of the ships, and hidden between the tents. The following day, the marshal sent a troop of his men to skirmish with the enemy: his men were to pretend to be fearful, and then to flee and apparently retreat. The Saracens were of course delighted, and pursued our men as far as the banner of Our Lady, then withdrew again. But by now it was midday and the sun was high; the enemy retired to the gardens to rest out the heat of the day, with the intention of returning to battle later. When the wise marshal saw that they had relaxed and were concentrating only on enjoying the fresh grass and the shade, he had the eighty horses brought out, mounted by good knights armed with lances; he had the company divided into two, one under his own command, the other under the command of Châteaumorand; he also deployed a company of lightly armed dismounted men-at-arms, archers and varlets. When these dispositions were in place, as he had long planned, he and Châteaumorand surrounded the gardens. Our foot soldiers threw themselves so abruptly into the fray that the Saracens – who had taken off their armour – did not have time to rearm. The other men of our forces then assailed them, and killed all of them with arrows and swords. [228] If you had been able to see how bewildered those rats of Saracens were you would have had a good laugh: they had no idea how to defend themselves, and they dared not venture out for fear of the mounted men who were waiting for them. Even so, many of them took to their heels, only to be received on the points of our men's lances; in that way, all of them were killed, with the exception of a few who were able to gallop through our ranks and find hiding-places. This was how the lord of Candelore and his whole army were reduced to such a state of terror by the heavy losses they sustained, including the very best of their forces, that they fled into the hills and kept carefully out of sight. The brave and worthy marshal, on the other hand, following this defeat of the Saracens, rallied his men, preferring not to waste much time pursuing the enemy; rather, he ordered his forces to resume battle-order, not knowing if the lord of Candelore would be able to gather together his own troops and launch what could be a brutal counter-attack. The marshal therefore ordered his forces to take up defensive positions, and set his dispositions accordingly: he would take command of one battle,[49] and Châteaumorand another that would be ready to reinforce the main company if needed. He had the standard of Our Lady raised over his forces and made ready to defend the gates of the city, then, with everything in order, he waited very patiently – but his precautions were quite unnecessary, for the Saracens had no thought of anything other than flight. So passed that day – until the following morning when the marshal commanded a select company of men-at-arms [229] to capture a hill occupied by the fleeing Saracens; however, when the infidels saw our men coming, they fled in the opposite direction and hid in the forest. At that our men returned to the plain and laid the whole country to waste: there were elegant palaces, good manor-houses and fine gardens, all of which they set on fire.

When the lord of Candelore saw that our men had no intention of withdrawing, he sent envoys to the marshal to say, plaintively, that he was astonished to find himself the object of such vicious attacks, for he had done no harm to the marshal in person or to his men; he had indeed done no harm even to the Genoese, nothing that would justify the marshal's actions. If the latter would negotiate a peace with him, he would ally himself permanently with the marshal and with the Genoese, would offer him every amenity, and put his own power and authority at the marshal's service against the king of Cyprus, or against any other foe the marshal might name. The marshal in his wisdom, wishing to seize every advantage, acknowledged that he did not know if he would indeed end up at war with the king of Cyprus; if this were to happen, then Candelore would constitute a safe haven close enough to give his forces some respite, and to provision his army for an assault. He discussed his future moves with his council, and they agreed that the best option would be to make peace – especially as the lord of Candelore was showing such humility. And that is what they did – and immediately thereafter the marshal, who had spent fourteen days in Candelore, embarked his whole army on his galleys.[50] [230]

XVIII: How peace was made between the king of Cyprus and the marshal, and how the marshal decided to set sail for Alexandria.

The marshal had no sooner re-embarked his troops than he heard that peace had been declared between himself, the king of Cyprus and the Genoese, always provided

49 A 'battle' in this sense referred to one of the divisions of the army when arrayed for combat.
50 The French probably embarked on 9 July 1403.

that he, the marshal, approved the terms.[51] He called his council, and they agreed that the terms and conditions of the proposed peace were just what they would have wished. Peace was therefore agreed, and this freed him, to his delight, to turn his attention to the infidel; his wish was to go to Alexandria, in Egypt. He summoned all the patrons[52] of his ships and galleys, and laid out for them what his intentions were and what he hoped to achieve; he hoped that a part of the fleet would make up an advance party. The patrons told him that from Candelore their route to Alexandria could not be direct, because the winds would be against them; they would have to return to Rhodes and pick up following winds from there; [231] the marshal gave them his approval. He and his galleys meanwhile returned to Cyprus to ratify and confirm the peace treaty as negotiated by the grand master of Rhodes with the king of Cyprus. He sailed as far as a galley-port called Pandaïa [Pandee][53] where the grand master and the councillors of the king of Cyprus were awaiting him, and he and they signed and confirmed the treaty. When this had been done, he acceded to the wishes of the grand master and the king's councillors and proceeded to a meeting with the king of Cyprus himself. The king came out to escort him lavishly and with great honour, and conducted him to his castle where extravagant preparations had been made. He offered the marshal fabulous gifts – some twenty-five thousand ducats – but although the marshal thanked him warmly, he refused the gift, saying that such generosity was undeserved, and besides, he had no need of the king's bounty since the king of France, his own sovereign lord, had provided him with quite enough; if on the other hand the king would agree to furnish him with men-at-arms and soldiers from his own country, and to lend him galleys to transport him to infidel territory, that he would accept with great pleasure and gratitude. The king acceded gladly to this request, and provided two galleys manned with men-at-arms – although one of them absconded, since its crew turned pirates. The marshal had now spent four days on Rhodes, and he was eager to depart; he took leave of the king, with an exchange of jewels, [232] embarked his men, and set sail for Alexandria. Soon they were at sea, but not for long: as the mariners set a course around Cyprus for Alexandria, to follow the ships that the marshal had sent ahead, such a fierce head-wind blew up that they were unable to continue, despite all the skill and experience that the mariners brought to bear, and despite all their efforts. This reverse lasted for some three whole days, although had they had more luck they had barely six miles to make before they would have picked up favourable winds. The mariners, seeing that none of their expertise was allowing them to make progress, said that never in their lives had they seen such a phenomenon: in their opinion it was a sign from God that for

51 The terms of the peace were agreed on 7 July 1403 and Boucicaut was presumably informed on 8 or 9 July.

52 'Patron' was the title for the captain of a merchant vessel – that is, of a *nave* (see above, part II, note 48). Venetian military vessels were captained by a *supracomito*, though the author was probably not clear on the distinction.

53 This is Pandaia on the north coast of Cyprus.

their own safety they should go no further; their experience suggested that these adverse conditions would last for many days. The marshal took counsel and agreed that they would change objectives and head for Tripoli, in Syria;[54] there would be no navigational difficulties, for they would have following winds. He was unwavering in this ambition, even though the Genoese advised him to return to Genoa, telling him that he had done quite enough. But this he refused to do, and sailed on as far as Famagusta, [233] although he did not put into port. He did, however, take a galley there and arrived before Tripoli the following morning.[55]

XIX: How the Venetians had warned the Saracen states that the marshal was preparing an attack, and how the marshal fared before Tripoli.

Now, in order to explain events, we must return to what I mentioned earlier, the sullen veiled hatred between the Venetians and the Genoese: the Venetians' envy meant that they would make every effort to damage Genoese prosperity, but so underhandedly that no-one would realise their treachery. They came to the conclusion that they could do so by no better means than to deprive the Genoese of the wise governor that they had acquired, whose wisdom and valour were enhancing their reputation by the day – but they would not of course contemplate, or perhaps dare, to do so openly, even though they had the advantage militarily; the fact that they had gathered a large army, [234] for no other obvious reason, might have suggested that that was their ultimate intention if no other means presented itself. To achieve their ends, however, they had devised another and most treacherous scheme, one that they thought to be watertight – but who God keeps is well kept. They had sent messages to all ports and harbours throughout the lands of the Saracens, from Egypt to Syria, to warn them of the marshal's approach, and to caution them to be on guard for he was looking to lead a large army against them. That they did indeed employ this subterfuge was well known, as we shall explain. And indeed that the Saracens had been forewarned, and well beforehand, was obvious in those regions, for the whole of the Tripoli foreshore was manned with Saracen warriors, armed to the teeth and ready to repel the Christians – and this would never have happened had they not had prior warning, for they were arrayed ready to fight, in great battles[56] of cavalry and infantry. Tamerlane had provided some six hundred horses caparisoned in velvet and cloth of gold [235] and other luxury fabrics, finer than anything previously seen on the field of battle, and their riders were wearing fine plate armour and rich surcoats:

54 The port of Tripoli, around 125 miles south-east of Famagusta, is now the largest city in northern Lebanon.

55 6 August 1403.

56 See above, note 49.

the Saracens were clearly most honourably prepared and eager to give battle, and it seemed that among them were people of high honour and great estate.

When the valiant marshal saw these unexpected dispositions, he was astonished yet undaunted: impervious, he said that with God's help he would not be deterred from making a landing, even though his council considered this most unwise, for they were few in the face of the Saracens. Nevertheless, the marshal declared he would persist, and sent Mountjoy Herald from galley to galley, telling his troops to prepare to disembark in good order, as his prior orders had instructed. That done, he had his ships beached. The trumpeters sounded their horns, and the crossbowmen, drawn up on the galleys, began to inflict heavy fire on the Saracens to make them withdraw so that our men could land. Their archers meanwhile fired on our men, but their rate of fire and their range were less than ours. [236] Oh God ...! How nobly our men responded to the challenge; they were like lions in the fray, full of courage and daring. The old saying, 'Like master, like man', was never more apt, for the good marshal encouraged them to be bold and fearless by his own admirable deeds. Had you been there, you would have seen brutal combat between those first ashore and the Saracens, who came at our men to contest their possession of the port and to repel them at lance point. But you would have seen our men-at-arms throw themselves into the sea up to their necks to come to the aid of their fellows. Ah God! We owe them and others like them our prayers, for when they fulfil their duty, they do so to protect their country from all enemies. Indeed, we cannot honour a brave man-at-arms enough, or reward him enough, for this is a most dangerous occupation: the more arduous and the more dangerous the conflict, the more worthy he is of great honour and generous remuneration.

As you can imagine, the battle was fierce, for the Saracens defended themselves with great ardour, and the Christians attacked vigorously. I can assure you that there were many fine individual and collective deeds of arms. It was there that one could see who was stalwart and expert in arms, [237] and who was worthy of a prize – for it required more than a little force to take the harbour in the face of such opposition: there were at least six Saracens to every Christian. Our people had much to endure, and there were many dead and wounded – but they were sustained by their faith in God and Our Lady, and by the valour and bravery of their tireless leader who thrust into the thick of the battle and did all that could be asked of a man of courage. In this way, with God's help, they performed with such vigour and fortitude that in spite of enemy resistance, they landed and took the harbour; the crossbow and cannon fire that they loosed from the galleys drove back the Saracens, who retreated from the port and left it to our men.

XX: Of the fine battle-order established by the marshal, and how he defeated the Saracens before Tripoli.[57]

At this point the Saracens rallied their men in very good order. They placed the mounted men that I mentioned earlier on the left and right flanks [238] of the foot soldiers, and there they stood firm. The valiant marshal allowed his men a short breathing space, for they were exhausted from the assault on the harbour; he ordered water brought to refresh them, for it was very hot. Then he exhorted them to renewed efforts, for his hopes for victory rested with God and the Virgin Mary. Then he ordered them to their assigned ranks, and they advanced in close formation, at the trot, their lances upright on their shoulders, on the Saracens who were drawn up ready on the field. When they were close enough, the trumpets blared, and arrows flew from bowmen on both sides. But in the face of fire, our men continued their advance with the most steadfast courage, so much so that the Saracens were dismayed. Ah! This is surely the definition of the man of valour: he is worth a thousand men less valiant, and a thousand weaklings add up to less than he. Valerius Maximus, speaking of the Romans, was absolutely right: five hundred men of courage can often take on as many [239] as ten thousand.[58] And that a small force of picked men can prevail against a horde of adversaries was obvious here, as the outcome showed. For they showed their mettle from the moment of engagement, with no sign of alarm at the number of their enemies, even though their small numbers were obvious. They charged the Saracens with great courage, and their leader and captain fought among them, showing them by example what he expected of them – but the Saracens also fought wholeheartedly. The battle was brutal and cruel, and there were many losses on both sides. But the Saracens had very much the worst of it: the courage and endurance of our men, and the hail of fire from the crossbowmen, killed great numbers of them in a long-drawn-out battle. How could I possibly describe the deeds of arms that each of the Christians performed, or the blows exchanged on each side? My account would take far too long! Briefly, however, the brave marshal fought with a courage that could not be surpassed. He was matched by the grand master of Rhodes, Philibert de Naillac; by my lord Raymond de Lescure, the grand prior of Toulouse; by my lord Pierre de Bauffremont, knight of Rhodes; and by all the company of the grand master. Others too fought with valour: Châteaumorand, that man of heart and courage; Guillaume de Montrevel, the Hermite de La Faye, whose gallantry never faltered; my lord Louis de Culant, marshal to the army; and so many other good and valiant knights, [240] too many to name. There too the squires did valiant service: Tercelet

57 Less glorious accounts of this encounter were given by the Egyptian chroniclers al-Makrizi and Ibn Hajar al-Asqalani, as well as by the Venetians Emmanule Piloti and Bernardo Morosini. D. Lalande, *Jean II le Meingre, dit Boucicault (1366–1421): étude d'une biographie héroïque* (Geneva, 1988), pp. 111–14.

58 This echoes the comments in Simon de Hesdin's translation and gloss of Valerius Maximus, I, c.1, in BNF MS fr. 282, fol. 106d.

de Chelles, Jean de Neuvy, Richart Monteille, Guillaume de Tholigny and his brother Hugues (Huguelin), Guillaume de Labbesse, the Bastard of Rebergues, Jean d'Ony, Renaud de Cambronne, Jean des Barres (known as Le Barrois) and so many others of equal valour: all of them, those I have named and the rest, deserved eternal praise and honour for their force of arms and their signal bravery. And to be brief, their merit can be read in its result: they were no more than two thousand men steadfastly defying more than fifteen thousand Saracens who, in spite of their costly horses and trappings, in spite of the magnificent armour of the riders – some seven hundred of them – did everything to damage our men and to break their battle-order. But they were unable to withstand the fire of the crossbowmen or the blows dealt by our good Christians: gradually, they gave ground and then started to flee from the battle, for by this point they had sustained very grievous damage: so many of them were dead or wounded. The Saracen retreat gathered pace, with those able to flee doing so: our men chose not to pursue them, but rather to remain firmly on the field. And either by main force or out of treachery, the enemy withdrew from the foreshore, [241] believing that the Christians would engage in pursuit, and that when they had distanced themselves from their ships, the Saracens would be able to cut them off from the sea and surround them. But the wise marshal, who had nothing to learn about military tactics, guessed what trick they were intending, and therefore declined the pursuit.

But now let me tell you about the courage, the hardihood and the determination of the valiant leader! Once the Saracens were some distance away, he had his battles[59] regroup, and forbade any in his army, on pain of death, from returning to the ships or deserting his post. He withdrew his fleet and swore that he would engage the Saracens a second time. He could not be dissuaded from this, although many advised him that he should do no more, for he had already acquired, they felt, honour enough – but he refused to listen. He mustered first his vanguard, then the main body of his army, then the rearguard, and made sure that the captains knew exactly what they were to do; he exhorted them to further great deeds. When the Saracens saw the wise dispositions and great determination of their opponent and his men, they became very fearful, and obviously so for they withdrew from their positions and took up station near the Tripoli gardens which are very thickly grown, so that if flight became necessary, they could retreat into the undergrowth. There they mustered their foot, with their cavalry on the two wings. The marshal sent the vanguard first into the attack, [242] under his marshal my lord Louis de Culant; he followed closely behind with the main army. When they were close to the Saracens, they greeted them with a hail of arrows, as did the Saracens the Christians, and then rapidly engaged them; the Saracens mounted a fierce defence. But our men engaged them so closely and pressed them so hard that they soon began to waver. When the Saracen horsemen saw that their army was beginning to falter, they tried to surround the marshal's forces – but

59 See above, note 49.

the Christian rearguard fired on them so thickly that they failed to do so. At that, the valiant marshal attacked them with his entire force; the battle became hand-to-hand, and very many men and horses fell, never to rise again. By this time both armies were fully engaged, and there was a desperate mêlée, with many dead and wounded on both sides. But why should I prolong the story? In the end, the Saracens were unable to withstand the attack, and they fled for their lives. By this stage they had need of a retreat into the gardens – and they plunged into the undergrowth, defeated and overcome. The flight became a rout, but many left it too late and were killed; all however either fled or lay dead on the field. The marshal was furious to see them escape to places of safety, and he would have liked to follow them into the gardens. But those who were close to him begged him for God's sake [243] not to do so, for the ways through the gardens are difficult to follow, and they were afraid that if once he ventured in, he would never find his way out. So he halted the army on the field, and waited for some time in case the Saracens might emerge and offer him combat, or in case they rallied – but they had no spirit for such a thing. And when he had waited long enough, everyone said that he should withdraw to his ship after so glorious and successful a day; he and the army withdrew in good order, the vanguard in front, the main army next, the rearguard last – and with his forces so disposed, giving thanks to God, he withdrew to his ship.

XXI: How the marshal and his men discovered incontrovertibly that the Venetians had warned the Saracens that the marshal was coming, and how the marshal took the cities of Batroun [Botun] and Beirut [Barut].

Even now, the valiant marshal had not tired of damaging the Saracens, although everyone was telling him that given his remarkable exploits, he could make a most honourable return to Genoa. But he did not agree – and it seemed as if he was determined to gain even more admiration. He left Tripoli, as we have said, having heard news [244] that a Saracen nave was heading for Beirut. He deputed Châteaumorand to go there, with a good force of men-at-arms and two galleys. Châteaumorand and his contingent sailed to meet the Saracens; they engaged them in so fierce a sea-fight that the infidels were all killed and their ship was taken, then rejoined the marshal's fleet to celebrate joyfully. The marshal himself headed for Batroun, a large country town which his Christian forces pillaged, and where they killed all the Saracens they found; from there he sailed for Beirut.[60]

But that brings me back to my previous topic, how it became known for certain that the Venetians had warned the Saracens of the marshal's coming: as the marshal

60 Boucicaut probably raided Batroun, some fifteen miles down the coast from Tripoli, on 9 August 1403. He arrived at Beirut, twenty miles south of Batroun, the following day.

was nearing Beirut, he saw one of those vessels known as a *gripperie*[61] making out to sea, thinking to slip away unnoticed before the marshal arrived; to make a quick getaway it headed for the open sea. But the marshal saw it and sent a galley that soon overhauled it, and it was brought back to the marshal; he asked who was manning it and was told it was Venetians. He had the captain of the vessel brought before him and questioned him closely, with a mixture of threats and blandishments, as to why he was fleeing. And briefly, although the captain was initially very cagey, the marshal pressed him, without any harm or mistreatment, until he admitted [245] that he had been quartering the eastern Mediterranean, across all the Saracen territories there, to warn the Saracens, those of Syria and Egypt and neighbouring countries, that they should make preparations to resist the Christians who were bringing a large army against them; he had, he said, warned Beirut and everywhere else; he had returned to Beirut to see how things were progressing. The marshal was astonished by a wickedness that he could never have imagined; for a moment he contemplated throwing the captain and his crew, who were responsible for the warning, into the sea. But he soon reconsidered, for they had confessed very openly, and besides, the fault was not so much with them as with those who had sent them. So he listened to his own noble and generous impulses – never deigning to seek an easy revenge – and set them free. Few other commanders would have done as much, but he did not want to be the cause of a further rift between the Venetians and the Genoese. On the other hand, once he arrived before Beirut he realised immediately the damage that had been done by the warning, [246] for he saw before him the whole port swarming with Saracens drawn up in battle-order to deny him landing. But their preparations were in vain, for the marshal, like a lion scenting prey, beached his ships, and had his crossbowmen fire a hail of arrows into the villains who by this time were howling like mad dogs; the arrows skewered many of the defenders, who were driven willy-nilly into retreat. Our men then issued from the ships and attacked with great speed and courage. When the Saracens saw the disciplined forces assailing them, they did not dare linger and fled; our men stood there armed for the attack, but had no-one to engage with. The marshal led his men to the walls of Beirut and attacked the town with such vigour that the Saracens remaining there were terrified and many of them fled off to the landward side; those who remained fought back as best they could. In the end, however, they could not resist, and the town was taken and all the remaining Saracens were put to the sword; the town was plundered and pillaged of all its goods, although little was left since the warning had allowed the inhabitants of the town to cart away anything of value and any commodities and to hide it all, the marshal was told, in the forests and the mountains. So the Christians set fire to the town itself and to the ships in the harbour, and withdrew to their galleys. [247]

61 A *gripperie* seems to be a lateen-rigged oared vessel, smaller than a galley, whose name would be a variant of the Italian *gripos* used by Pietro Bembo in 1530–40 for a vessel used to carry soldiers for an amphibious operation.

XXII: How the marshal set sail for Sidon [Sayete], and of his great valour and gallantry in the face of the Saracens.

Now the marshal left Beirut and headed for Egypt, passing by Sidon which he intended if possible to capture.[62] When he arrived there, as in the other Saracen ports he had visited, he found that it was garrisoned with a great number of Saracens drawn up in good order: there were more than twelve thousand of them, on horse and on foot. The good marshal was undaunted, for his faith was in God; he stormed ashore and met the Saracens with good crossbow bolts and missiles from bombards[63] to such effect that they would never have known so deadly an encounter. There were soon so many dead that the shingle was heaped with bodies – but even so, the Saracens steadfastly refused to beat a retreat. Very soon, however, they had no option: it was that or lose their lives; had they lingered much longer, their numbers would have shrunk very considerably, so they had no alternative. Our men were not backward: they raced out in pursuit with the greatest courage, and leapt like wild boar into the sea, up to their bellies, to get at the enemy. [248] The first to make the leap was the good squire Jean d'Ony whom I mentioned earlier, who thus set an example to his companions. The Saracens meanwhile, still confronting the Christians courageously, did all they could to repel the invaders. But now a considerable misfortune befell our forces, but which nevertheless afforded them great praise and honour: a great wind rose, so unfavourable that the crews could not land all the galleys to give reinforcements to those who were engaged on the shore, and who are worthy of the greatest acclaim: there were moments when the sheer number of the Saracens bade fair to drive the Christians back into the sea. But at those moments the ships standing off resorted to crossbow and bombard fire, which killed even those of the highest rank. The battle raged on, but I need not prolong my account: our men bore themselves so valiantly and so proficiently that in spite of their losses they finally took the port. Ah! What a triumph and an honour this was for a mere handful of men, no more than five hundred, against the Saracen horde!

What can compare with this heroic act? [249] Surely only the long-ago Greek knight Leonidas, who with no more than five hundred knights overcame the army of Xerxes, high king of Persia, by surprising him in his tents? Never could Xerxes have imagined that Leonidas, with his tiny force, would be so daring, yet it is a feat that is now celebrated, rightly, in all the histories.[64] But why should we not equally celebrate the valour and daring of the marshal and his splendid men, who did not,

62 Boucicaut arrived at Sidon, referred to by its Arabic name Saïda by the French writer, on 12 August. Sidon is around twenty-five miles down the coast from Beirut.

63 A large-calibre, muzzle-loading artillery piece used to throw stone balls during sieges or naval battles.

64 Leonidas I, king of Sparta (d.480 BC) famously fought Xerxes of Persia (519–465 BC) at the battle of Thermopylae in 480 BC. This account derived from Simon de Hesdin's translation and commentary upon Valerius Maximus, III, c.2, ext. 3, in BNF MS fr. 282, fols 146a–c.

certainly, surprise the Saracens in their tent, but were rather themselves surprised, few in number but great in courage, and confronted by a great multitude of adversaries, and yet managed to take the port when even the elements were against them? And yet against all the odds the marshal was victorious! Let me tell you more stories of his strength and courage: he was undaunted to find himself with so small a force ranged against some ten thousand enemies; he faced up to the Saracen army which was drawn up overlooking the harbour in full battle-order; he advanced until the Saracens could get a good view of the bowmen stationed in the middle of the battle of our men-at-arms. And there he stayed, fearless despite any threat from the enemy, for five full hours, until the sea calmed down enough for the remainder of his men to disembark to give battle to the Saracens and launch the planned assault on the town. [250] He was naturally very uneasy that the wind was preventing his ship from landing, but despite this, he stood his ground so steadfastly that the Saracens did not dare launch a frontal attack: they merely made occasional attempts at a charge, or attacked from the flanks or from the rear; but the marshal's dispositions were such – his two hundred or so archers, his men-at-arms scarcely more numerous, all standing in serried ranks like a wall – that the Saracens never got up enough courage to launch a full-scale attack. If they did risk something of that nature, it led merely to their destruction, for large numbers of them were killed and wounded by arrow-fire and by casting spears. As you have heard, the marshal maintained position until near nightfall; seeing at that point that the sea was not calming down enough to allow reinforcements to land, he withdrew in excellent order and led his men into his ship. Now I leave it to you to judge whether the marshal should receive every honour for his steadfastness in the face of so many of the enemy: the latter were so alarmed by the Christians' resolve and stoicism, and by their evident determination, that in spite of their far greater numbers they were filled with fear and shorn of courage. And yet there is not a shadow of a doubt that had the marshal and his men shown any signs of weakness or fear, the Saracens would have attacked mercilessly and slain all those drawn up onshore. [251]

XXIII: How the marshal arrived before Latakia [La Liche], and how the Saracens had set ambushes for him.

At this point the marshal left, and sailed up wind to a large town on the border with Armenia, inland about a league and called Latakia.[65] But he arrived before the port with less than a quarter of his galleys: the contrary wind that night had split up the

---

Hesdin's commentary had added the story of how the Spartans managed to penetrate Xerxes' tent to Valerius Maximus's account.

65 Latakia, identified by its medieval name 'La Liche' by the French author, is now the principal port of Syria, and is around 140 miles north of Sidon. It is not inland at all, and nor is it close to the border with Armenia.

fleet and sent the other galleys off course; the Saracens having built great watch-fires on the shore, it was difficult for the marshal to see the whereabouts of the missing galleys. But he stayed anchored offshore all day: he did not wish to disembark unless with all his men, for many of them were sick or wounded; he stayed at anchor until low vespers [at around six o'clock], waiting for the arrival of the rest of the fleet; he was very disappointed, for he could see that there were no more than three thousand Saracens onshore, and he felt very capable of defeating them. Finally the missing ships arrived – but it was too late to disembark.

Ah God! How right is the old saying which claims: 'Who God keeps is well kept,'[66] [252] and so too the Holy Scriptures which say: 'If God be for us, who can be against us?'[67] For everything about this episode tells us that God wished to keep His dear servant the marshal safe, and also his army, as you will hear. The marshal had high hopes that the following day he would see action; he assigned my lord Giovanni Centurione d'Oltramarino of Genoa and my lord Hugues Cholet to one of the galleys, with a mission to spy out the two towers which guard the harbour of Latakia – he intended to launch an assault on them the following day – and he himself retired to a little distance, as God in His wisdom had counselled. When the Saracens saw him withdrawing, they thought he was leaving, so they emerged from their ambush which had been set up in two locations, one behind a hill, the other in a wood lying between the port and the town: there were, it transpired, some three thousand Saracens, and all of them poured onto the shore yelling and screaming like devils from Hell. And when the marshal and his men saw how many they were, they gave thanks to Our Lord for His mercy in preventing the Christians from going ashore, and thought it a miracle that Our Lord had saved them. [252]

XXIV: How the marshal decided to return to Genoa, for winter was coming on.

The marshal now left Latakia, realising that with so few men he could not prevail against so numerous an enemy; he was also conscious of the number of his own men who were enfeebled by illness and injury. So he returned to Famagusta, in Cyprus, the city which had been, as we saw, a bone of contention between the king of Cyprus and the Genoese; it had remained peacefully under Genoa's control. It was thus important that he should make a visit.[68] He spent time hearing complaints and grievances, and settling disputes to the best of his ability in the short time – only eight or ten days – that he could make available. He appointed officers and charged them with administering justice. Then he went to Rhodes where the grand master

66 The biographer had previously used this maxim on p. 119 above.

67 Romans 8: 31.

68 Boucicaut was at Famagusta from at least 21 to 28 August 1403.

welcomed him and did him honour, and stayed there ten or twelve days, during which time he ordered three of his ships to be prepared, and had loaded onto them all the sick and wounded; there were a great many of them, [254] knights and squires, crossbowmen, foot soldiers and sailors alike; once they had left, this meant he had only a small company at his orders, for he staffed the departing ships with most of his own men-at-arms to act as crew and guards. He himself was left with forces so small that, along with his few men-at-arms, he had barely a dozen crossbowmen for each galley. Of the three ships, two set sail at the same time as he did, even though he would be able to offer them very little protection; the third waited a further month in Rhodes, but then on its voyage home it sank off Sicily: a great loss, and a tragedy for the good men on board. It was thus that the marshal parted from the grand master; his councillors urged him to return immediately to Genoa, and he resolved to do so with no further military exploits for that season: it was the time of year – the winter, that is – when the seas can often be very rough because of changes in the wind. He set off from Rhodes with the much-reduced company we have described, and arrived in the Morea unhindered.[69] He expected to sail on without incident, but when he was in harbour in Cape Maleas [Cap Saint Angel] he was joined by two of the ships he had left in Rhodes, crewed by many good men-at-arms and crossbowmen;[70] he left them on the ships because he hoped not to need them. [255]

XXV: How the Venetians, to have an excuse for their later actions, complained of the marshal's capture of Beirut.

Now I must return to the Venetians, to complete my previous remarks by explaining how the envy that had festered and suppurated like a sore for so long in their hearts finally burst and oozed out a vile and ugly poison. When the Venetians saw that all their intriguing against the marshal had been in vain, they resolved that, at all costs and at any opportunity, they would reach their goals: once he reached home territory, in Genoa, they would be powerless to do so. They would never, they knew, have so good an opportunity again, given that the marshal had so few forces at his command having divested himself of so many of his galleys and other ships from his fleet, for he did not suspect that there might be any attack. The Venetians were very well aware of the situation, having nothing better to do, in pursuit of their ends, than to spy on the marshal's intentions. [256] But in their duplicity, to cover up their secret aims, they wished to find a plausible excuse for their actions; so they went around grumbling to anyone who would listen that the marshal had provoked them, as shown by his taking of Beirut where he had done serious damage to the great quantities of their merchandise and goods warehoused there, and without having given the Venetians

69 Boucicaut departed from Rhodes with eleven galleys towards the end of September 1403.
70 Boucciaut arrived at Cape Maleas on 4 October 1403.

prior warning of their intention; they claimed to have been robbed, and to have sustained very heavy losses.[71] These accusations came to the ears of the marshal's friends and allies, and thus were transmitted to him in the Morea; he would do well, they advised, to beware of the Venetians, for it was to be feared that they wished him ill. The marshal was astonished by this, and replied that he really could not believe that they bore him any ill will, nor that they were accusing him – for never had he done anything to provoke them, and had in fact, always and everywhere, treated them as favourably as his own Genoese, thinking them his friends and allies; besides, he wanted to preserve peace between them and the Genoese, and in addition, wherever he had had dealings with the Venetians, they had been so gracious to him that he had become very attached to them. As for Beirut, he could not believe that they were resentful, [257] for they knew perfectly well that, more than a year previously, he had sent a challenge to the sultan over the fact that he had seized Genoese merchants in Cairo, Damascus and Alexandria and ransomed them against the terms of the safe conduct that he had granted; more than ten months before setting sail, he had sent word of his challenge to the Venetians so that they could remove their goods and merchandise from the city of Beirut; that they had received the warning, he said, was clear from the fact that when he and his men ransacked Beirut, there were no Venetian goods stockpiled in their empty warehouses. Moreover, in all the time that he was in Beirut, and indeed before or after, no Venetian or any other person had mentioned that he had laid hands on Venetian property: had he been notified that the Venetians or any other Christians held anything there, then he would not have allowed it to be touched, for he had no intention of damaging Christian interests, merely those of the infidels. Moreover, if they were malcontent, and if they could let him know just what losses they had suffered, he would ensure that everything was restored to them; any complaints – and so far none had been made to him personally – would be dealt with in the same way.[72] And moreover again, had he intended to do them harm, or known that they might intend harm to him, he would never have sent ahead four of his galleys and other ships from his fleet, given that his forces were few and that he had lost many of his crossbowmen. From which it was obvious, he said, that he had not intended an attack of any sort, and that he had not expected an attack on himself. [258] Had any such suspicion crossed his mind, he would have kept more forces at his disposal, having ample time to do so. All he wished was to sail on peacefully, having no other ambition; he was sure that no-one wished him any harm. Such were the replies that the marshal made to any warnings he was given.

---

71 According to Italian sources, the Venetians had lost five hundred bundles of spices, valued at 30,000 ducats, as well as a vessel belonging to Bernardo Morosini.

72 There is no evidence that Boucicaut did pay compensation to any Venetian merchant harmed by his attack upon Beirut.

Very soon, he arrived at Porto Kagio [Port des Cailles], and anchored there overnight.[73] During the night, just before dawn, there arrived in the harbour a small Venetian brigantine; its crew thought that the galleys they could see there were Venetian – the Venetian fleet, as you will hear, was not far away. The brigantine carried messages from the Venetians to the captains of their galleys and the crews, and the messages were put accidentally into the hands of the captains of the marshal's galleys.[74] No sooner had the Venetians handed over the messages than they realised their mistake; they were so dismayed that they did not know what to say or do. When the skipper of the marshal's ship saw the messenger so dismayed, he asked him where he had thought he was: he replied that he had thought he was on a Venetian galley, but he could now see that that was not the case. So the skipper took the letters and brought the messenger to the marshal, who questioned him a little; once, however, he saw how dismayed the messenger was, out of his liberality, guilelessness and nobility of spirit, [259] and so that the Venetians would have no cause for complaint, he said graciously to the messenger: 'Friend, have no fear, you are among friends and you will have your letters back untouched.' At that he returned the letters to the messenger, in a bundle just as they had been handed over to him, and said to the messenger that if there was anything he needed he had only to mention it; he gave him into the care and protection of the skipper and his crew, and thus the messenger departed.

At daybreak, the marshal resumed his journey; nothing of note happened that day.[75] He anchored for the night at Modone, close to the island of Sapienza; on arriving, he dropped anchor, and immediately a barque[76] appeared bringing a Venetian spy and five or six other men; they asked who it was who was at anchor, wanting to see what the marshal was up to, whether he suspected anything, and what his forces might be. The crew replied that this was the marshal and the Genoese: what was the news ashore, and was there anything that the marshal could do for them? The spy and his companions thanked them, but said they had no other news; they were served drinks, and then left. [260]

73 Boucicaut arrived at Porto Kagio on 5 October 1403. The French writer uses the name Port des Cailles (Quail Port), the medieval French name for the small town known to the Venetians as Porto Quaglio, located on the eastern side of the Main Peninsula, three miles north of Cape Matapan.

74 These were almost certainly messages being sent between Carlo Zeno, who had set sail from Crete to intercept the Genoese fleet, and the Venetian senate, who had received news of the sack of Beirut on 19 September 1403. The senate wrote to Zeno on 25 September 1403, urging him to be wary of triggering a war that would be disastrous for trade and instructing him not to attack a Genoese fleet unless his force was clearly superior, but their instructions arrived the day after the battle of Modone.

75 Boucicaut departed from Porto Kagio on 6 October 1403 and arrived at Sapienza that evening.

76 A barque is a smaller open boat which could use oars or sail for propulsion. Richard Unger considers that the *DMF* entry, 'bateau à fond plat ou convexe utilisant les rames ou la voile', is too specific (personal communication).

XXVI: How the Venetians attacked the marshal and a ferocious battle ensued, and how the marshal was victorious.

On Sunday 7 October, very early, the marshal left the port of Sapienza off Modone, and set a course straight for Genoa. But the moment had arrived when the treachery of the Venetians could no longer be kept secret. This seemed to them the time and place to put their plans into effect, for they saw the marshal's forces as poorly armed whereas they were many and well equipped, and had planned for this moment. The marshal had sailed no more than a couple of miles when out from behind the island of Sapienza came sailing the captain of the Venetians, with a fleet of eleven galleys; the captain headed straight for Modone, and joined up with two great galleys[77] that had been anchored there and that were packed with as many as a thousand men-at-arms, as well with eighteen or twenty vessels known as *palestarmes de naves*[78] and brigantines, [261] packed with men-at-arms and crossbowmen.[79] With all these reinforcements and with their eleven galleys, these latter already fully laden with men-at-arms and crossbowmen, they set off at full speed in pursuit of the marshal, having first taken up position in full battle-order. And meanwhile, on land, the Venetians had stationed a host of men-at-arms on foot and on horseback to follow the marshal along the foreshore, in order to prevent his company from escaping if by any chance – for fear or for any other reason – they should head for land. The marshal could see all these manoeuvres from a distance, but he had no suspicions of the Venetians: he thought that they were sailing out in this formation in order simply to head straight for Venice; it never crossed his mind that they would attack him with no prior formal declaration of war.[80] The Venetians sailed at full speed so that they were very soon close to the marshal's galleys – and at that point the marshal's men, seeing them come on in formation, told him that they were undoubtedly hostile, and coming to the attack: there they were, in battle formation, with men armed to the teeth, crossbowmen with their weapons ready to fire, men-at-arms with their lances

77 *Grosses galées*: from 1294, the Venetians developed 'great galleys' propelled by sails and oars and which were 'longer, wider and deeper ... enabling them to have room for a sizable amount of cargo': Gardiner and Morrison, eds, *The Age of the Galley*, pp. 125–6.

78 The precise meaning of the term *palestarme de nave* is unclear. Some sources suggest that it was a large rowing boat used as a tender for a larger vessel, whereas others suggest that it was a synonym for a brigantine.

79 Carlo Zeno and the Venetians had arrived at the bay between Modone (nowadays Methoni) and Sapienza on 6 October 1403, the same day as Boucicaut, but had given no sign to the Genoese fleet of their hostile intentions. Zeno's eleven ships were supplemented by two huge merchant vessels commanded by Almoro Lombardo that had been planning to sail for Tanais on the Black Sea, as well as a number of smaller vessels.

80 In a letter that Carlo Zeno sent to Venice on 9 October 1403, immediately after the battle, the Venetian admiral blamed the Genoese for initiating the encounter by advancing upon his ships without first sending an envoy to negotiate, which Zeno viewed as a necessity on the part of Boucicaut, given that the Genoese fleet was in Venetian waters.

raised, and everything entirely ready for an attack and for battle; by God, they said, he should consider his options so that he would not be taken by surprise unarmed and unprepared. [262] When the marshal saw what was up, and that there was no mistaking the intentions of the Venetians, he was consumed with anger. He had his men take up arms immediately: the few men he had at his command, for he was now bitterly regretting the fact that two days previously he had sent two of his ships ahead packed with men-at-arms and crossbowmen; had he known then what was to come, he would never have done so. The Venetians, of course, were perfectly aware of his decision, and had been able to take him by surprise. The marshal assembled his forces, and especially his few crossbowmen; he had his galleys swung round to face the Venetians, and take up battle-order in case of need. However, he expressly forbade anyone from firing missiles from bombards or other sources, because he still could not believe that the Venetians were approaching with hostile intent, and wondered if they were simply intending to parley with him over compensation for the taking of Beirut – which he knew to be a bone of contention for them – or over some other matter; he was intent therefore on ensuring that he did not launch the first attack. When the Venetians' ships were close enough to the marshal's, they hove to in order to prepare for battle, as is customary on the high seas; they had the sails lowered to avoid damage,[81] and set everything for battle. The marshal too had hove to in order to set his forces, as best he could, in battle-order. At this point he realised that battle was inevitable, and he exhorted his men to defend themselves with all possible force; he had faith that God, [263] Who had always helped them, would not abandon them in such an emergency, and he sent word to this effect to all his galleys. When once the Venetian ships were in battle-order, they made full speed towards the marshal; he in turn, undaunted, made for them also at full speed. The Venetians shouted: 'Battle! Battle!' and greeted our ships with a good volley from bombards; that was their opening move. But our men were undeterred; they responded with a hail of fire from bombards and other weapons. So the ships closed with each side firing on the other, until they were close enough to engage with lances and board the enemies' ships. At that, battle was engaged with lances on both sides, vicious and deadly, and many were killed; this was followed by hand-to-hand fighting with daggers and axes and swords. Had you been there, you would have seen our men sustain very violent assaults, but their outstanding bravery, so often seen on the field of battle, stood them in good stead; they defended themselves with remarkable and great vigour. The odds were very much against them: our men were outnumbered four to one, and the enemy had nearly double our shipping. Our men were very pressed by the enemy's supremacy in numbers of men-at-arms and bowmen, but the way they fought back was a marvel; many of them were killed and wounded; [264] but they sold themselves dear, throwing many of the enemy into the sea in full

81 The captain of a galley would order his sails lowered before engaging with the enemy in order to clear the decks for action.

armour to swim with the fishes. You'd have seen our men fling themselves valiantly over onto the enemy galleys and ships, in the face of the two great galleys which were far taller than their own, and which were therefore able to do them much damage. But their fury and resentment at being ambushed in this way lent them courage and made them all the more eager to exact revenge, and they performed wonderful feats of arms. Alas! Had they not been so heavily outnumbered, the battle would not have lasted long! But their enemies were too many, and they had recruited too many good men-at-arms and soldiers, for the Venetians knowing the calibre of the marshal and his men had hired elite troops, the best they could find. The battle lasted long, due to the vigour of our men's resistance – but it involved much suffering for them; the enemy did not find them easy to overpower. By this time the galleys had grappled, and the crews were fighting hand-to-hand; it was painful to see the two adversaries who had never previously done harm to each other suffering so many deaths, for they were attacking as ferociously as if they were avenging the deaths of a father or a mother, or to right a wrong long past – and all this the result of the wickedness and jealousy of one of the parties, as we have seen. Alas, perfidious Envy! [265] What dreadful results you have brought about! Was it not you who caused the deaths of Alexander the Great, Pompey and Julius Caesar, and who brought so many to ignominy? But with God's help, for this time at least and hopefully for many more, God spared the valiant marshal! For God has the marshal in his keeping, and may He long do so!

How can I best describe the marshal's courage, and that of his men, as his galley grappled with that of the Venetian captain? For God alone knows how valiantly they fought, the marshal to encourage his men, his men to follow his example and defend their leader and lord. The battle was nothing short of a marvel: the enemy, just as battle-hardened as our own men, were as eager in the attack, but you would have seen the men from the marshal's galley fighting like wolves starving or rabid, hurling themselves onto the galley of the Venetian captain, wounding all who opposed them so badly that if the wounds were not quickly treated, the wounded would die. But they were assailed from both sides by the two great galleys, and this was a serious hindrance to our men – for the enemy crews towering over them could shoot downwards, and in this way killed many.

I shall not prolong my account: the battle lasted four full hours, and a bystander would have been astonished it could last so long! As you have heard, this was the fiercest of battles, but the marshal and his men fought with such courage [266] that, in the end, victory was theirs. It would take me too long to detail all the acts of valour performed by all the combatants – but for the sake of their reputations during their lifetimes, and of their descendants, and as examples for those who hear of them, it is right that the names of certain of the principal men of valour should be recorded here. The first we should name is the marshal himself, whose courage, hardihood and sense of strategy gave him all honour. We shall now name the following knights: present were the good Châteaumorand, whose courage, as his adversaries discovered, was unalloyed, my lords Louis de Culant, Jean Dôme, Robin Fretel and Jean Loup; present also were the following squires: Guichard de Mage, Robert de Tholigny, Renaud de Cambronne, Richard Monteille, Jean de Montrenard, Charles de Fontaines, Odart de La Chassagne and Jean d'Ony – this latter distinguished himself so much in the battle that by general agreement on both sides he received the greatest praise, as was obvious from the many near-mortal wounds that he received in spite of being well armed. And there were many others, too many to list, who fought with great bravery: all the French, and many of the Genoese.

In the end, the enemy became exhausted and realised that all their efforts and all their trickeries were in vain and that they were losing too many men; [267] had they been able to retreat with their honour intact and having made a modicum of gains, they would have been pleased to do so.[82] At that point they encircled three of the marshal's galleys which had become separated from the others, and they commandeered all three and sailed them off, leaving the field of battle to the valiant commander and his men, who are due all honour. And although not all the Venetian galleys were able to sail off – the marshal was able to capture one – the others abandoned the field of battle and retreated to the harbour at Modone; they were dismayed and shocked to have failed in their plans. And the marshal and his men for their part remained on the field of battle until the Venetian ships disappeared from sight.

XXVII: How the marshal retired to Genoa very resentful of the Venetians, and of the prisoners taken by each side.

As you have heard, victory on the field fell to the marshal and what remained of his men; the Venetians, defeated, retreated and left him victorious. But the marshal remained dismayed and angry at these events of which he had had no suspicion, [268] at his having been taken by surprise, and at the loss of his men; his resentment towards the Venetians was beyond description. That said, he had every intention of exacting his revenge for their treason: he would do so as long as God spared him. He left that part of the world, gathering his ships and his men around him as best he could. But the fleet had nothing of a party leaving a feast or a dance: the men were, unsurprisingly, exhausted, wounded, dejected. The marshal, full of pity and love for them, rallied them and encouraged them to the best of his ability. And then, four days later, on his voyage to Genoa, the marshal came across two Venetian ships, and chose to avenge part of his losses on them; he ordered the attack and captured them and took them with him to Genoa. The two ships were laden with

82 In his letter dated 9 October, Zeno explained that he had not been able to pursue the Genoese fleet because his men were wounded or tired. The Venetians may have suffered 153 casualties in total, and the Franco-Genoese fleet over six hundred men, in addition to the four hundred who were captured.

merchandise, and provided him with valuable prisoners whom he retained, intending to exchange them with prisoners held by the Venetians. But he was sick at heart at the thought of his much-loved knights who had been taken prisoner during the first major battle, the principal victims being that valiant knight Châteaumorand who had performed so well in the battle, and with him some thirty-four knights and squires, all picked men known for their honour and repute, and also a certain number of good and distinguished Genoese, and others who had been taken prisoner on the two galleys captured by the Genoese.[83] Fortunately, however, [269] there had been many noblemen of honour and distinction on the galley which, as I said, our own men had captured – and these would become valuable when questions of ransom and release were being negotiated, as you will hear. In this way the marshal arrived back in Genoa, where he was received with joy and honour not only by the dignitaries of the city but also by the common people: no governor had ever been greeted with such warmth.[84] But now I shall stop speaking about the marshal, and turn to Châteaumorand and the other prisoners who were being taken to Venice.

XXVIII: Of the pitiful fate of the French prisoners.

When Châteaumorand and the other prisoners arrived in Venice, they were sent to a secure prison; as is usual in such circumstances, I don't imagine they were made particularly comfortable, with hard beds and scant meals. Alas! They had need of comfort, for many of them were wounded or sick; they had been used to comfort, pleasure and rest, but now they lacked all three; this is often the fate of those who seek honour and renown, [270] and such men should be honoured for the price they are prepared to pay. Their thoughts were filled with apprehension, for they knew that the marshal was, quite rightly, so indignant with the Venetians that nothing would persuade him to make peace with them or to abandon his revenge; they did not know what best to do, for they had heard said that the Venetians, when engaged in war, would customarily refuse to release any prisoners until peace had been negotiated, and that imprisonment might often last a lifetime. You can imagine how our good and noble men must have felt! The good Châteaumorand, wise and steadfast as he was, replete with all the virtues proper to a man of courage and integrity, as undismayed by misfortune as he was equable in good, was their leader. He gave them great comfort with his good guidance, [271] and his pleas – for he was a man of piety – that they remember God: they should turn to Him and trust Him to save them from death; they should show themselves strong and tough, resist despair, remain hopeful. Such

83 The prisoners included Jean de Châteaumorand, Louis de Culant, Jean Loup, Jean Dôme, Robin Fretel and Jean d'Ony.

84 One Genoese merchant reported that Boucicaut returned to Genoa on 29 October 1403 with just five ships, and the chronicler Antonio Morosini asserted that the Genoese were deeply upset that Boucicaut came back with just one of the two galleys that he had originally taken.

comforting words he gave them often, and they were much cheered. But you should not imagine that the good marshal had forgotten his good friends, even if they were now imprisoned and out of sight – unlike other princes, sadly, who so often forget the men who are ruined in the wars they have themselves waged. Certainly not! On the contrary, as soon as he possibly could, he sent them comforting words and encouraging help – for he sent them ample funds, and told them not to despair: he would be true to them as long as he lived; they were much consoled by this.

XXIX: How the prisoners sent urgent letters to the lords of France pleading that the marshal not declare war on Venice so that their release might not be delayed.

It is normal that anyone suffering illness or loss [272] should seek their salvation or their cure by any means possible; accordingly, the prisoners frequently took counsel with Châteaumorand to consider how they might win release from the cage where they found themselves. Everyone gave his opinion, and some thought it would be good to write pleading letters to the marshal begging him before God to have pity on his beloved friends and followers, and therefore to moderate his desire for vengeance for the wrong the Venetians had done him; they beseeched him therefore, for the sake of the prisoners who would otherwise be ruined, or might even die from long imprisonment, to desist from war against the Venetians.[85] Others thought it better to write to the princes of the blood in France pleading with all humility, and for God's sake, that they negotiate peace with the Venetians, failing which they, the prisoners, would be shamed and lost. Both initiatives they thought good, but some of the wisest of them doubted that the marshal's fury, and his determination to wage war on the Venetians, could be appeased, even out of compassion for the prisoners or out of any pleas from any prince; they saw only one prospect of peace, a direct order from the king of France, something which the marshal, they knew, would not dream of disobeying. If such an express royal order, in writing, could be elicited, they would be saved. [273] The proposal seemed good to them, so it was agreed to seek such an order – although they also agreed that the first project should first be tried, and so they set to immediately, writing letters to the marshal requesting that he make peace, some writers reminding him of the mutual affection between him and his men, others of the compassion he had shown in so many different circumstances, yet others of the well-founded reasons for him to pursue peace, and yet others again that to make peace would be a signal act of mercy and goodness. Their letters gave so many reasons for the marshal's compassion that as he read them, he could not for very nobleness of spirit prevent his tears, so greatly was he moved to pity and

85 Following his return to Genoa, Boucicaut called for a declaration of war against Venice, though he was overruled by those who preferred a peaceful resolution to the dispute.

affection. But he could not abandon the war he proposed to wage, for which he was making rapid preparations. He did, however, send messages of comfort to the prisoners and opened negotiations with the Venetians to arrange ransoms, as would be customary in France; the Venetians remained unwilling, for they said that this was not their custom. At that, you would have seen the poor prisoners write letters to those in whose service they were: some were in the king's service, others in that of the dukes of Berry, or Orléans, or Burgundy, or Bourbon, or indeed in that of others. Each of them humbly begged his lord and master not to forget them [274] and not to let them rot in prison. These supplications moved the lords to the deepest pity, so much so that they sent hasty letters on the subject to the marshal, and petitioned the king to such effect that he wrote to the marshal forbidding him from making any move until he had agreed with the council on the way forward. The marshal was deeply disappointed by this, but he had no thought of disobeying; he therefore ceased his preparations. Meanwhile, certain people engaged in peace talks, out of sheer pity for the prisoners. The negotiations were long and arduous, for the marshal refused to appear in person; since, however, the king and his council wished it, he agreed that the Genoese should conduct the process, and he would not contradict their judgement. In the end, peace was indeed negotiated, much to the delight of the Venetians who had been very much afraid of war; it was agreed that there should simply be an exchange of prisoners. And at that our prisoners were freed, [275] having spent eight full months in prison in Venice.[86] And we should recognise God's hand in this good outcome, for the process prevented a war that would have been deeply damaging and destructive.

XXX: How the Venetians sent word to the king begging forgiveness for what they had done.

After these events, the Venetians, not wanting their actions to put them in the bad graces of the king of France and the French princes, nor to be blamed for their having taken French knights and squires prisoner, sent their accredited ambassadors to the king bearing letters of the republic of Venice with their credence; the purport of the letters, as conveyed by the ambassadors, was that they wished to offer excuses for the event, saying that they had been provoked by the marshal who had done great damage to their interests in Beirut, and had purloined their stockpiles of goods and merchandise; when thereafter they had approached him [276] to lay the case before him and ask that their possessions be returned, he had launched an attack,

86 A provisional agreement was signed on 22 March 1404 in the palace of the doge in Venice, and Châteaumorand was allowed to leave with the Genoese ambassadors to help facilitate the completion of the terms of the peace. The remaining prisoners were allowed their freedom within the city of Venice, but not released until 17 May 1404.

unprovoked; they had had no option but to defend themselves, for which reason God had afforded them victory, as the king could see; there was no reason why the king and the princes should bear them any resentment.[87] They proffered such excuses, and other lies, to the king and the princes, but they were not believed, and no-one had any great trust in them, so they left the court rather doleful, and with a tepid response. The marshal heard of these developments from his friends and allies in France, who actually sent him copies of the letters that the Venetian ambassadors had delivered to the king; he was beside himself with anger, and it seemed to him good cause to foment anger with the Venetians – precisely the excuse he had been looking for. For that reason, and to lay bare their lies and deceptions, he wrote the letter that follows, to which the Venetians never dared to offer a reply. And in all truth, just as he had demonstrated his valour in arms, and in government his prudence, so the content of his letter shows his wisdom and learning; he dictated it with no professional help and, as we shall see, with coherent arguments and an elegant and remarkable style; no clerk rhetorician could have done better in expressing his thoughts with the clarity and lucidity required in the pursuit of arms. From which we must conclude that the marshal was as accomplished in letters as he was in arms. [277]

XXXI: Here follows the content of the letter that the marshal sent to the Venetians.[88]

'In the name of God through Whom all things were made, to Whom all secrets are known, and Who loves truth and hates falsehood, I, Jean Le Meingre, known as Boucicaut, marshal of France and governor of Genoa, to you, Michele Steno, doge of Venice, and to you, Carlo Zeno, citizen of the said city: I acknowledge receipt of a copy of the letter sent by you, Michele Steno, to the king my sovereign lord, and written in Venice on the last day of October. Had I not been acquainted with the habits and customs of you and your predecessors in your office, I should have been astonished at their content, given that they are based on lies and contain not a word of truth; I should have responded earlier, had I not feared for impediments to the release of the French and Genoese whom you were holding captive in defiance of all justice and reason. Now, however, I respond to the articles contained therein, and in the following terms. [278]

'First, as concerns what your letters claim, that on or around the tenth day of last August, I, sailing along the coast of Syria in alliance with the Genoese, did appropriate goods and merchandise, the property of your fellow Venetians resident

87 The Venetian senate had sent a letter of justification for their actions to the king of France on 30 October 1403.

88 The letter of defiance addressed to Michele Steno (1331–1413), doge of Venice (1400–13) was written at Genoa on 6 June 1404.

in Beirut, despite those Venetians claiming such assets were theirs and those of other Venetians, and that I also appropriated ships belonging to the said Venetians: I respond as follows. I maintain that my ambassadors having negotiated peace with the king of Cyprus, I found myself in Cyprus with my then army; I wished not to waste the campaigning season, and remembering the injury and violence perpetrated by the sultan against the merchants and the possessions of Genoa and against the citizens of Genoa (of which city I have the honour to be governor, on behalf of the king my sovereign lord), persuaded that I had good and just cause to inflict injury and loss on the said sultan and on his lands and subjects, wished therefore to proceed to Alexandria; wind and weather were against me, and I was obliged to head for Syria; on disembarking, I found that Syria was warned of my coming with my army via messages and letters sent by your Venetians, which letters were an affront to God, to loyalty and to the duty of all Christians. On the date stated in your present letter, I came ashore in Beirut, or in its environs; prior to my coming ashore, I saw a *gripperie* leaving port; I commanded one of my said galleys to apprehend it, and the said *gripperie* was taken captive; [279] it was a Venetian vessel, which by order of your council in Nicosia had been sent to notify the Saracens of my coming with my army. Nevertheless, very soon thereafter, and to demonstrate goodwill beyond my duty towards you, I freed the *gripperie* and its crew and passengers with no damage to them or to the vessel itself. It was a matter of good conscience that I did not have all the Venetians hanged or thrown overboard, given that their actions were a betrayal of God and of Christianity. As for the goods and merchandise found in the said city of Beirut, you should know that the Venetians, warned of my coming, had ample time to take goods and possessions to a safe place. I concede that finding myself in enemy territory I took possession of what goods were found there – but there was very little to take. After a fitting time spent in the city, I ordered the city to be burnt and withdrew to my galleys; during my sojourn in the city, and before returning to my galleys, I received no embassy, Venetian or other, [280] requesting that I return any such goods and merchandise, nor any of the other articles which you falsely claim were stolen by me. For God knows that had such measures been requested, I would willingly and happily have returned such things, for I had no wish to damage Venetian interests or those of other Christians, but simply to do injury to the sultan, his lands and subjects, with whom I was at open war.

'And in response to what you add, that after the taking of Beirut I captured some of your ships: were I not accustomed to the lies and falsehoods in which you indulge beyond any other people or nation on earth, there too I would have been amazed; for you yourself know, and cannot deny, that what you write is the very reverse of the truth. Had I so wished, I could indeed have captured such vessels, for in Candelore, in Famagusta, in Rhodes and in other places, as I came and went, I found many of your ships and other vessels which I could had I wished easily have seized; yet wherever I found them, I afforded them the same generous treatment as I did the Genoese vessels.

'And as for your claim in your letter that on the seventh day of last October, I with my eleven galleys found myself off Modone, and that you, Carlo Zeno, captain of the Venetian galleys, chose to confront me and my fleet [281] amicably over the claim that goods and merchandise had been purloined from Venetian merchants by me and my company in Beirut and elsewhere, and that without warning I had my galleys turned, with every sign of hostility, to face yours, and that you, seeing no other recourse, did as much with your galleys against mine, and that this, by my fault and culpability, led to a battle during which three of my galleys were taken while the remainder of my fleet were put to flight. I respond as follows. I concur that as I returned from my voyage east, I landed briefly in Rhodes, after which I set sail with a force of eleven galleys to travel home; my galleys were much depleted after so long a voyage which had seen many of my men killed or wounded or sick, and were seriously short of mariners, of crossbowmen, and of men-at-arms. So I needed to resupply and rearm, knowing as do you that there was ample provision of provisions and arms on Rhodes; and I had no suspicion of other Christians let alone of you Venetians, for I believed in the lying civilities that you, Carlo Zeno, [282] had proffered so often to me, cognisant though I was that you were moored at Modone with the Venetian galleys. So, with my eleven galleys, I proceeded to Modone, off the coast of which – that is, on the island of Sapienza – we anchored on Saturday the sixth day of October, thinking ourselves in friendly waters. To demonstrate to all my firm intention and resolve not to offer hostilities to any of your galleys or ships or other Venetian possession – where I could, had I so wished, easily have done so – I point out that only a few days before arriving in Sapienza, I had sent to Chios two of the galleys from my fleet, plus a further galley and a galiot belonging to the lord of Mytilene, plus a galley and a galiot from Pera [Peire], and a galley belonging to the lord of Ainos (Esne];[89] I had also sent another of my galleys, and two or three galiots, to Alexandria. Had I had any hostile intentions towards you, I would naturally have kept all these galleys and galiots with me; a mere command would have sufficed. Moreover, the day before I arrived on Sapienza, while I was off Cape Maleas, there came two of my ships loaded with men-at-arms and crossbowmen – in one ship at least eight hundred men-at-arms – and had I wished, I could have retained all those men and distributed them as needed [283] across my galleys. And in addition, again while I was off Cape Maleas and on watch, just before dawn, I saw a brigantine or a *gripperie* of yours making out from Heraklion [Candie][90] and approaching my ships under the impression that they were yours; it carried several letters to you, Carlo Zeno, and to others of your commanders. When the messenger came aboard my galley, those letters were handed to my skipper who asked me what I wanted to do with them; I replied that I wished him to return them without reading them, that I did not wish the messenger or the other Venetians to be offended or displeased, and

89 The lord of Ainos (now known as Enez) was Niccolò Gattilusio (d.1409).
90 Candia was the Venetian name for Heraklion, the largest city on the island of Crete.

that the messenger should be set free with courtesy. And so it was done. On the very night I arrived at the port of Sapienza, and very soon after my arrival, one of your barques approached, and when I had some of my own men hail it and ask for news, I was told that you, Carlo Zeno, were at Porto Longo with eleven galleys, and that there were a further two great galleys at Modone with a number of other ships large and small;[91] the barque, I was told, came from one of the great galleys, and after offering it every courtesy, I let it go free. The following day, Sunday 7 [October] as said, I left the port of Sapienza early with my own galleys, heading towards Genoa and intending to take on water at the port of Zonchio [Jon], for my galleys were much in need of it. I had gone no more than two or three miles, [284] on course direct to Zonchio to take on water as I said, when you, Carlo Zeno, with eleven galleys from Porto Longo appeared heading for Modone; I thought nothing of it, and when you halted at Modone briefly and then emerged with all eleven of your galleys and in addition, unexpectedly, the two great galleys that I have already mentioned, I still had no suspicions and assumed relations were friendly. My own galleys, as I have said, were poorly armed and manned and could therefore only move slowly, but I was in no hurry, thinking that you were headed to Venice, or perhaps that you had something to say to me; I had no inkling of the treachery and the deep-rooted malevolence with which you had long plotted against me, and before very long your superior speed brought you very close to me and my galleys. I soon realised that you were closing on me very fast, and that your eleven galleys and two great galleys – thirteen ships in all – were coming up in line of battle, and that you had a disproportionate number of men-at-arms whose lances and armour could now be seen clearly; I also saw that you had cleared your decks ready for action,[92] and that you yourself, Carlo Zeno, were on your own galley flanked for your greater security by the two great galleys [285]; I also saw that your fleet was augmented by seven or eight brigantines or *palestarmes de naves*, loaded with men-at-arms and crossbowmen; this did not look like the sort of approach to request restitution that your previous letter had described, but rather like preparations for an outright attack which, without prior warning, was about to be launched on us unexpectedly. This seemed all the more likely because onshore we could see that you were mustering large numbers of men-at-arms, on horse and on foot. By this time we were close to land, and I had no choice but to turn the prows of my vessels towards you; I nevertheless ordered that none of my galleys should launch an attack with bombards, crossbow-fire or other weapons, or indeed by any other means, without my express orders; these orders were strictly followed. But you had planned your treachery carefully over some time, and accordingly you had crammed

91 Porto Longo was the harbour of the island of Sapienza.

92 The French author says that Zeno had prepared his *chetimeres* and *abillemens* for battle. *Chetimere* remains puzzling; Lalande and the *DMF* (for this single instance) paraphrase 'préparatifs de combat (dans la marine vénitienne)', and Richard Unger draws a possible parallel with Venetian *schieramento,* also referring to the disposition of troops for battle (personal communication). *Abillements* appears also to mean preparations for combat.

your brigantines and *palestarmes* with a very large number of soldiers, men-at-arms and bowmen, some from Modone, some from Corone,[93] some who were intended for the garrison at Heraklion in Crete, others, in great number, part of the garrison then stationed in Modone, [286] and all of them armed with bombards, crossbows and other battle weapons, all properly drawn up for battle before I could get the few men that I had standing to – especially since, having shown you every sign of friendship and alliance, I had hoped that you had no hostile intentions towards me. Seeing your preparations, however, I ordered my own men to stand to and be ready to do their duty in all eventualities.

'From this account everyone who hears or reads it, and who is concerned with truth rather than with lies, will see that the outcomes were brought about by your ill will and malice aforethought; you were not, in other words, as you claim in your own letter, forced into action, and if I and my men engaged battle, it was through your culpability and your fault, not mine: we were merely defending ourselves. After all, had I intended hostile action towards you, I could have gone on the attack against you in Porto Longo when you had only the eleven original galleys, and when you had not had time to reinforce your forces with the two great galleys and the *palestarmes* I mentioned earlier; this would have been easy for me to do had I so wished.

'And further, to respond to the accusation that after our battle three of my galleys were captured and the others put to flight, I refer you to the realities of the battle and the description that you, Carlo Zeno, [287] would provide if you were at all truthful, for you know that your own galley was twice chased down and close to capture; you know that had the fight been simply between your galley and mine, had I not needed to deal with other galleys as well as yours, I would have had no difficulty in boarding and defeating you, whatever your treacherous plans and your long-standing hostility, despite your large number of men-at-arms and crossbowmen and weapons, far more, as I have said, than would have been a normal complement. Turning to the capture of galleys, I concede that my galleys took one of yours, and your galleys three of mine; it is actually rather surprising that all my galleys were not captured by you, given that you had the advantage in men of three to one, and double the number of ships, and that you had had so long to make preparations whereas we were taken by surprise, running low on supplies and equipment, and completely unaware of your treachery. But God, Who will not let treachery and evil go unpunished, guarded and saved us – thanks to our own courage and efforts – from the fate that your pride and treachery had planned. I am astonished that you claim so deceitfully and so publicly in your letter that my other galleys fled: the real truth is known to so many, that is that it was you, Carlo Zeno, [288] and your galleys who, once the fleets had disengaged – and it was you and your ships that initiated the disengagement – but when we were still within striking distance, bolted, shamefully and disgracefully, for the port of Modone

93 Corone was the Venetian name for Koroni on the south-west peninsula of the Peloponnese on the Gulf of Messina.

while we stood to until we saw you enter port, some nine miles away; we did not withdraw until you entered port and we lost sight of you. And all your actions should be a source of shame and humiliation to you and all your followers, showing as they do signal cowardice and disgrace.

'In conclusion, I maintain that if it be the case that you, Michele Steno, ordered, authorised and instructed Carlo Zeno to act as he did towards me and my company, at a time when there was peace between the commune of Genoa and your own, then you acted falsely, treacherously and wickedly, you and all your councillors. If however it be the case that you, Carlo Zeno, acted without the instruction and authorisation of the said Michele Steno, your doge and superior, then I charge you as I did him and all his councillors. And given that it is incumbent on any man of nobility, born of a free and noble lineage, [289] to give sure and certain effect to his words especially if his honour is impugned, I wish to act accordingly, to demonstrate the guilt and culpability of those responsible, and also in order that the public knowledge of such wickedness may dissuade any other person from behaving in such a way; I say therefore, and shall continue to say, to prove and to maintain, as any noble man must, that all that you, Michele Steno, have written to my sovereign lord the king and that is contrary to the pure truth contained in this my letter, or that you, Carlo Zeno, might have written to others on the same subject, is a tissue of false and wicked lies; that you have lied wickedly and treacherously; that you will continue to lie insofar as you contradict, in word or in writing, the facts as I have narrated them. And in witness of this, if either of you dares or wishes to assert the contrary, I offer to prove my contention in a trial by combat, that you might with God's help acknowledge and confess the truth of my account. And if neither of you wishes to accept my challenge – as I believe may be the case – then in earnest of my truthfulness and honesty, and affirming my faith in God, Our Lady and my lord Saint George, then I offer that my five should fight against your six, my ten against your twelve, my fifteen against your [290] eighteen, my twenty against your twenty-four, my twenty-five against your thirty. I stipulate only that my opponents be all Venetians, while I and my companions be French and Genoese, given that your act of treason was directed against the French and the Genoese. And as for who should organise and be judge for this combat – always assuming you accept my challenge – I would welcome above all the king my sovereign lord, if by his grace he would accept the role. If however he did not wish to do so, or if you yourself did not accept him, I would be content with any other Christian king whom you might designate, or indeed anyone of a lesser rank than king. And if indeed the battle takes place – as it will, please God, if you do not default – I would wish each combatant to be armed with weapons and armour that he is accustomed to have normally in war and battle, with no malice or underhand trickery. And if you should refuse both these challenges, on the grounds that your wars have always been naval rather than land-based, then I accept that and offer an alternative: that one of you should take to sea in a galley, and I in another, your galley having been inspected first by one of my trusted men, and mine having been inspected by a chosen man of yours, to ensure the parity of the two galleys; that each of us be licensed to arm his galley as he prefers, [291] with as many men-at-arms as he wishes, provided simply, as outlined above, that those in your galley be Venetian and those in mine be French and Genoese; that we assemble at a given place with our two galleys and give battle until one or the other galley be overcome and defeated. However, before this battle takes place, in order for me to be confident that no-one, yourself or any of your men, plot disloyalty or treachery, or intrigue to bring more than one galley against me, or to attack me with more than the men on your single vessel [. . .];[94] I shall do likewise. And if you choose to accept one or the other of these challenges, I urge that it be fulfilled within a short time, for war and battle are best pursued by deeds not words. And your response once received, I hold myself ready, with the help of God, Our Lady and my lord Saint George, to put the challenge swiftly into effect. And to show that every clause of this challenge stems from my own knowledge and my own wish, and that as far as in me lies, I shall fulfil my role entirely, I seal this letter with my personal seal. Devised and written in the royal palace of Genoa, the sixth day of June 1404.'[95]

Here ends the second part of this account.

94 Lalande points out that a main clause is missing here in the manuscript.

95 On 13 July 1405, French ambassadors ordered Boucicaut to suspend all hostilities with Venice, and a new treaty was signed on 2 July 1406.

[295] I: Here begins the third part of this book, which describes the marshal's deeds from the time of his return from Syria to the present.

And first, the Italian lords who sought [296] the acquaintance of the marshal because of all the good things they had heard of him.

Once matters had been brought to a peaceful conclusion and the marshal had returned to Genoa, his high reputation for virtue and benevolence spread throughout Italy, and certain lords of that country were impressed and wished to make his better acquaintance. Among these was the lord of Padua, who was himself of great benevolence, valiant and expert in arms; for this reason he was much attached to the marshal, for, as the old saying goes, 'Like attracts like'.[1] And because of his love for the marshal and because he very much wished to see him, he wrote to him a number of times and finally made a visit to Genoa. The marshal received him most honourably and made him very welcome; the lord was so impressed by his reception, and felt such affection for the marshal, that he was drawn to all the French for the marshal's sake. The loyal marshal, for his part, always eager to advance the honour and the interests of the king of France, lost no time in offering the lord such warmth of affection and such wise advice, that the lord pledged himself to the king and accepted his sovereignty over the two great cities of Padua and Verona, as well as over all of his land, paying homage to the king [297] through the person of the marshal; the marshal received this homage with delight.

Just as the lord of Padua had done, so the lady of Pisa and her son Gabriele Maria Visconti approached the marshal and of their own accord paid homage to the king, via the marshal, for the lordship of Pisa and its region;[2] they offered him every possible service should he require it; the marshal thanked them most heartily and gave them most honourable hospitality throughout their visit. And any king or prince should rejoice in having in his service a servant and lieutenant and military leader so devoted to furthering the interests and the honour of his lord!

---

1 Francesco Novello da Carrara (1359–1406) succeeded his father as lord of Padua in 1388.

2 Gabriele Maria Visconti (1385–1408) was the illegitimate son of Gian Galeazzo Visconti (1351–1402), duke of Milan. Pisa had been annexed by Milan in February 1399, and so, following the death of Duke Gian Galeazzo, it was inherited by his son Gabriele who ruled as lord from 1402 to 1405. Gabriele paid homage to the king of France on 15 April 1404, principally to secure Fench protection against the threat posed by Florence.

II: How the young duke of Milan declared war on the marshal, and got the worst of it.

Around this time it happened that after the death of their father, the first duke, [298] the young duke of Milan and his brother, the count of Pavia, opened hostilities with the Genoese and ultimately declared war.[3] They employed in their service Facino Cane who, as many people know, was for many years the greatest *condottiero*,[4] the best known and the most feared that there had been in Italy for many a long year, and the one having the most hardened of men. But despite the strength of his forces and his own personal courage, despite all that he could do, despite the might of the duke of Milan, the Genoese were not much injured by him, for they had at their head their good governor who was able to lead and protect them; after all, the Milanese were not up against some child, but rather against someone who had long been a master in games like these, and who had nothing to fear from them. The marshal immediately gathered his troops against them, and, without waiting for them to attack, he took the fight into their territory, and engaged them in ways so warlike that very soon he had terrorised all their lands, and done much damage to them. Briefly – for it would take too long to describe in detail all the attacks and counter-attacks – the marshal and the Milanese engaged in a number of hand-to-hand battles, but these were always to the detriment of the Milanese, who lost a large number of their men. In spite of anything they could do, the marshal laid siege to their castles and fortresses, and took many of them by expert assault in the face of any Milanese defiance, [299] and in spite of several attempts by Facino Cane to lift the various sieges: nothing that the Milanese could do was successful. And so the marshal pursued his cause with such vigour that in the end, briefly, the duke of Milan was only too pleased to treat for peace – although a treaty took some time to negotiate, for it was he who had, so wrongly, initiated the war. In the end, however, the marshal, who is known for his sound judgement, condescended to treat with the duke, and in this way peace was made between the Milanese and the Genoese: a peace that was favourable to the king, honourable for the marshal and beneficial to the Genoese.

III: How the marshal made great efforts to bring about peace in the Church, so that the Genoese would declare for our Pope.

Among the many good acts that the marshal did on this earth, we should not forget something very worthy of remembrance: the great efforts and personal investment

3 Gian Maria Visconti inherited the duchy of Milan from his father Gian Galeazzo Visconti in 1402. His brother, Filippo Maria Visconti (1392–1447), became count of Pavia in 1402 and succeeded Gian Maria as duke of Milan in 1412.

4 Facino Cane da Casale (1362–1412) was a famous mercenary or *condottiero* who had joined the service of the Visconti rulers of Milan in 1401 and effectively controlled the duchy from 1402 onwards following the succession of the young Gian Maria Visconti.

that he devoted to the good of Christendom, that is to say to the Church which had for so long – sadly – been divided as everyone knows by a distressing schism.[5] But which other person today, prince or commoner, has worked more assiduously to promote [300] unity and peace within the Church than the marshal? None, certainly, and this is something commonly recognised. And to achieve this goal – peace in the Church – he showed exemplary faith, prudence and wisdom, and operated shrewdly in its pursuit, as is perfectly well known. But to ensure that in time to come his efforts stand as an example to all, it will be proper to give a full account of his actions.

The marshal was not one to be idle, and so, after he returned from his expedition to Syria as we have seen, and once he had a little leisure, he resolved to put into effect an ambition that he had long cherished, to find some way, or at least to advance other initiatives, to restore unity and harmony to the Church. Accordingly, he decided that he should make every effort to achieve two aims. First, he wished that the Genoese, adherents of [Boniface IX] the anti-pope of Rome, might be led instead to declare for our Holy Father [Benedict XIII] and come to his obedience. Second, he wished to bring it about that our Holy Father, for the sake of peace in Christendom, would agree to resign whenever the path was opened up by the resignation of the anti-pope, whether his departure was forced or amicably agreed.[6]

He therefore decided on a time and place – as soon as possible – to address the Genoese on the subject.[7] [301] So one day he called a council of all the wisest and most notable nobles, burgesses and merchants among them. He told them, in a speech elegantly composed and finely expressed, that he had a proposition he wished to put to them, and which was inspired by his great affection for them. They were not to resent what he said, but rather to understand the good intentions that lay behind his words. He began by saying that just as a good shepherd in charge of his flock must make sure that the sheep do not stray, he who although unworthy had been appointed their protector and governor was filled with pity that they had for so long slept in error, an error in which they were still persisting: that was to believe in, offer obeisance to and have faith in the anti-pope of Rome; perhaps, he said, this was because they had previously been misinformed as to the truth of the matter,

5 The Great Schism lasted from 1378 to 1417. At the start of the fifteenth century, Benedict XIII (1394–1423) was pope at Avignon, while Boniface IX (1389–1404) and then Innocent VII (1404–6) were the popes at Rome.

6 Four interrelated solutions to the Schism were debated both within France and across Christendom as a whole. The *via facti* was a military solution aiming at the destruction of the anti-pope, popular with Louis of Anjou and other Valois princes who hoped to secure Italian kingdoms under papal auspices and with papal financing. More peaceful alternatives were the *via conventionis* which focused on diplomatic negotiations, the *via concilii* which hoped for a solution imposed by a general council of the Church, and the *via cessionis* which called for the abdication of both popes.

7 Early August 1404. At the same time, messengers from King Charles VI to Pisa, Florence, Lucca and the papal curia at Rome were calling for support for the *via cessionis*.

just as the French had been;[8] he was now determined to remedy this; were he not to instruct them, as duty, he said, dictated, in the truth of the matter, his failure to work for their salvation would weigh on his conscience; when all had been properly explained, [302] they could, he said, choose which path to follow; no-one should be forced into any act that has to do with conscience and the saving of his soul; such things should come from pure free will; God does not wish His people to be forced into His service; he himself, however, once he had fully laid out the truth, would feel he had done his duty to God.

IV: How the marshal summoned a council of the wisest Genoese, and what he said to them on the subject of the Church.

At that the marshal launched into his explanation. He started with the origin of the schism, and said that this pestilential split in the Church, which had already sadly lasted some thirty years, had started in the reign of the most Christian king Charles V whose righteous life, outstanding virtues and wisdom make him considered the most just of princes, the wisest and the most upright of French kings since King Louis [IX] himself, and indeed in his lifetime, of all known kings across the world; he was the most ready to heed advice – indeed he did not act without it.[9] [303] Consequently, when the first papal elections had been held, first in Rome and then nearby (and they were, as everyone knows, held very close together), King Charles received numerous letters from the cardinals explaining what had transpired, and what reasons had brought about the results.[10] Despite the fact that the cardinals declared that the second election had been just and true, and that the first had been valueless, the wise king was not satisfied; he resolved, dutifully, to have himself informed as to the conduct of both the elections, in order to determine which of the candidates he should endorse. Wanting to be fully and accurately informed, he deputed certain wise prelates from his council to go to Avignon to meet the cardinals who were at that time in the city, and question them on the subject; the cardinals were to swear the truth of what they said, and to say, without fear or favour, which

8 This is presumably a reference to the fact that Charles VI had temporarily withdrawn France from the obedience of Benedict XIII on 27 July 1398. Boucicaut's brother Geoffroy had occupied Avignon and laid siege to the papal palace for five years, until Benedict was able to escape on 12 March 1403. On 28 March 1403, Charles VI and an assembly of the French clergy at Marseille had restored France to the obedience of Benedict XIII.

9 The Great Schism had started in 1378, towards the end of the reign of King Charles V (1364–80), a descendant of King Louis IX (1226–70).

10 Bartolomeo Prignano was elected as Pope Urban VI at Rome on 8 April 1378, and Robert of Geneva was elected as Pope Clement VII at Fondi, around seventy miles south-east of Rome, on 20 September 1378.

of the two candidates should be considered the true pope. The envoys duly carried out their mission to the cardinals, who swore one after the other, by the holy body of Christ, [304] and on pain of damnation to their souls, to speak the truth. Thereafter they said that as they sat in conclave in Rome, determined to elect a pope without fear or favour, according only to the dictates of God's will and the Holy Spirit, the Roman mob was infected by malign influences and gathered outside the palace and began to shout out, with copious threats, that they wanted a Roman pope, or at the very least an Italian. The Romans held the cardinals besieged there, yelling at them constantly, and they became so distressed and so corrupted by the uproar, so afraid that they would be killed, that they resolved to pretend to elect the archbishop of Bari, who was an Italian.[11] That is what they did, and the Romans were pacified – but their intention had always been to take their departure as soon as possible, abandoning the pope elect who had been enthroned by force of circumstance, and not by proper vote. They did not consider him pope, even though they had performed all the proper ceremonial; they had been forced into doing so. They did as they had determined and abandoned him indeed. When they arrived in Avignon, they found themselves free to act. [305] They therefore met and after due and holy deliberation elected another pope who they asserted, on pain of their eternal salvation, to be the true and real pope whom all Christendom should obey as its true shepherd. To the truth of this endorsement letters sealed and signed by all the cardinals bore witness, and the said envoys returned to the king and reported on their findings. But the king, ever conscientious, was not yet satisfied; he wished to hear in person from some of the cardinals or other prelates who had been present in person at the elections, preferably those with the highest reputation for righteousness and wisdom. So he sent for them and had them make the journey to his court entirely at his expense. To hear their words, he gathered a council of all the prelates and most expert masters in theology in the whole kingdom of France and elsewhere.[12] The cardinals were much challenged at that council on all points that had to do with the election, and they responded to each point so fully that there was no more to be said. The matter was properly, fully and lengthily discussed, as was proper in a question of such concern, so that there could be no error, no hidden meaning [306] and no remaining scruple. In the end, all the prelates and all the learned masters in theology and all the sages present agreed, after long scrutiny and discussion, that the king and the whole of Christendom should declare themselves for the second of the two elections; they swore to the truth of this resolution, and staked their immortal souls on its veracity. The king was rightly convinced, saying that it was most unlikely, indeed inconceivable, that so many upright men would call down damnation on themselves simply to favour a single candidate. Hence he declared publicly for the pope elected

11 Bartolomeo Prignano was briefly archbishop of Bari from 1377 to his election as pope the following year.

12 This assembly took place in the Bois de Vincennes on 16 November 1378.

in the second election, and wrote to this effect to all the kings and princes who were in alliance with him, those of Spain, Aragon and Scotland among others. And these, persuaded by his worthy reputation and his wisdom, expressed their confidence in the enquiry he had directed, and made the same public declaration.

The marshal relayed all this information to the Genoese, and made other observations that I shall leave aside for the sake of brevity. Finally he concluded by saying that it was not without careful thought and wise advice that the French had condescended to lend obedience to the second election; [307] if the Genoese considered that someone of such probity as the wise King Charles had investigated fully, as he had outlined and as could be attested by many people still alive, and indeed by the marshal himself for these events had taken place in his own lifetime (he had certainly been very young at the time, but the events had been recounted to him many times), then they too should follow their consciences and declare for our side. When the marshal had finished his speech, the Genoese – who had listened attentively – replied that they had heard his account of the whole affair but that it was new to them, it touched on matters of conscience and needed very careful discussion. They would consider his words, and give him their reply; he happily accepted this. At that they departed, but in the aftermath they held a number of meetings, and in the end, briefly, they reported that since God wished it for the sake of Christendom, they would declare for our faction and render obedience to our pope.[13] The marshal received this news with great pleasure, and gave thanks to Our Lord.

And so it was that he achieved his aim, with great sagacity and foresight; [308] the Genoese, notably, had been the nation of Italy that most assiduously, since the schism, had supported the party of the anti-pope. And all the wise men and clerics of Genoa agreed and affirmed that without the marshal's intervention, they would have resisted all calls to support the pope, despite all sermons or gifts or offers from all the kings, princes and prelates of the world. And this triumph should be counted among the deeds of the marshal as near miraculous, for over in Italy they consider it the most remarkable outcome to have been achieved in Italy for the last two centuries.

V: How the marshal argued that the Church should be reunited under the obedience of a single pope elected by a general council.

The marshal had thus achieved one of the goals he had long set himself, to get the Genoese to accept the authority of our pope; now he was to turn to the next of his ambitions. [309]

He was very much aware of how before his death the wise King Charles, as a good and just and Christian king, had been saddened that he could not bring all

13 This was the result of an assembly held at Genoa on 22 October 1404.

Christendom, as is right, under the obedience of a single pope; such divisions were bringing great harm to Christendom. He came to the conclusion that to bring an end to the accursed schism, it would be wise somewhere to hold a general council of all or nearly all the prelates of Christendom, where those present would discuss the matter fully; it would be determined that the two popes elected resign – if not voluntarily then by force, with the assistance and aid of the secular princes.[14] Thereafter a single pope would be elected, in due and dignified process, under the guidance of the Holy Spirit. Such was the design of the good king, and he would no doubt have brought it to fruition had he not died – a great loss to Christendom, and most of all to his own kingdom. The marshal was aware of this project, and knew also that our present monarch, the king's son and heir, and our lords the princes of France, had ever since [310] favoured this solution to bring about unity in the Church. And because he felt that there was no better or more just way to bring about peace in the Church, he determined to do everything in his power to promote reconciliation. This was what had prompted him to put such effort into ensuring that the Genoese would declare for our pope; he believed that if once, with God's help, he could bring the Genoese to obedience, then thereafter with their help (for they have great influence in Italy) he might be able to convert others to the same action – as indeed he did with the lords of Padua and Pisa whom we spoke of earlier, and with others to whom we shall come later;[15] he would then be able if necessary to launch an attack on the Romans if they refused to allow the anti-pope to resign, or if he himself declined to do so.

The marshal was able to do even more – for as we have already said, his high reputation and his goodness attracted the affections of many noble men. Even one of the most important cardinals in Rome to have adopted the cause of the anti-pope, Cardinal Fieschi, felt such affection towards him and thought so highly of him that he desired his acquaintance, and they exchanged several epistles – as a result of which, ultimately, the cardinal abandoned the cause of the anti-pope, [311] thus renouncing sixteen thousand francs-worth of benefices that he held – and rendered obedience to our pope.[16]

But to turn to the other goal he had in mind, through both of which goals he wished to bring about Church unity: the first goal led to the second. The Holy Father was marvellously grateful to the marshal for having brought the Genoese – formerly the group most hostile to him in the world – to give obedience to him; he blessed him and

14 There is some evidence to suggest that Charles V did declare shortly before his death that the Schism would need to be discussed by a council of the Church. See, for example, Christine de Pizan, *Le livre des fais et bonnes meurs du sage roy Charles V*, ed. S. Solente, 2 volumes (Paris, 1936–40), II, pp. 185–6.

15 Gabriele Maria Visconti, lord of Pisa, submitted to the obedience of Pope Benedict XIII on 1 September 1405.

16 Ludovico Fieschi, cardinal from 1383 until his death in 1423, abandoned the obedience of the Roman pope Innocent VII and joined the obedience of Pope Benedict XIII until his deposition in 1409.

prayed for him. But the marshal did even more for the pope, for in order to further their mutual affection, he lent him large sums of money, and helped him out from his own fortune; some time thereafter, the marshal and the pope met in Genoa, and the marshal rightly paid him great respect and honour.[17] And during their meeting, the marshal urged him, for the good of Christendom and the harmony of the Church, to engineer, by force or by love, that the pope of Rome stand down, and to send him messages to that effect: this was something he had promised the lords of France to work towards, and the marshal himself promised to do everything he could to bring it about. The marshal pressed the pope [312] so persistently on the subject that the latter swore that he would definitely do so. It was thus that the marshal achieved his two goals, and from them stemmed great success: the Romans, having heard of the marshal's intentions, were so nervous of his valour and his capabilities, and of the forces at his disposal, that after the death of the anti-pope who recently died, they agreed of their own accord, quite unforced, to get the cardinals, with the consent of the city, to have their newly elected pope stand down and renounce the papal throne, provided always that the pope of Avignon would do the same, in order to allow a proper and holy election for a new shepherd of the flock.[18] My own opinion is that this resolution in the cardinals' faction – to seek unity by resignation – was the work of the Holy Spirit, taking pity on the woes of His Bride our Holy Church, and wishing to restore the unity which will, please God, soon be brought about; I do not claim it can be the work only of mortal man, although we must acknowledge the marshal's contribution, for, until his intervention, the Romans had refused to countenance such a move, and it may be that the marshal's actions were indeed decisive. In any case, it seems, thank God, that war will be unnecessary, and unity will be achieved – God grant that it be so! [313]

As against that, the false hypocrite that the cardinals of the Roman faction had elected – who had passed himself off as a most good and holy man – having initially promised to stand down once our own pope had done so, having confirmed that intention by letters under his seal to all the kings and princes of Christendom, then showed his true colours as a hypocrite and a cheat, for every word he said, it turned out, and as I shall show later, was a tissue of lies.

VI: How the Pisans rebelled against their lord, and how the marshal sought to make peace.

Much as I might wish to, I cannot tell all my history tidily; I must deal with matters one at a time, even though many of those that I wish to recount were happening

17 Benedict XIII arrived in Genoa on 16 May 1405 and remained there for many months. His opponents in Venice, Siena and Florence believed that Benedict and Boucicaut were trying to gather military support to attack Rome in order to implement the *via facti*.

18 Pope Innocent VII (1404–6) died on 6 November 1406 in Rome

simultaneously. So I turn now to the Pisans who in 1405 rebelled against their lord and expelled him from the rule of Pisa – [314] as is not unusual in Italy where the people, once they feel they have the upper hand, refuse to countenance any long-lasting regime.[19] When the lord found himself thrown out of the city he had inherited by his unruly subjects, he realised that he did not have at his command the forces that would allow him to retake it; so he resorted to the marshal in his role as lieutenant of his sovereign lord the king of France, to whom he had paid homage for his inheritance; he asked his help in the king's name, as a vassal requesting due help from a lord. When the marshal heard the news, he was much disturbed, and replied that before resorting to a punitive expedition he himself would prefer to do everything to restore amity and good order; he would be reluctant to destroy Pisa by act of war, for the damage would be serious and long-lasting; he could not counsel it, and would open negotiations with the Pisans. The marshal therefore set off from Genoa, and headed for Porto Venere [Portum Vendre],[20] from where he sent word to the Pisans that he had come to open discussions with them. The leaders of the rebellion came to meet him with a large number of followers, and the marshal said to them, affably, that he was disappointed to hear that they had rebelled against a lord who had been nothing but good and gracious to them; [315] [Gabriele Maria Visconti] and his mother the lady Agnes had loved them and protected them, to the best of their ability, from all troubles (as was right in a lord for his subjects), and who intended to do more in the future; [the marshal] had come to tell them that they should reconsider and approach him in a spirit of contrition and ask for forgiveness, in which case he, the marshal, would make every effort to have the lord in his mercy pardon them; it was to act as a mediator for peace that he had come. Such were the words of the marshal, and he expressed them warmly. But the Pisans replied, briefly, that they wanted nothing to do with such a plan; they wanted no more of the lord's rule; rather, they implored [the marshal] to become their lord himself and to accept sovereignty over Pisa and its domains, for only in him did they have confidence; they were confident that he would be able to guard them and protect them; if he would accept, they would offer him their obedience, their loyalty and their love, as true subjects should their true lord; let him not refuse an offer made in good faith.[21] The marshal replied that they should never entertain such a hope, for it was not the way of the French to enter into such machinations; he would rather die than do such a thing; he begged them to follow his advice and return to their true lord, and become good and loyal and obedient subjects; he promised that if they would do so, he would be their friend and offer them the same protection that he would [316] if

19 The uprising against Gabriele Maria Visconti started on 20 July 1405, three days after he had met with a Florentine envoy to discuss an alliance that would have been deeply unpopular amongst the citizens of Pisa.

20 Porto Venere is a town around seventy miles east of Genoa along the Ligurian coast.

21 The delegation of Pisans hoped to secure French support against Florence by placing their city under the sovereignty of the French crown, just as Genoa had done in 1396.

they were to become his own subjects, even, if necessary, against their own lord if he, the marshal, heard that their lord was mistreating them. What more can I say? The Pisans responded, briefly, that his words were in vain; nothing he could say would make Gabriele Visconti agreeable to them; they would prefer to be torn limb from limb rather than accept him; since he himself did not wish to become their lord and master, they begged him to go to a castle on the coast called Livorno [Ligourne], the port for Pisa, and they would come to him and pay homage to the king of France himself, just as had the Genoese.[22]

VII: How the Pisans pretended to the marshal that they wished to become sworn subjects of the king of France, and how this was a hoax.

When the marshal saw that for all his fine words and persuasions, for all the offers he could make, the Pisans were refusing to put an end to their ill will towards their lord, and that there was no possible remedy to the situation, he left and called for my lord Gabriele [Maria Visconti], explained all that had transpired [317] and that the Pisans had responded that they refused adamantly to have Gabriele return to Pisa as their lord: it would never happen. Hearing this, Gabriele was deeply saddened; the marshal told him to consider his options; if there was indeed no remedy and if the Pisans continued to refuse obedience to him, preferring to submit to the king of France, then perhaps it would be better for that king to rule rather than some other foreign lord, given in particular that [Gabriele] had already paid homage to the king; on the other hand, he stressed that the king would not want it said that he had alienated the lands and lordships of his own vassals and loyal subjects; accordingly, if he, the lord [of Pisa], would agree of his own volition to resign from the lordship of Pisa and place his county in the king's hands, and to cede all rights to the king, he, the marshal, would ensure that Gabriele received compensation for his lands and his lordship and his other revenues; because the marshal had engaged his own responsibility, the lord [of Pisa] declared himself content and in agreement.

In this spirit, the marshal repaired to Livorno as the Pisans had requested, expecting them to meet him to render themselves to the king and to pay him homage.[23] But the treacherous dogs had never had any intention of doing so; their only thought was wickedness and betrayal [318] and deceit – as later events were to show. Once they arrived at the port, they said that before they submitted to the king, they wanted my lord Gabriele, who was installed in the citadel of Pisa, to leave; they wanted the marshal to take command of the citadel; once this was done they would do as they

22 Livorno (known in English as Leghorn) is a port on the western coast of Tuscany, just over ten miles south-west of Pisa.

23 Boucicaut arrived at Livorno on 4 August 1405.

had promised; they would do homage, they swore, without any trickery on their part. The marshal agreed to their demand, expelled those who were in charge of the citadel, and installed his own men, under the command of Guillaume de Meuillon.[24] The citadel's supplies were almost exhausted, so he had a galley and a barque loaded with all sorts of stores. On top of that, to reinforce the garrison, he sent his own nephew [Louis] des Barres and a great number of the gentlemen from his household, and also a large number of gentlemen and citizens of Genoa; they took with them much of the marshal's clothes and personal effects (for he expected to follow), and two thousand golden écus as pay for my lord Gabriele's men to keep them happy and persuade them to leave the citadel without feeling hard done by. After he had made all these arrangements, he sent off the galley and the barque, expecting there to be no hindrances. [319] But when they entered the river of Pisa, [the Arno], and were close to the citadel, the treacherous Pisans as soon as they caught sight of the ships gathered so secretly that no-one saw what they were doing, and set up a secret ambush.[25] Our men reached harbour and disembarked with no thought of trouble, believing that the Pisans, whom they now thought of as allies and to whom they had never done any harm, would come to their aid if any outsider threatened them. But no: some six thousand of the Pisans went on the attack, and the whole population of the city ran up yelling and bellowing foul things against the king of France, against the marshal and against the French; they surrounded the French like a pack of mad dogs, surprising our men who had had no inkling of the trap. The Pisans took many of our French prisoner, beat them, wounded them and even killed some of them, and hauled them off to dark and filthy prisons; they pillaged the ships; to add insult to injury, they purloined the standard of the king of France which flew on the galley and dragged it through the mud, trampled it and spat on it, uttering, as we have said, foul-mouthed insults to the king and to the French. And to complete their wickedness, they paraded in large numbers in front of the citadel which was still garrisoned by the marshal's men, French and Genoese, and uttered vile threats and said that they would do to the garrison what they had done to the marshal's new arrivals. This is an example of their great wickedness and deceit, for the marshal and his men had never been anything but good to them; [320] on the contrary, they had often shown them benevolence, for those of Florence, hearing that the Pisans were in conflict with their lord, had immediately launched an attack, and the garrison of the citadel had come twice to their defence; this was something that those ingrates knew perfectly well,

24 See *Faits et gestes de Guillaume de Meuillon, publiés d'après le manuscrit original*, ed. E. Maignien (Grenoble, 1897), pp. 15–16. Guillaume (d.1429?) enjoyed an energetic diplomatic and military career in the service not only of Boucicaut but also of the dukes of Anjou, Orléans and others.

25 This attack occurred on 13 August 1405. The biographer does not mention the fact that three days earlier, Boucicaut had apparently been contemplating a double-cross of the Pisans when he appointed two Genoese, Battista Lomellini and Cosma Tarigo, to meet with a Florentine envoy at Pietrasanta. Meanwhile Gabriele Maria Visconti was meeting with another Florentine, Maso Degli Abruzzo, at Lavajano.

just as they knew that the marshal and his men had pursued the well-being of the Pisans – and this was his reward!

VIII: How the marshal continued to make every effort to have the Pisans swear allegiance to the king of France.

The disloyal Pisans, having behaved in this way, feared the marshal's anger, and particularly that he might lead a force against them to annihilate them – as indeed they richly deserved. But to conceal their treachery, and indeed to compound it, they sent him an embassy composed of their most prominent citizens, who begged him, for God's sake, not to be angry with them; they recognised that what had happened had been wrongly and egregiously mistaken, that everything was the responsibility of the people and nothing to do with the prominent citizens, who for their part were more than ready to make amends in any way he wished and to give their consent, as promised, to recognising the sovereignty of the king of France. The marshal listened to them; he preferred not to inflict [321] hard penalties on them, since he still hoped to persuade them to submit to the king. He replied that they had behaved as badly as could be imagined; he was more saddened that they had caused offence to the king than that they had damaged himself and his men; if, however, they submitted to the king as they had promised, their treachery would be forgiven. They responded that they would do so without fail. They would, they said, take cordial leave from him and return to the citizens of Pisa to tell them about the marshal's benevolence; the ambassadors would, they said, return to the marshal to confirm everything, but they begged him not to launch an attack of any sort on them during negotiations – something the marshal agreed. At that the perfidious deputation departed; their sole motive had been to keep the marshal talking while they plotted their next act of treachery. For while these talks were ongoing, they threw all their forces into the attack on the citadel, day and night, with siege engines, crossbow-fire and cannons. And worse yet: every day they used their catapults to hurl into the fortress a hundred or more barrels of night-soil, poisons, rotting carcases and other filth. They dug great trenches between themselves and the citadel, cutting it off from the town. And because the citadel stood over to one side of the city against the walls – as does for instance the Bastille Saint-Antoine in Paris – they encircled that section of the walls, on the outside, [322] with trenches and with bastilles[26] so that the garrison could not be relieved. In this way they besieged the garrison from all sides and made repeated efforts to force the citadel – but this was not easy to do for it was very well fortified. And as well as all this, they made strenuous efforts to guard any exit so that no word could be sent to the marshal.

26 A bastille was a wooden tower on wheels built for siege warfare.

They had in mind even greater treachery – for they sent ambassadors to Florence with letters of credence to offer the republic of Florence their choice of four castles owing allegiance to Pisa, and freedom from taxation on any exports to the city, in return for which the Florentines and all their armies would join in the siege of the castle of Livorno occupied by the marshal and their lord Gabriele, assist in capturing the two of them, and hand them over to the Pisans. But the Florentines refused to consent to such an enterprise.

While the citizens of Pisa were pursuing this scheme, the Pisan ambassadors returned to the marshal to prevent his realising what was going on; while talks were proceeding, they hoped to take the citadel and find a means to besiege the marshal himself in Livorno. They explained that the Pisans were still intending to fulfil their promise and submit to the king of France, but, before they would comply, they wanted the marshal [323] to hand over the three castles then in his hands: the citadel, the castle of Livorno and the castle of Librafatta [Lipe-et-faite] which was still in the hands of my lord Gabriele. The marshal replied: 'What do you intend to do with the citadel?' The Pisans responded: 'We want to demolish it, and take possession of the other two castles.' 'In that case,' said the marshal, 'what powers will the king retain over you, and what authority will he have to exercise justice?' 'We do not wish him', said the Pisans, 'to be anything other than our nominal lord.' 'The king', said the marshal, 'would consider such powers and authority negligible. He will require you to submit as did the Genoese, or as you did yourselves to Gherardo de Piombino whose title then passed to the duke of Milan.'[27] The Pisans replied that under no circumstances would they do so, and then left. At that the marshal realised that all the negotiations had been a trick, and that the Pisans had perfidiously drawn out the talks for twenty-two days. My lord Gabriele, seeing at this that the Pisans' intentions had been entirely deceitful, opened negotiations with the Florentines to sell them Pisa and all his rights over their territories. But the marshal was undaunted, and saw it as his duty to prevent the Florentines from doing any such deal. He sent six of the principal citizens of Genoa to those of Pisa [324] to tell them that they should not be party to their own destruction, for their lord was in negotiation to sell their city to Florence – which, they knew, was hostile to them and would treat them badly; they should take note of this and offer their fealty to the king of France, as they had promised; this would bring them great benefits, and they would be able to live in peace and security.

While the ambassadors were in Pisa, the Florentines sent the marshal a copy of the letters of credence that the Pisans had given the ambassadors to Florence, which, as we have said, were intended to persuade the Florentines to take up the siege of the marshal's forces in Livorno.[28] And on that very day the marshal had news from his

27 Gherardo Appiani (c.1370–1405) had been lord of Pisa briefly until 1399 when he sold the lordship to Gian Galeazzo Visconti, duke of Milan. Appiani was also lord of Piombino from 1398 until his death.

28 The Florentines informed Boucicaut of the offer that they had received from the Pisans in a letter written on 21 July 1405. They also wrote to Guillaume de Meuillon on 31 July 1405.

nephew [Louis] des Barres and the other prisoners, saying how badly they were being treated and that they had been held to ransom, and begging him, despite the large size of the ransom, to get them freed from their prison, for they were suffering from great want and in mortal danger. The marshal was much distressed, and incensed, at the treachery and wickedness of the Pisans. Had it not been for the fact that he had already sent word to the king of France and his council that the Pisans had already submitted to him, he would have hurried to attack them and punish them for their treachery and wickedness, but, in the circumstances, he preferred to suffer rather than give those who were jealous of him – and there were many such in France and elsewhere – grounds to say [325] that the marshal's arrogance had lost the king his sovereignty. So he simply ordered the immediate release of the prisoners, and the messages sent by the Genoese to Pisa never had a considered response; the Pisans simply replied: 'We shall not accede to any of your requests, and we do not want to hear any more of them. Rather, you should do better: revolt against the sovereignty of your king, kill Boucicaut and all the French, govern yourselves as we have done. Then we may live, the two of us, as brothers – which would be a wise course of action.' This was the response that the ambassadors brought back, nor were they able to extract anything different.

IX: How the marshal sent word to the Pisans to say that if they did not submit to the king, their lord was planning to sell them to Florence.

The lord of Pisa could now see that there was no chance of the Pisans accepting the rule of the king of France, and he was even more determined to pursue his negotiations on the sale of the city to Florence, thinking to transfer his entire authority to them. The discussions continued until both sides were agreed that Florence would give four hundred thousand florins to my lord Gabriele. But the Florentines insisted that before any other moves were made, the marshal should give his consent, [326] and his agreement and endorsement, otherwise the agreement would be void. At that, my lord Gabriele came to the marshal and asked him to relinquish the citadel of which he was still in possession; the marshal had sworn and promised to do so unquestioningly once an agreement had been reached with the Pisans, so he could scarcely refuse the request. The marshal responded that he would keep any promises he had made – my lord Gabriele could be sure of that. But as concerned the arrangements Gabriele had made for the sale of Pisa, he would never agree to the king's losing a sovereignty for which he, Gabriele, had himself at one time sworn fealty; he insisted on seeing the treaty and the agreements that Gabriele had made with the Florentines, and these were given him. And when the marshal had received them and studied them, he sent copies to the Pisans saying that in spite of all the acts of treachery and wickedness that they had done him, or plotted to do him, he nevertheless felt great compassion for them for the misfortunes that were to come, and for the ruin which their folly was inviting; so that they should understand the situation, he was sending them a copy of the treaty that had now been signed and sealed between their own lord and the Florentines; he himself had not so far consented, determined as he was that neither God nor man should be able to say that he had not fulfilled his duty, which was to warn them of their folly before they were utterly destroyed; [327] once again he invited them to submit to the king of France as they had promised, in which case he would save them from ruin and restore peace; this was, he said, his last warning, for henceforward he would be unable to do anything to prevent the said sale; if they did not send their submission within two days, they would be unable to change their minds, for he had promised their lord that he would cede Pisa to him unless they submitted; Gabriele was pestering him over that promise so untiringly that he could not renege; they should understand that once he had given his word and sworn, he would never go back on his promise; they should consider very carefully, and for the last time, what their decision was to be. To which the Pisans replied that, once and for all, they would not submit, and that they wished to hear no more on the subject.

X: The agreement made between the marshal and the Florentines on the status of Pisa.

At this point my lord Gabriele wanted to agree a final version of his treaty with the Florentines, but the marshal disagreed and said that he would never agree that another power should receive sovereignty over a territory that had already done homage to the king; he would rather wage war on the Pisans and conquer them. When my lord Gabriele saw this, [328] he took counsel with the Florentines; they decided jointly that in order to satisfy the marshal, the Florentines would swear fealty to the king for the sovereignty of Pisa, as my lord Gabriele had done. They then took the proposal to the marshal, who replied that whatever else he might agree to, they could rest assured that he would never let the castle of Livorno be alienated or pass to a foreign power, for that would be to the detriment of the Genoese for whom his own duty was to maintain or increase their jurisdiction and authority; he would, however, consider their proposal, and they should return to hear his response the following day.

At this my lord Gabriele said that he himself was ready to consent there and then to the marshal's terms: that in whatever negotiations he might have with the Florentines, the castle of Livorno would remain absolutely and inalienably in the possession of the marshal, for the latter had done so much for him that he had deserved it; the Florentines replied that they would not dispute the claim.

During the following night, the marshal considered the proposals carefully; he concluded, in summary, that in what the Florentines proposed, the king would lose nothing; in fact, he would gain, for rather than one sovereignty he would have two:

Pisa itself (whatever the wishes of the Pisans), and with it the Florentines, themselves a major power and who would become vassals of the king.[29] [329] He decided that he would agree to the proposals, provided that they would in addition agree to certain demands – among which, good Christian as he was, he remembered to include our Holy Mother Church, the unity and reconciliation of which he cherished hopes for day and night, as we have described.

The following day, when the envoys returned, he told them that he would agree to their proposals – that is that the Florentines would become possessors of Pisa itself, the citadel and all the associated territory of the county with the exception of the castle of Livorno; that they would do homage to the king for these territories and become his liegemen; that they would agree, swear and undertake that they would never trade by sea other than using the ships and vessels of Genoa and the Genoese.

Item: that a month after they had acquired the city, by force or negotiation, they would declare for our Holy Father the pope, and undertake to get the Pisans to do likewise.

Item: that six months from that date, if the pope of Rome still clung to his error and refused to resign, they would commit themselves to join with the French and the Genoese to engage if necessary in war against the pope, and make it clear that they were his enemies.

Item: that if once they agreed to all these conditions, then a full digest of their accords and agreements would be drawn up and sent to the king of France and his council, without whose agreement he could not come to a final agreement, nor did he wish to be solely responsible. They needed, he said, to agree this last condition, [330] for if the terms had been ratified by the king and his council, they themselves could feel more secure; if they did agree, he would undertake to have the king, his council and the lords of France indite and seal formal letters to this effect.

When the marshal had given his response, the Florentine envoys replied that they would go and ascertain the wishes of their own authorities, and return with a formal response. Briefly, they came back with letters of credence allowing them to sign the agreement, to the entirety of which they acceded. Present were my lord Gabriele and more than a hundred of the most important gentlemen and citizens of Genoa who had been brought by the marshal, for he wanted them to be present and to show that the agreement had been made freely. Those concerned then entirely agreed, swore and promised to hold to the settlement in perpetuity, in earnest of which formal letters were exchanged, sealed and certified between the two parties.[30]

---

29 In the final agreement, the Florentines promised to send a white horse once a year to the governor of Genoa, as representative of the king of France, in recognition of the homage that they owed to the French crown.

30 The contract for the sale to Florence of Gabriele Maria Visconti's rights over Pisa was agreed on 27 August 1405. Gabriele received 80,000 florins, and Boucicaut 126,000 florins.

XI: How the marshal sent word to the king of France, to our lords and to the council, of the agreement made with the Florentines [331] on the subject of Pisa; how the king and the lords sent formal letters conveying their own agreement; and how the Pisans – deceitful as ever – wanted to transfer their allegiance to the duke of Burgundy.

As soon as the accord had been agreed, the marshal wrote to the king, his council and our lords the dukes, presenting in writing all its clauses and stipulations.[31] He begged the king that if the council agreed that the accord was good, advantageous and honourable, and if the lords were agreeable, then he, the king, would ratify and confirm it via formal, sealed letters, agreed with the council; he requested that the members of the council certify it with their own authentic seals, in the presence of the king's said uncles the dukes, so that the matter would be durable and confirmed in perpetuity because no opportunity had been left for any party to the agreement to renege or to repudiate it. When the messages reached the king, the matter was discussed in council. The marshal was much praised by the king, by our lords the dukes, and by all the wisest of the council, for the prudence and wisdom with which he had brought the king not one but two lordships which offered such advantages to France, which would bring honour and benefit to the Church, and profit for the lordship of Genoa. And the marshal was showered with praise for all these successes and all the other deeds that he had performed and indeed was still performing every day; [332] everyone was much beholden to him, and said so. The king confirmed the agreement in every clause as it had been negotiated by the marshal, by formal letters patent; it was endorsed by our lords the dukes and by all the peers, who swore never to counter it and certified their consent by letters sent to the marshal.[32] He in his turn handed them to the Florentines who were overjoyed, and declared themselves content. These formalities completed, the Florentines immediately forwarded the vidimus[33] of the contract of sale to the Pisans, enjoining them to obey – as was their duty – their new masters, failing which they, the Florentines, would declare war and impose their authority by force; their reprisals would be the more savage the more rebellious the Pisans had been. The Pisans ignored all this, and replied that they would repudiate the agreement in its entirety; if anyone declared war on them, they

31 Pope Benedict XIII also wrote to Charles VI on 15 August 1406, praising the agreement that Boucicaut had negotiated.

32 The contract of sale was ratified on 6 March 1406 by the French royal council led by the duke of Berry, but in the absence of the dukes of Burgundy and Orléans. In a letter to Boucicaut dated 15 July 1406, Burgundy reported that the royal council had approved the agreement with Florence and Gabriele Maria Visconti, but noted that this had been concluded without the knowledge and consent of King Charles VI, who was ill at the time of the original discussions.

33 Vidimus: the attested copy of a document.

would fight back unstintingly; they were afraid of no-one. At this, the Florentines did declare war on Pisa; they attacked the city and quickly did much damage; finally, they besieged the city, although the Pisans fought back so tirelessly that it was not easy to subdue them.[34] [333]

After the war had lasted more than a year, the Pisans realised that they could not hold out against the Florentines and their allies, and resorted to the tricks and betrayals that they had employed previously. They therefore sent messengers to Ladislaus, self-proclaimed king of Naples, to say that they would submit to his rule as long as he brought a large army to lift the siege.[35] He replied that he would do so – and fortified by this hope they resisted even more strongly. But their hopes were dashed, for Ladislaus was distracted by other events so that he could neither come himself nor send reinforcements, and the Pisans had fewer and fewer resources. Indeed the Pisans' resistance was quite extraordinary: they had been suffering the miseries of the siege for two whole years, constantly under attack. Their garrison was diminishing by the day, for they were enduring famine within the city, and war outside it. They no longer saw any solution – indeed they said that rather than surrender they would submit to the Saracens: they would rather die than surrender to the Florentines.

So once again they resorted to treachery, hoping by such means to escape from the predicament in which they found themselves. [334] They sent ambassadors to France primed with fine words, and told the duke of Burgundy that they would surrender themselves absolutely to him provided he would send them help against the Florentines and lift the siege.[36] The duke demurred initially, remembering the agreement he had personally signed and which he did not want to contravene. So the ambassadors – who were clever as a cart-load of monkeys – repaired to the duke of Orléans, the king's brother, and promised him the world if he could engineer a cure for the situation. The result was that, urged on by the ambassadors, the duke of Burgundy and the duke of Orléans went to the king and begged him to allow them to accept the Pisans' offer, and to transfer to them any authority that he might hold.[37] To be brief, they hammered away at him until, since he was always reluctant to refuse his brother anything, and since some of his councillors urged him to do so too, he acceded to their demands – at which the dukes wrote to the Florentines to say that they should lift the siege and cease to wage war on the Pisans.[38] [335] At the same time they wrote to the marshal to say he should no longer ally himself with the

34 The Pisans revolted on 6 September 1405 and captured the citadel. The Florentine siege of the rebel city began very shortly afterwards and lasted until October 1406.

35 In December 1405, the Pisans sent envoys to Ladislaus (1377–1414), king of Naples, who refused to assist them. They also sought help from Pope Innocent VII, from Venice and from Martin I, king of Sicily (1390–1409).

36 The Pisan envoy to John the Fearless, duke of Burgundy, was dispatched on 11 February 1406.

37 The two dukes attempted to intervene between May and July 1406, and paid homage to Charles VI for the lordship of Pisa on 27 July 1406.

38 This letter was dated 10 July 1406, and received in Florence on 12 August.

Florentines, but rather take up the cause of the Pisans who were now their lieges, and lift the siege.[39] When the marshal received this message he was astonished, given that the dukes themselves had endorsed the agreement and promised their entire support; he himself, as a man of honour, would rather die than perjure himself.[40] He replied that in honour he could not do as they asked, and that even if he were prepared to do so, to take on a major power like Florence was no easy task, for the city had at its disposal large numbers of men-at-arms whereas he for the moment was short of men, and the Florentines had access to very large funds whereas he did not. If they wished him to embark on such initiatives, they would need to ensure that he was better provided with both men and money.[41]

The Florentines took no notice of the dukes' letters and made no move to end the war;[42] they pushed the Pisans harder and harder, even though a number of French captains and men-at-arms deserted the siege and the alliance with the Florentines to avoid trouble with the dukes. Briefly, the war continued unabated until the Pisans were unable to hold out any longer; they sent to the dukes for help on many occasions, but unsuccessfully. [336] The dukes simply sent more letters to the Florentines to request that they lift the siege on pain of creating enemies at the French court. But the Florentines were unmoved – in fact they laughed at the threats, saying that conceding and rescinding was child's play, and that it did the house of France no honour to renege on an agreement signed and sealed. They persisted in their refusal, and pursued the war until they achieved their objective and took Pisa by force; they entered the town in the face of Pisan resistance, in spite of the fact that the king, urged on by the dukes, declared his hostility to them.[43] And it must be said that it was the Florentines' responsibility to decide whether or not to keep the previous agreement, the king for his part having broken it; they themselves achieved their objective. And this is the true story of how the Pisans came to be under the rule of Florence, and I defy anyone to deny its truth.[44]

39 The envoy of Jean Sans Peur, duke of Burgundy, arrived at Pisa at the start of July, announcing that the duke had accepted the lordship over the city. On 7 July, the Pisans raised the banner of Burgundy over the city walls.

40 Boucicaut tried to delay things by saying that he would follow the instructions to challenge Florence if the dukes did so too. Burgundy responded in a letter dated 15 July 1406, demanding action.

41 The biographer does not mention the fact that, as agreed in the contract of 27 August 1405, Boucicaut had also received payments from Florence: 29,680 florins (2 October 1405), 20,000 florins (early January 1406), 27,000 florins (around 20 February 1406) and a further payment on 21 April 1406.

42 The Florentines wrote to Charles VI on 15 August 1406 defending their actions; copies of this letter were also sent to the dukes of Berry, Burgundy and Orléans. But when French ambassadors arrived in Florence in September, they were unsuccessful in their mission to persuade the Florentines to put an end to the siege of Pisa.

43 On 9 October 1406, Pisa surrendered to Florence whose troops entered the city.

44 On 10 January 1407, the Florentines rejected Boucicaut's request that they honour their promise to place Pisa under the obedience of Pope Benedict XIII.

XII: How the noble lords the dukes of Orléans and Burgundy resented the marshal's [337] refusal to help the Pisans against the Florentines.

On this account, the noble lords the dukes of Orléans and Burgundy bore a grudge against the marshal, and they and their followers spread blame in France. Because of such talk, many people who, as so often, had no real knowledge of the affair considered it to be the marshal's fault that the dukes had lost the sovereignty of Pisa which would have brought them considerable advantages. But they are attempting to blame him for something that actually redounds very much to the marshal's credit; had he behaved otherwise, he would himself have attracted much blame, for anyone who reneges on an agreement made after due discussion and consultation, and duly signed and sealed, will be accused of faithlessness and transgression. On the other hand, if the dukes spoke in such a way, and if they harboured a grudge against the marshal, I do not believe that this was their initial impulse; I believe that they were seduced into such a stance by the spiteful flatterers – there are always so many at any court – who surrounded them, and who were determined to find any means to undermine the marshal's good fortune and his prosperity; I am confident that, with God's help, they will not succeed, for God will protect his humble servant and they will suffer for their malignity.[45] And you who read this book should note that no-one [338] can be so perfect in word and deed as to be universally beloved; envy, which is everywhere, will see to it that valour, merit, loyalty and goodness will fail to attract the praise and honour that they deserve; those who are envious will always attempt to recast anything that the admirable do for good and worthwhile reasons as improper and ill-intentioned. But Our Lord Jesus Christ, Whose blessed life was lived in this world for our own betterment, allowed Himself, as an example to the virtuous, to be reviled and calumniated by the envious – as we see in the Gospels which tell us that the jealous masters of the law dismissed the miracles that He did by His divine power as the work of evil spirits and of the Devil, and called Him evil for the works that He did.[46]

And it would be gross ingratitude, and a scandal, to hate so worthy a man as the marshal, whose wisdom was responsible for saving from destruction the noble city of Genoa: not merely for saving it, but for leaving it more prosperous than it had ever been since its foundation. But it is nothing new that the influence of the envious should damage the virtuous, for our writings are full of examples of just such eventualities. [339]

45 On 17 May 1407, Boucicaut was named a member of the council of Jean Sans Peur duke of Burgundy, and on 18 July, Boucicaut paid homage to the duke in writing, acknowledging the debt that he owed John for saving him in the aftermath of the battle of Nicopolis in 1396.

46 Matthew 9: 34 and 12: 22–8; Mark 3: 22–30; Luke 11: 14–22; John 9: 16.

XIII: Here we give examples of how the virtuous are often the target of envy.

A pertinent example is provided by Valerius: that of Scipio Africanus the Younger who extended the possessions of Rome to such effect that the city subjugated Carthage and the whole of Africa, which for many years had been at war with Rome so damagingly that the city was close to being destroyed. Scipio's valour, however, and his courage turned the tables to such good effect that Carthage was subjugated and destroyed by the Romans. But so great were the valiant Scipio's virtues that many of the Romans became jealous, so much so that the citizens in their ingratitude repaid his worthy deeds with insult and malice: the citizens were readier to listen to the slanders of the jealous, accusing him falsely of invented transgressions, than to remember the great deeds he had performed on their behalf.[47] Accordingly, they sent him into exile in a mean city situated between marsh and desert, called Liternum [Luitterne],[48] and it was there that this noble man – once the soul of honour – lived out his life; all this was the result of envy, [340] for nothing annoys the envious more than hearing a virtuous man praised.

But to return to the marshal: even today, there are those who say that the majority of the Genoese disliked the marshal; some of them, they say, were betrayed and imprisoned by him, and in the end they threw him out; the jealous conclude from this that he was neither just nor benevolent, since had he been so and governed them as was proper, they would all have loved him. This argument, however, is faulty: it is no surprise to find that the majority will have disliked him, for in any community there are more of the wicked than of the good, and the wicked hate nothing more than justice itself and those who administer it. There is no doubt that all the upright citizens of Genoa were devoted to him – and why would they not be? He had, after all, saved them from destruction at the hands of the wicked. And even if he had been hated by the whole population, that does not prove that he was cruel or culpable – as many examples will show.[49] Take, for example, the story that Valerius tells of Lycurgus, king of Sparta [Lacedemoine], who was so worthy that wise men

47 Publius Cornelius Scipio Africanus (236–183 BC) secured his agnomen Africanus for his great victories against the Carthaginians culminating in the victory at Zama in 202 BC. Scipio Africanus was accused by enemies led by Marcus Porcius Cato the Elder (234–149 BC) of having received bribes from Antiochus III king of Syria (222–187 BC). This account was taken from Simon de Hesdin's translation and commentary on Valerius Maximus, V, c.3.2b, in BNF MS fr. 282, fols 221a–222a.

48 A town on the coast of Campania, in Italy.

49 In late 1409, Pileo de Marini, archbishop of Genoa, sent a memorandum to Charles VI denouncing the violence of Boucicaut while governor and other failures of his rule. D. Puncuh, 'Il governo genovese del Boucicaut nella lettera di Pileo de Marini a Carlo VI di Francia 1409', *Mélanges de l'École française de Rome. Moyen Âge, Temps modernes*, 90:2 (1978), pp. 657–87, and 'Il maresciallo Boucicaut e l'arcivescovo Pileo de Marini', *Il maresciallo Boucicault, governatore di Genova tra Banco di San Giorgio e Magistrato della Misericordia* (Genoa, 2002), pp. 15–31.

have said that his nature was more divine than human.[50] In his wisdom he devised for the Spartans well-grounded laws and institutions [341] – they had had no such system previously, and had lived like wild beasts; he defended them from all sorts of hardships, and greatly extended their possessions. But despite all the favours he bestowed on them, and despite his admirable character, nothing – his virtuous life, the affection in which he was widely held, the excellence of the legal system that he had instituted – protected him from a citizenry that was so hate-filled and ill-intentioned towards him that on a first occasion they expelled him from the palace, on another threw him out of the city, and finally hounded him from the whole country. On which subject Valerius says: 'Who then can have confidence in the citizenry of other countries, when the Spartans, who prided themselves on their moderation and their sense of gratitude, showed themselves so ungrateful to one who had done so much good for them?'

And still on the subject of ingratitude among citizens, let me give another example as a warning not to trust one's own judgement, nor to treat such men with hatred or to send them into exile. Valerius, again, gives the example of the Athenians' ingratitude towards Aristides, a man of saintly and upright character, and who is spoken of in all the histories of the Greeks as someone of the greatest virtue; [342] the reward for his virtue was, however, that his fellow citizens drove him out of the country – precisely because he was too fair and too impartial.[51] And Valerius concludes: 'Aristides, the source of justice for all Greece, the very soul of dignity and virtue, was thrown out of Athens, and with him went all righteousness.'[52]

XIV: Here we prove by example that one should not always rely on or believe popular opinion.

I give these examples as proof that one should not always have faith in the judgements of the majority, for they are frequently to be dismissed as irrational. True, an old proverb says that 'the voice of the people is the voice of God' – but I consider that the voice of the people is sometimes the voice of the Devil, as was shown when the inhabitants of Jerusalem cried out against Our Lord Jesus Christ: 'Crucify Him, crucify Him!'[53] [343] And as further proof that popular opinion is often perverse, Valerius, among other examples, cites the case of the celebrated musician Antigenidas who had trained his disciple so well in all the sciences of music that the young

50 Lycurgus was the legendary lawgiver of Sparta who allegedly lived between the ninth and eighth centuries BC. This story was taken from Simon de Hesdin's translation and commentary upon Valerius Maximus, V, c.3, ext. 2, in BNF MS fr. 282, fol. 225a.

51 Aristides (530–468 BC) was a statesman in ancient Athens.

52 Rather than a direct quotation, this is a paraphrase of Simon de Hesdin's commentary on Valerius Maximus V, c.3, ext. 3, in BNF MS fr. 282, fol. 226d.

53 Matthew 27: 22–3; Mark 15: 13–14; Luke 23: 21–3; John 19: 6 and 15.

man played excellently on the flute.[54] The master then had his disciple come and play before the people so that they would recognise his talent – but the common people, low-born and ill-educated as they were, unused to hearing such mastery and untrained in melody, failed to acknowledge the disciple's expertise. When the master saw this, he said to his disciple: 'Ignore them and sing for me and for the sake of the music itself,' by which he implied that the people are brutish and unworthy to hear such things. And it is true to say that it is often the fate of the valiant, the courageous or the wise to find themselves unrecognised and not esteemed as they deserve; on the other hand, the virtuous and the wise in those communities, seeing the excellence of their words and deeds, and well versed in such things, pay them praise and due honour; virtue and courage, excellence in science or in art, may be trampled on by the misdeeds of Fortune, but never lose their fundamental value; [344] they will always receive the acclaim of the few, and will leave the virtuous confident in their virtue. It is worth noting, says Valerius's translator, that he speaks of Fortune's misdeeds; for just as the populace takes no account of virtue, so Fortune herself often rewards the vicious and the wicked, as I have shown with the example of the disciple who was grand master of his art but could not please the people, most of whom are brutish and ignorant.[55]

XV: How the valiant marshal undertook an expedition to capture Alexandria, and of the messages he sent to this effect to the king of Cyprus.

In the year 1407, the good marshal, whose sole wish was to further the good of Christianity and bring honour to knighthood, [345] saw the suffering and shame imposed on the Christians by their subjugation to the Saracens in the noble lands of Outremer[56] which ought by rights to be the heritage of the Christians had they not been lost through wickedness and cowardice. Accordingly he resolved on a bold new deed: he considered it possible, and not too difficult, for someone courageous, and with the appropriate forces, to capture the noble and renowned city of Alexandria and wrest it from Saracen control; to achieve such a triumph would bring great honour to the victor and great advantage to Christendom.[57] He determined to devote himself bodily, and with all his resources and influence, to the cause; he

54 Antigenidas of Thebes, discussed in Valerius Maximus, III, c.7, ext. 2, translated and commentated upon by Simon de Hesdin in BNF MS fr. 282, fols 167a–b.

55 Simon de Hesdin had cited the story of the disciple in his gloss on the story of Antigenidas from Valerius Maximus, III, c.7, ext. 2, in BNF MS fr. 282, fol. 167b.

56 See part I, note 62 above.

57 Alexandria was an important port in the eastern Mediterranean held by the Mamluk sultanate, and had been, for example, the target of a failed crusade led by Peter I of Lusignan in October 1365, described by Guillaume de Machaut in *La Prise d'Alexandrie*.

would dedicate a whole campaigning season to the endeavour, or if necessary even longer. At that time there was in Genoa the ambassador of the king of Cyprus, the right reverend lord Raymond de Lescure, Hospitaller grand prior of Toulouse and commander of Cyprus, a man of outstanding honour, wisdom and worth, and expert in all sorts of things.[58] The marshal decided to confide his plans in him, partly to seek his advice given that he knew the country well and had spent much time with the Saracens in Alexandria; he would, the marshal knew, have good advice to give. The marshal preferred never to undertake any enterprise [346] without having first called on God's help, so he made a pilgrimage to a most holy shrine, not far from Genoa, called Nostra Signora Incoronato [Nostre Dame la Couronnee],[59] and from there he sent for the prior of Toulouse. After he had heard high Mass, he told the prior in confidence his intentions in that regard; the prior was delighted and gave him great encouragement, saying that in his opinion what the marshal proposed was entirely possible; he himself would be very willing to offer his support, in terms of his own presence, of men and of supplies and resources, for the proposed enterprise was pleasing to God and valuable for Christendom, and would bring great honour to all participants. This was very reassuring for the marshal. When he had carefully considered and weighed up the modalities, he identified those he thought would be most appropriate to undertake embassies to any court liable to look favourably on his enterprise, as we shall explain later, and sent for them – a particularly prominent religious of the Order of Saint John, called Brother Jean de Vienne, and his own squire Jean d'Ony, whom we have mentioned before; he told them what he had in mind, and explained the mission he had for them. But of course no man's memory is able to recall everything said to him in sufficient detail, so to ensure that no item of his message would be forgotten, he gave them a written memorandum to reiterate [347] what he wanted them to do. And I copy here this very memorandum, as given to them and later handed to me in person, so that I am not tempted to add anything of my own – as follows:

'There follows a memorandum of the commission drafted and given by me, Jean Le Meingre, known as Boucicaut, at the place specified below and on the 7th day of August in the year of Our Lord 1407, to you, noble religious Brother Jean de Vienne, commander of Belleville, and to you, Jean d'Ony, our loyal and well-loved subjects.

'First, we wish and direct you to keep the enterprise secret such that no-one can guess it, and that it be divulged to no-one except the king of Cyprus to whom we send you, and certain members of his council; should it become public, this could be highly damaging; we also enjoin upon you, after your departure and with God's help, charged with my instructions, that as my most trusted envoys you employ all due

58 Raymond de Lescure (d.1411) was named grand prior of Toulouse on 27 February 1396 and grand commander of Cyprus on 22 October 1405. He visited Genoa in April 1407.

59 The church of Sainta Maria and San Michele Arcangelo in Cornigliano, Genoa, used to be known as the sanctuary of Nostra Signora Incoronato (Our Crowned Lady).

diligence and determination in pursuing, to the best of your abilities, the mission I shall entrust to you.

'Although you have been informed in full, as I wished, of your mission, [348] and although I know that you will have done everything to register my wishes and to put them into effect with all due diligence, nevertheless to ensure your safety, and to make certain that you remember perfectly all that I have said, I give you this memorandum of what I wish you to convey in the course of your mission.

'First, you will go to Venice, and from there take ship to Rhodes. We expect you to stay there for eight or nine days, according as it will seem useful; you will pay our respects on our behalf to the grand master of Rhodes and his lords; you will give him news of our deeds, of the situation here in Genoa, and explain that your embassy to him concerns an urgent matter which closely concerns us, namely the jewels of the king of Cyprus given by him, as he knows, to the Genoese as surety during our absence in Cyprus, in recompense for the thirty thousand ducats in expenditure that the said Genoese paid for the army of Famagusta, the city that the king had thought to appropriate and usurp from the said Genoese. Under the terms of the peace agreement that we made, he consented to renounce it, and to give us the sum mentioned here for our missions.[60] You are to detail for him the agreement we have made with the prior of Toulouse, and the amount of money we gave him to buy back the jewels in the king's name. While you are in Rhodes you will also negotiate for a ship to take you to Cyprus; [349] if you are unable to do so, you will ask the grand master in my name to organise it for you.

'Once you leave Rhodes, and when with God's help you reach Cyprus, then you will go straight to the house of Saint John in Nicosia; you will enlist the lieutenant of the prior of Toulouse to take word of your arrival to the king of Cyprus, and to tell him you will present your respects to him at his convenience. Once you have word from the king, and once you are in his presence, you will present yourselves to his majesty and to my lords his brothers; you will then present your letters of credence.

'When he deigns to accept your credence, you will ask him on my behalf to give you a private audience, during which no-one will be able to overhear you; you yourselves should make sure that your talks are so secret that overhearing will be impossible. You will beg him first to keep what you are about to say entirely secret because of the dangers that would ensue if the matter came out, and also in order to guard his own honour and reputation which are involved in the matter.

'Thereafter you will begin your account, prefacing it with remarks as to the high reputation that he enjoys in France and across the world, the number of damaging assaults he has led, and still leads, against the Saracens, in the course of which, unsparingly, he sets at risk his own person, his own goods, his very life – for which reason [350] he is held today to be among the young princes of the world whose

60 Janus, king of Cyprus, had pledged the jewels as security for the peace treaty signed on 7 July 1403; these jewels were held by the grand master of Rhodes. See part II, note 51 above.

early reigns seem so promising, and so admirable. All of which encourages the hope that he has every intention of devoting himself to the pursuit of honour, as did his predecessors who so ardently sought honour in this world through their outstanding virtues and merits, through worthy wars and noble enterprises that they waged in person against the unbelievers and the enemies of the Christian faith, and for which they will be everlastingly remembered as exemplars of goodness and valour. For this reason, we who wish with all our hearts to bring him honour and enhance the nobility of his estate and his reign, and who are ready to devote ourselves body and soul and with all our possessions to such a cause, we who admire him and love him more than any other prince in the world, always of course excepting the king of France and those of the royal blood, we who are cognisant of the good that flows from his just and capable reign in neighbouring lands and everywhere, we who hope to see the virtues of his youth more and more enhanced, have devised a high and noble enterprise which, if he agrees to take part, and should it, as is probable, be successful, will see his fame resound down the ages.

'And it is in pursuit of this enterprise – that is, to announce it to the king after due deliberation – an enterprise which seems to us pleasing to God and advantageous for the whole of Christendom, that we have sent you to his royal highness. [351]

'After this you will, as our ambassadors, explain to the king of Cyprus all the plans that we have drawn up as to the taking of the city of Alexandria. And you will stress repeatedly, as necessary, that we are so impressed by his zeal that it is in his company that we wish to venture our own person, and those of our kindred, our friends and our liegemen and to engage our resources, and this for four principal reasons. First, our love for Our Lord, in Whose service and that of the whole of Christendom we wish to engage ourselves. The second, for the good of our souls. The third, to ensure, as we have said, that in the very flower of his youth he should undertake the good deeds which will give him an enduring reputation. And the fourth, something to which any knight and man of breeding should aspire, the acquisition of honour and renown in arms.

'*Item*, when all this has been said, and to strengthen the king's desire to agree to our proposal, you will show him how favoured by God he must be to be offered a purpose so high but which he can pursue with little expense on his part, and the details of which will largely be organised by the efforts of others; you will stress also that if he refuses, he should dread God's displeasure, and fear that no-one will believe him to be courageous, or daring.' [352]

XVI: On the same topic: the instructions that the marshal gave his ambassadors as to what to say to the king of Cyprus.

'Once you have said all these things, in good order, to the king of Cyprus, you will take careful note of his expression even while you are still speaking to him; in that way, you will judge how far your proposition is pleasing to him, and adjust what you say accordingly. If he asks you how it is possible that such an enterprise could be prepared without its becoming known, or how the generous funding necessary could be acquired, you will reply that he can gather an army of his own on the pretext that he is pursuing his war with the sultan, and thus be ready at a date set by himself, so that as our own fleet approaches, he can set sail and pretend to be heading for Rhodes. We shall precede him to Kalaat Yhamour [Chastel Rouge][61] where we will rendezvous with him, and from there, in the name of God, we shall set sail with our combined forces for Alexandria. [353]

'*Item*, it would be good if he could find means to send a Cypriot or an Armenian to live in the said city of Alexandria, and who would be able to send news of all developments there; it would be useful for him to tell this person that he, the king, wanted such news because of his war with the sultan.

'As for the money and resources that would be required, you will tell the king that we perfectly understand that he could not invest on the scale that his predecessors did and which formerly allowed the taking of the city, for since that date his country has had much to suffer.[62] For that reason, just as we are willing to assist him in our own person and with our men, so we shall do so with our own resources.

'And so that he understands that we have planned every detail of the expedition, you will tell him that in our opinion – subject however to his own advice and experience – the following forces will be needed: first, a thousand well-trained men-at-arms, a thousand foot ('varlés armez'), a thousand crossbowmen ('arbalestiers'), two hundred archers and two hundred horse in addition to those that we shall requisition in Egypt.

'*Item*, a fleet: five large naves, two galleys, and two *galees huissières* [354] carrying provisions for six months. You will then tell him what the cost will be for these vessels, stressing that it will not be great when one considers their value to the enterprise: it should reach no more than around 132 thousand florins.

'*Item*, the monthly cost of charter for the two galleys and the two *galees huissières* should be around five thousand florins, and thus the cost, for four months, would be twenty thousand florins.

'*Item*, the monthly cost of a thousand crossbowmen is five thousand florins; for four months therefore the cost will be twenty thousand florins.

'*Item*, the monthly cost of two hundred archers is a thousand florins, so the overall cost for four months will be four thousand florins.

'*Item*, the monthly cost for a thousand men-at-arms, with the thousand foot and the two hundred horse, is twelve thousand florins; the overall cost for four months will be 48 thousand florins.

---

61 Kalaat Yhamour (also known as the 'Chastel Rouge') was a French fortress on the Syrian coast, near to Tripoli.

62 See part III, note 57 above.

'*Item*, the overall cost of provisions will be ten thousand florins, and for artillery and other necessities ten thousand florins.

'The total outlay will therefore be one hundred and thirty-two thousand florins. It would be necessary to accumulate the total sum in the city of Genoa, so as to have it all available as from the month of December next, so that the necessary provisions can be acquired; on the other hand, to allay suspicion, it will be important not to have all supplies and other resources stocked in Genoa. The fleet and the army would need to depart around the month of April [1408].

'Of these considerable expenses we are happy to contribute our share; [355] but given that the enterprise will bestow such honour and fame on the king, we consider it only right that he should contribute at least half: that is, a total of sixty-six thousand florins. If, though, he cannot envisage such a sum, then he should contribute sixty thousand. It is essential, however, that the sums be sent as soon as possible to Genoa: the sooner the better. If sixty thousand is still too much for him to send in time, we shall be happy to subsidise his contribution, from embarkation until he returns to his own kingdom, to the tune of eighteen or twenty thousand florins; it is vital that there should be no shortfall in advance of the expedition. On that point you will stress to the king that my lord the prior of Toulouse, eager for love of the king to enhance his honour and reputation, considers this enterprise to be most worthy, and one to which he can subscribe financially without any reservations. And indeed if the king cannot see his way to finance on this scale, the said lord the prior of Toulouse is willing to provide finance on his behalf providing that he is authorised to do so by the king; the king's word will be sufficient to raise the money, and indeed more, should it be required.

'This is the message that you will convey to the king of Cyprus. Should he respond that he hesitates to leave his kingdom because of possible seditious elements, you will reply that he should recruit into his army any person of whose loyalty he has any doubts. [356]

'*Item,* if he responds that he knows the Genoese are no friend to his interests, and that he is therefore wary of the preponderance of Genoese in the army, you will reply that he need have no fear: all the men-at-arms, all the foot, and all the archers will be from France, all of them under his, the king's, own command and authority.

'Finally, you will tell him that if he wishes to participate and then to invest more of his own resources – more men-at-arms and more ships than are listed here – then he can rest assured that the more he invests, the greater will be his share of the booty, as would be only reasonable given his investment. You will convey all that we have written here to the king of Cyprus; if there are issues that require your immediate response, we rely on your discretion, and stand ready to put into effect any decisions that you may make.'

XVII: Of the warm welcome that the king of Cyprus afforded to the marshal's ambassadors, and of his positive response.

Such was the memorandum of the marshal's commission to the commander of Belleville and to Jean d'Ony, the ambassadors sent to Cyprus in pursuit of an alliance to take Alexandria. [357] The two ambassadors left Genoa, and to cut a long story short, they sailed to Cyprus where they fulfilled their whole embassy as they had been commissioned to do. It is now our duty to say what was the king's response.

When the king of Cyprus heard of the arrival of the ambassadors, he sent for them and received them honourably and with great warmth. When he had made the conventional enquiries as to the health of the marshal and the prosperity of Genoa, and when he had heard their embassy in full, he responded joyfully, as follows, with very warm words:

That he thanked God for the noble and valiant enterprise proclaimed by a man of such valour as the marshal; that he recognised the marshal's affection for him and his care for his reputation, and his eagerness to allow a young man still without much experience or chivalric reputation to take part in an enterprise which promised such renown; that the marshal's own willingness to contribute his person, his friends and allies, and his wealth were evidence of his commitment. That he could not give praise or thanks enough to the marshal for even a hundredth part of the invitation to the enterprise, nor could he envisage ever being able to do so. That he was overjoyed at hearing of so great and noble an enterprise – but that he could not engage himself without careful thought and deliberation; that he would strain every sinew to consider how best to engage in it, [358] and that he would furnish them as soon as possible with a response that would content them. That in the meanwhile they should be content, that he welcomed their coming, and that, if they lacked anything, all that was his was at their disposal.

The ambassadors then asked the king if he was content that one of the councillors closest to him, Perrin Le Jeune, be informed of the enterprise; if so, they would convey to him a letter that the marshal had written concerning it; they knew that the king had great faith in him. The king replied that he was indeed content. Perrin studied the letters, and was able to confirm to the king that the marshal's proposition had been conveyed to the king complete in every particular; Perrin gave every sign of enthusiasm for the enterprise, thanked the marshal for the affection he had shown, for his having singled out the king for so honourable a venture, and for his having chosen Perrin as worthy to know the secret; he could not but advise the king to accept so flattering an offer, because the news of a refusal would soon become known.

Very soon thereafter, the king summoned the ambassadors and set out for them the reasons for his war with the sultan. Previously, the sultan had allowed the king's merchants to come and go peacefully in his territories; this state of affairs had continued until my lord Raymond de Lescure, prior of Toulouse [359] and commander of Cyprus, was taken prisoner in Alexandria and taken to Cairo [Kaire].[63] The king had then written to the sultan to ask him, in the warmest of terms, to free the prior; the sultan had taken no notice whatsoever of the letter. 'For this,' said the king, 'I was very indignant, given the courtesies that I had extended previously to the sultan. But I could do nothing further until the prior was released against twenty-five thousand ducats in ransom. Once he had been released, I sent a challenge to the sultan – but he ignored it. At that, I sent a galley to attack the sultan's territories; it did him much damage, and in particular my galley took the finest of his ships which was fully laden. My galley continued down the coast, pillaging and laying waste, as far as some fifteen miles up the Nile – and the ease with which it did so proved the cowardice of the sultan and his men. I give thanks to the Lord God Who afforded me the occasion to make war on them, an enterprise which has allowed me to fear them less in advance of the proposition that you have made me; I am a hundred thousand times less fearful of them than I was previously. Indeed, the more I have to do with them militarily, the less I fear them, for I find them more and more cowardly, more and more ineffectual – in spite of their great numbers – to such an extent [360] that in spite of the multitudes they can muster, I feel that a small number of good and well-trained men could overcome them. I recognise that however unworthy a sinner I am, God loves me and wants me to revive the reputation and the fame of my valiant predecessors who themselves achieved just such an enterprise; I ask nothing better than to emulate them. May God give me the grace to do so! For I take no account of the expense, nor of any other impediment.'

XVIII: How the king of Cyprus sent his excuses to the marshal via the ambassadors, explaining that he would not be joining the attack on Alexandria.

This was the way in which, to start with, the king of Cyprus addressed the marshal's ambassadors. But only a few days later, he was no longer quite so eager to talk to them about the project. The ambassadors came to believe that contrary advice had carried the day, and that the Perrin whom we mentioned earlier, to whom they had given the marshal's letter, had failed to keep his promise. They then began to beg the king to give them a settled response as to his intentions, for they had already spent too long in Cyprus; they repeated the request on several occasions, and on several occasions the king sent a response that gave them hope that he would give his consent, [361] but that he needed more time to consider something so taxing; on other occasions, however, he sent a much more off-hand response, citing his own doubts.

63 Lescure had been taken prisoner in 1404 by the sultan, Nasir-ad-Din Faraj (1399–1411), while in Cairo to negotiate on behalf of King Janus.

Nevertheless, the ambassadors pressed him so hard that on the 23rd day of October of that year, he returned the following considered response. He said that since the arrival of the ambassadors, he had not stopped thinking about the proposition they had put to him, feeling it to be the most tempting in the world; he had been torn, thinking that to find such an enterprise dangerous and burdensome might result from his own inexperience: another, he felt, might consider it trouble-free, not requiring long thought, whereas he, young and inexperienced as he was, found the proposition perturbing and perplexing. His conclusion therefore had to be that although the enterprise had been elaborated by his dear friend the marshal, who was very courageous, and although the invitation he had received arose from the marshal's selfless desire to enhance the king's reputation, nevertheless he would have to refuse it, and for three reasons. First, the great danger in which he would be leaving his own country, given the threat from his neighbours the Turks who command great forces able to overrun Cyprus and even dethrone him. He might, he said, have been able to overcome his doubts on this subject, [362] but more troubling was the second reason: he was more afraid of an undercover war than of open war, for he knew that if he left the country, many of those he considered his closest friends and allies could not be trusted; they would have no hesitation in organising a coup, which would mean his trading his assured position for one which would be much more vulnerable. The third reason was his distrust of the Genoese who had for many years, notoriously, harassed him; they might well have done worse, he believed, and much to their disgrace, had it not been for the protection of his good friend the marshal. To these three principal reasons he added another possible consequence: the uncertainties of war – the outcome of which no-one save God can predict. All these things in conjunction made him feel that the enterprise was too dangerous and too uncertain for him – and he was also swayed by the fact that the marshal would be absent from Genoa and therefore unable to protect him and his country from possible depredations from the Genoese. The ambassadors should understand that his decision did not arise from lack of courage or from cowardice, nor from unwillingness to contemplate such an expedition; the marshal should understand that although he could not envisage such an action at the present time, the king would remain tempted to it for the rest of his life; with God's help, he would attempt so to order the affairs of his kingdom that a time might come when he would indeed embark on it. He therefore begged the marshal, whom he trusted more than anyone else in the world, [363] not to abandon his project, but to afford him every possible help to organise his affairs – something the marshal was entirely qualified to do – so that he would eventually be able to absent himself from his kingdom; he and the marshal would then be able to devote their lives to the service of Our Lord; the marshal should consider the king his son, for he thought of the marshal as a father, and would seek his advice in the government of Cyprus. In conclusion, the king expressed himself so grateful to the marshal for his care, and for the exceptional invitation that he had issued, that he would never be able sufficiently to merit the marshal's regard, to thank him, or to repay him.

At this the king fell silent, and the ambassadors took leave and returned with all speed to the marshal in Genoa, where they told him what the outcome had been. [364]

XIX: Here we talk of the affairs of the Church, and of how the marshal tried to prevent King Ladislaus from taking control of Rome.

What I have described above are the ways in which the good marshal employed his time, intent on living day to day more virtuously – something of which he has never tired and will never tire as long as he lives, knowing that, as the saying goes, 'A good life leads to a good end.' I could not hope to recount all his good and outstanding deeds and sayings, things which he continues to demonstrate every hour of every day: there is an endless supply. I confine myself therefore to his major enterprises [365] and ventures, which serve to illustrate my intention: to show his valour which will stand as an example to anyone of noble or chivalrous stock who might wish to show himself virtuous in deed or in conduct. Earlier, I recounted how among the many ambitions he had to perform noble deeds, he particularly wished to work for peace and reconciliation in the Church; this was a wish that has never left him, as his efforts have showed, and show to this day. But he has been thwarted by the false covetousness ignited and promoted by the Devil in so many of the hearts of prelates of the Church, blinded as they are by evil ambitions and backstabbing; whatever the efforts of the good marshal and his well-intentioned associates, they have been unable to bring about the change that they have sought. Oh, false covetousness, pitiless and bottomless pit of hell, how have you been able to blind a man's heart so completely that although he recognises that his days are numbered, he fails to take account of God's punishment awaiting him? [366] We see the effect of this when two old men, approaching the grave, take their seats on the papal throne which was, as they know, designated by God for one man alone at any one time, and are so consumed by accursed covetousness and pride that they prefer their own eternal damnation, and choose to reduce their flock to doubt and suffering and to inflict damnation on an infinity of souls, rather than to renounce the fleeting and undeserved worldly honour that their followers confer on them! Oh bottomless pit of Hell, last resting-place of Cain and Judas, why do you not call them home to you? This festering wound in Christendom, so long-lasting, so constant, must surely be the result of the sins of the unworthy: it must be the will of God.

But to return to our purpose, which is to show how our hero, the good marshal, [367] has always done everything he can to reunify the Church: we cannot hope to recount everything at once, but many people know that when, in the year 14[07],[64]

64 The full date is not presented in the French text. On 21 April 1407, Benedict XIII and Gregory XII (1406–15) had promised to meet at Savona, around forty miles west of Genoa, to negotiate

our Avignon pope and the other pope elected in Rome came to an accord, this was the work of the good marshal and a number of other good lords who had negotiated the agreement, or rather the professed agreement, between the two of them: I say 'professed' because, as we saw, the agreement was a sham. Each of the popes had promised that to restore peace to the Church he would stand down if the other did the same. But the two deceitful hypocrites – and it is right to call them that, given their acts – had come to an understanding: they had been in touch about the wicked subterfuge that allowed each of them to say of the other: 'As long as he stands down, I'll stand down.' It is a game of tit-for-tat: each of them prefers to be pope of a part of Christendom, rather than to stand down and allow a third to stand – but it is a game, pray God, which will eventually destroy both of them. Meanwhile, however, they spend their time on such ploys, and leave the princes of the world bemused at their weasel words. [368] They had agreed, when the promise was made, that el Papa Luna, the Avignon pope,[65] would retire to a castle called Porto Venere, at the mouth of the river Scrivia; the Roman pope would retire to the city of Lucca [Luques]; the two places are a short day's journey apart.[66] From there, they would agree a place where they would meet for each to renounce the papacy, in the presence of the cardinals and the general council; then the Holy Spirit would direct the election of a single pope, as God Himself had ordained. As things turned out, the rival popes were harangued to such effect by the marshal and by other men of goodwill that they could not in good faith refuse to be present. But their promise turned out to be pointless: briefly, it was so difficult to find a location for the ceremony that the two popes could not agree; when one of them insisted on a particular condition, the other would veto it, and vice versa. The two damnable popes were in cahoots. It is perfectly obvious that they had plotted an immoral arrangement by which to pull the wool over the eyes of the rest of the world by pretending that they could not give their consent.

It would take too long to tease out all the causes of their idle excuses. [369] Suffice it to say that each of the devils was more malevolent than the other, and each of them intended to cheat the other (however earnestly they declared themselves allies): our Avignon pope, el Papa Luna, contrived to have all the blame for their lack of agreement attributed slanderously to the Roman pope. For which reason all the cardinals of the Roman pope deserted his cause and left for Pisa; soon no-one, in the whole of Italy, was supporting him.[67] At which point the Roman pope sent for help

their joint resignations. Boucicaut played a major role in organising the planned encounter which never took place.

65 Pope Benedict XIII, Pedro Martínez de Luna y Pérez de Gotor, was known as 'el Papa Luna' in Spanish.

66 Following the cancellation of the meeting at Savona, the two popes concluded a new agreement on 10 January 1408. Benedict XIII had been at Porto Venere on 3 January 1408, and Gregory XII arrived at Lucca on 28 January, but negotiations then stalled on the location of their meeting.

67 Nine cardinals abandoned Gregory XII between 11 and 16 May 1408.

to King Ladislaus of Naples, who readily agreed, intending to use this as an excuse to seize the city of Rome and its province – which indeed he later did, as we shall see.[68] Meanwhile King Ladislaus promised to use every endeavour to assist the Roman pope against all and every foe. Fortified by this, the Roman pope was so emboldened that he refused obstinately to cede to the wishes of the synod of bishops. The alliance between Ladislaus and the anti-pope of Rome advanced so far that they came to an accord that in ways agreed between them – which we shall explain later – Ladislaus would make himself ruler of Rome, then once he was in possession with a large army [370] he would go to Lucca and bring the pope back to Rome. And this was settled.

XX: On the same subject, and how the Roman Paolo Orsini was bribed to install Ladislaus in Rome.

News of what was afoot – that King Ladislaus was to offer aid and succour to the Roman pope and take possession of the city of Rome – came to the ears of the marshal; he was very angry, for he could see that such a plan would run counter to his own wish to bring peace and reconciliation to the Church; he was also dismayed on account of the city of Rome, which is rightly the patrimony of the Church, but which was to be seized and commandeered tyrannically by someone who was a renegade Christian, an enemy to France and a major foe to King Louis, cousin to the king of France.[69] Boucicaut was made aware that Ladislaus had already mobilised his forces on land and on sea, and was making for Rome to lay siege to the city.[70] [371] He racked his brains to see how Ladislaus's ambitions could be thwarted, and when he had come to a decision as to the best course of action, he summoned one of his entourage, Jean d'Ony, whom he knew to be valiant, wise, virtuous and conscientious – we have often referred to him in this history – and said:[71]

'You will make post-haste to Rome and speak to Paolo Orsini; you will give him my regards, and tell him that as de facto commander and governor of Rome, he should in the current emergency demonstrate the constancy, the righteousness and the valour that have always marked him and his noble ancestors, and employ his forces and his powers to demonstrate the constancy and the love that he rightly owes

68 King Ladislaus did have a great deal to lose from the negotiations between the Avignon and Roman popes; a resolution to the Schism would have led to the election of a new pope who might have supported his rival claimant to the throne of Naples, Louis II (1377–1417), duke of Anjou. But there is no evidence to support the biographer's claim that Gregory XII had colluded with Ladislaus. It is more likely that Ladislaus's seizure of Rome on 25 April 1408 forced Pope Gregory XII's hand.

69 Louis II d'Anjou had been king of Naples from 1389 to 1399, when he was ousted from the throne by Ladislaus.

70 At the start of 1408, Ladislaus blockaded the mouth of the river Tiber.

71 This occurred at the start of April 1408.

to the city of Rome by preventing, even if he should die in the attempt, that the city fall into foreign hands or the hands of a tyrant; should such a thing happen, it would be a heavy blow to the honour of the city and of the Romans; that he should show his mettle in aid of the Romans who have always been of high courage, rejecting servitude more consistently than any other city in the world; that I beg him, with all my heart, to do this; and that if he defends the city vigorously against Ladislaus [372] – something which will bring him everlasting honour – I promise that I will come to his aid with a large force within a fortnight.'[72]

Jean d'Ony hastened to Rome with this mandate, accompanied at the marshal's command by another shrewd esquire, Bourc de Larca, and gave the message to Paolo Orsini fully and sagely, just as he had been instructed. Having heard the message, Paolo Orsini, briefly, pretended to be delighted at the marshal's words, saying that he thanked him wholeheartedly; that nothing would prevent him from employing every effort, every resource, every man to resist Ladislaus's advance; that Rome was fully provisioned for five months, and had a garrison able to resist Ladislaus until the marshal was able to reach the city. He would resist the siege with every sinew of his being. Paolo Orsini promised all this to Jean d'Ony; he would, he said, defend the city fearlessly until the marshal arrived, but begged him to make haste. And to show the marshal how best he might access the city, with his own hand he made a sketch-map of the city and of the neighbouring city of Ostia on a sheet of paper, to show the marshal how he might best engage Ladislaus's fleet.

Item, he also set out how he intended to assist the marshal, gave him details of how the marshal would be able to recognise the fleet and outlined the way in which Ladislaus might be defeated on land. [373]

Paolo Orsini treacherously made all these promises – but he fulfilled none of them; for two days after Jean d'Ony had left to return to the marshal, he himself installed King Ladislaus in Rome in return for a bribe of twenty-six thousand florins and two castles.[73] However, Jean had left the companion I mentioned, Bourc de Larca, in Rome, so that he could transmit information to the marshal and also continue to petition Paolo Orsini. When, however, Jean returned to Rome, he found that Ladislaus's coup was further advanced than he and the marshal had thought: King Ladislaus was in full control in the city and was laying siege to the city of Ostia, which stands on the banks of the Tiber near Rome.[74] Ladislaus had with him some eight or nine thousand horse and some two hundred foot; he also had seven *galees soubtilles*,[75] two great *galees huissières* and up to seventy barques laden with military equipment and provisions.

---

72 On 2 March 1408, Florence rejected Orsini's request for aid against Ladislaus.

73 Ladislaus concluded a truce with the Romans on 21 April, followed by a treaty two days later. He entered the city on 25 April and established his residence in the Vatican palace.

74 Ladislaus laid siege to Ostia on 18 April 1408.

75 *Galees soubtilles* were narrow, streamlined war galleys designed to be fast and highly manoeuvrable. Gardiner and Morrison, eds, *The Age of the Galley*, pp. 202, 205 and 249.

Having seen all this, Jean d'Ony realised how important it was to make haste; he hurried from Rome to Porto Venere in just four days. [374] There he found the marshal who, having listened to his report, hastened to have all his forces, men-at-arms as well as ships, crossbowmen, provisions and everything else, also ready by the fourth day – and then he embarked in his galley.[76] His fleet consisted of eight galleys and three brigantines, as well armed and well manned with men-at-arms and crossbowmen as one could imagine; he had appointed as captains to the galleys those whose names follow here: himself, of the first; Lord[77] Jacques de Prades of the second; Jean de Luna, nephew of the pope, of the third; my lord Guérau Alaman de Cerveillon, the pope's marshal, of the fourth; Brother Raymond de Lescure, prior of Toulouse, of the fifth; lord [Gilbert] de La Fayette, of the sixth; my lord Robert de Milly, of the seventh; Jean d'Ony of the eighth. Among the noble and renowned members of the marshal's party were the following: my lord Guillaume Meuillon, my lord Luca Fieschi [count of Lavagna], my lord Gilles de Preuilly, my lord Béraut du Lac, Guillaume and Hugues de Tholigny, my lord [Amanieu] de Montpezat, Robert de Fenis captain of one of the brigantines, Gilet de Grigny, [375] Chabrulé d'Ony, nephew of Jean d'Ony, and too many others to list here.

The marshal had barely set off from port with this fine company than as God would have it, and no doubt for good reason, there arose a fierce headwind, and a storm so violent that the marshal's ships, much to his fury, could make no headway. He managed, by might and main, to beat upwind as far as Motrone [Moutron], but it was in vain:[78] This bad luck meant he had to retreat to harbour, and the storm lasted for three days, a source of more grief and frustration than I can describe. He stayed waiting for his luck to change, but because he was impatient to pursue his mission, he refused to allow any of his party to leave the ship until Bourc de Larca, whom Jean d'Ony had left in Rome and whom I have mentioned before, arrived post-haste and having survived many dangers:[79] he gave the news that, as I explained, Paolo Orsini had made Ladislaus the ruler of Rome. The marshal was much dismayed; all his party, however, thanked God that the storm, and their good fortune, had prevented their going any further, for if they had made it to Rome, they would definitely all have been betrayed, killed and slaughtered. [376] But God – always the Protector of His humble servants – had protected the marshal, although the latter remained saddened and disturbed by what had happened.

But this reverse did not subdue his burning desire to work for the good and the reconciliation of Holy Church, so having failed in his first initiative – to prevent the Roman pope being allied to Ladislaus – he considered other plans, and finally determined to use every means to make known across all those provinces of Italy which favoured Rome the many ills and misfortunes that the Roman pope's error,

76 Boucicaut set sail on 25 April 1408.

77 The French author, unusually, uses 'Damp' here; see *DMF*, *dan* (2).

78 Motrone was a river port near to Pietrasanta, ruled by Lucca.

79 Bourc de Larca must have left Rome on 24 or 25 April and arrived at Porto Venere on 28 April.

along with those of the Avignon pope, were causing Christendom. His efforts in this cause bore fruit and the eyes of the clergy were opened: they came to agree that it would be preferable for there to be a single shepherd of the flock, and for both existing popes to stand down.[80] With God's help, he also sent messages to all the kings and lands and countries who were obedient to the Roman pope – England, Germany and elsewhere – and to all those who subscribed to the Avignon pope – France, Aragon, Spain, etc. – [377] to say that all the princes of Christendom should work together to promote the reconciliation of the Church, and should cease to support either prelate. The process was time-consuming, so although nothing could be brought about overnight, and although he had to take account of a multitude of different opinions and loyalties, nevertheless within three years he achieved his aim: that all the princes of Christendom who had subscribed to one or the other, and all the different lands, indeed even Ladislaus himself, are all now in agreement that both popes should stand down and that there should be an election to nominate a new pope; everyone today is working towards that end.[81] A day has been allocated for this process – that is a particular day in the month of April in this year 1409[82] – in the city of Pisa, at which the general council will be assembled, and to which the two popes have been invited; there will be gathered the prelates and ambassadors delegated by all the princes and countries (foremost among them France, which is held in great honour, her king and princes, along with the noble university of Paris which has put considerable time and effort into ensuring the success of the occasion). And if the two popes should refuse to be present, then they will be damned and dismissed as heretics, and as impious; [378] they will be abhorred by all their cardinals, by the princes and by all men; they will be deprived of all their powers, and if they can be taken, they will be chastised. By the grace of the Holy Spirit, another pope will be freely elected. according to due process, by the college of cardinals; may God in his mercy swiftly bring this to pass, for the sake of the peace of Christendom, for it cannot be doubted that it is because of this schism that God has brought down on us the terrible ills that now afflict the world.[83] This that I have described is today, 6 March 1409,[84] the current state of the Church, and around this date the following are to set out for the council: the envoys of the king of France, the patriarch of

80 On 12 January 1408, Charles VI had issued an ordinance declaring that he would become neutral if there were not one single pope by 24 May. On 25 May, Charles VI publicly withdrew his obedience to both popes, and on 21 July 1408, Boucicaut issued an order forbidding all of his subjects from submitting to Avignon or Rome.

81 In reality, Ladislaus did not support the plan to withdraw obedience from the two popes.

82 On 23 August 1408, the cardinals agreed that a general council would open in Pisa on 25 March 1409. The French author gives the year as 1408, using the old system of dating.

83 On 5 June 1409, the council of Pisa deposed Benedict XIII and Gregory XII, and on 26 June they elected Alexander V (1409–10), who was succeeded by the antipope John XXIII (1410–15). As a result there were three rival popes until the council of Constance (1414–18) finally resolved the Schism.

84 The French author gives the date as 6 March 1408 in the old style of dating.

Alexandria,[85] other distinguished prelates and noble clerics of the university of Paris, and many men of authority. I shall now leave this subject, and speak of the other worthy deeds of the valiant knight who is our subject here.

XXI: How on the voyage from Genoa to Provence the marshal did battle with four Moorish galleys, and how a great many were killed.

Christ's great champion, that is to say the marshal who is with every fibre of his being the scourge of the unbelievers, [379] wished to return to Provence to see his lovely wife and revisit his lands. He left Genoa on 20 September 1408 on the Genoese guard-ship and set sail in the name of God. As he was sailing, he heard that his way was blocked by four Moorish galleys. He asked the advice of his noble companions as to the best course of action. They replied that as night was falling, he should, they suggested, spend the night at Porto Maurizio [Porto Morise] and send a detachment to discover where the galleys were;[86] the following day he could act on the information as he chose, but they begged him to have himself left on land, for if he were to be killed or otherwise harmed, the consequences would be very serious. The marshal acquiesced in everything they said – except the proposition that he be left on land: on this he refused adamantly to listen to them. Around midnight he heard that the Saracens were at anchor on his route to Provence, near a castle called Roquebrune-Cap-Martin [Roquebrune],[87] and were making no preparations for departure. The marshal heard the news, and, in spite of general misgivings, the Saracen ships heavily outnumbering his, he said that he would not be turned from his path by some Moors; he turned to his men and smiled and said: 'Now we shall see what mettle you're made of! Our enemy are strong, but it is in combat with the strong that we win the greatest honour.' [380] Then he cleared the decks for action: he took fifty archers onto his ship, and ordered them to take up battle stations on his galley. Stationed near him on the poop, to fight at his side, the most important were the following: my lord Hugues Cholet, my lord [Amanieu] de Montpezat, Guillaume de Tholigny, Pierre Castagne, the Genoese lord Thomas[so] Pansan[o], and a number of other gentlemen. At the prow were stationed Jean d'Ony, Macé de Rochebaron, the Bastard of Varannes, the Bastard of Auberon and a number of others. And on the deck he stationed Louis de Milly and a number of others.

85 Simon de Cramaud (c.1345–1423) was a French bishop and the titular Latin patriarch of Alexandria.

86 Porto Maurizio is now part of the coastal city of Imperia, around seventy miles west along the coast from Genoa.

87 Roquebrune-Cap-Martin, controlled by the Grimaldi family of Monaco, was around forty miles west of Porto Maurizio.

As day broke, the marshal weighed anchor and set sail; at precisely the hour of vespers he arrived where the Moors had spent the night; however, they had now left and were anchored off the port of Villefranche [Villefranque].[88] The marshal headed that way with all possible speed and came up with them an hour before sundown. He threatened attack with every sign of bravado; they did not dare to await his onslaught, and were indeed so afraid that many of them cut their moorings and fled as if their lives depended on it. After them came the hue and cry; he harried the Moors and came up with them at sunset off Nice [Nisse]. He boarded their vessels fighting hand-to-hand; many good feats of arms were performed, and every Christian showed his mettle. [381] But it would take too long to describe every individual feat of arms, so I shall simply say that a master can be judged by his creation: the Saracens were routed so completely that some eighty to a hundred of them were killed on the spot, and their bodies washed up onshore the following day. The remainder tried to flee, but they were too hard-pressed; nevertheless they defended vigorously, and threw themselves at our men. The skirmish between the Saracens and ourselves lasted all night, and our men released a hail of fire so dense that from the marshal's galley alone seven cases-worth of crossbow bolts were fired. The following day, still fighting, the ships arrived before the castle of Brégançon [Briganson], where the marshal spent the night.[89] The Saracens, on the other hand, withdrew to an island off the coast of Brégançon, and then at midnight slipped anchor and headed for the Barbary coast [Barbarie]. But the Christian prisoners taken by the Saracens, and who had escaped from the island, reported that the fighting had cost them more than four hundred wounded and dead, whereas the marshal had lost no more than nineteen wounded and dead; on the other hand, the Christians were, unsurprisingly, exhausted, as they had fought for a night and a full day. The marshal kept his course and came to find King Louis in Toulon [Thoulon];[90] the king greeted him with great warmth and honour, and with praise to God for his success. Once the marshal had reported his doings and his actions, [382] he took leave and repaired to his castle of Meyrargues [Marargues], to join his wife, who was so overjoyed that she wept for love and sheer happiness.[91]

88 Villefranche-sur-Mer, adjacent to Nice and around sixty miles west of Porto Maurizio, was controlled by the house of Savoy.

89 Brégançon is just over sixty miles west of Villefranche-sur-Mer.

90 Boucicaut met Louis II, duke of Anjou, at Toulon, twenty-five miles west of Brégançon.

91 Meyrargues is around forty miles north-west of Toulon.

XXII: How Gabriele Maria Visconti, bastard to the duke of Milan, thought to usurp the king of France as ruler of Genoa, and how he was executed.

I explained previously how Gabriele Maria Visconti, bastard son of the first duke of Milan, sold the city of Pisa to the Florentines, and how the marshal had always allied himself to Gabriele – so much so that he had several times saved his life, and preserved him from famine and other adversities. This was all perfectly true, but it turned out that Gabriele was so wicked and disloyal that he repaid the marshal by making strenuous efforts to usurp the king of France as ruler of Genoa; I shall now tell you how.

It is true to say that when Gabriele had sold off Pisa, he went back to the court of his brothers, the young duke of Milan and the count of Pavia, who received him very kindly.[92] Briefly, however, in spite of their brotherly kindness, he betrayed them by seducing many of their subjects to his cause with lies and by daring to make war on his brothers.[93] [383] He repaired to the fortified citadel of Milan, believing that he could hold out against them by main force. But this arrogance was his undoing: in the end, he was defeated by famine and had to surrender, which he did on condition that his life would be spared. The duke of Milan banished him for his crime, and exiled him for a fixed term to the city of Asti [Ast] which belongs to the duke of Orléans; Gabriele swore to respect his banishment. But he broke his oath, and indeed did precisely the opposite; he allied himself with Facino Cane, the great tyrant and *condottiero*, leader in Lombardy of a band of mercenaries, enemy of God and of man; for many years, Facino was the author of terrible deeds, killings and cruelties. Facino Cane is also a foe of the king of France, and a great enemy to the duke of Milan and his brother the count of Pavia. Gabriele took up residence for a year in a city called Alessandria [Alixandre de la Paille],[94] which Facino had usurped from its rightful ruler, and set himself to inflict the maximum of damage on his brothers.

And this was not his only act of treachery. He and his false brother in arms, Facino Cane, set in train what would have been an even greater wickedness had they brought it off – but God in His mercy (thanks be) prevented it. What they intended, out of their iniquity, was to seize the sovereignty of Genoa from the king for themselves, [384] slaughter all the French in the city and at the very least to sack the city: that is, to plunder and despoil it, and go off with the proceeds. They conceived the plot between themselves, and persuaded some of the Ghibellines to join them. The intention was that Gabriele would come and join the marshal – from whom he had had nothing but friendship and consideration – and demand

92 Gabriele took refuge in Milan after he had sold Pisa by an agreement dated 27 August 1405. See pp. 159–60 above.

93 Gabriele had supported the Ghibellines in Milan who were defeated by the Guelphs in 1407.

94 Alessandria is a city in Piedmont, around fifty miles south-west of Milan.

a letter of marque giving him redress from the Florentines over a certain sum of money that they still owed him for the sale of Pisa;[95] his visit to Genoa would allow him to discover how their enterprise could best be achieved. Once they had agreed this, Gabriele got in touch with the marshal for leave to visit him, and to this the marshal willingly agreed. On top of that, before setting out, Gabriele asked for a safe conduct, since the marshal would know that he had spent time with Facino Cane who was an enemy to the king and to the Genoese; this the marshal agreed, on the understanding that Gabriele intended no harm to himself or to the interests of Genoa.[96] Fortified by this agreement, Gabriele came to Genoa, and the marshal granted him the letter of marque as requested, and for his father's sake received him as affably as if he had been his brother; Gabriele stayed in Genoa at what seemed to be his own expense for some six months, pretending to pursue the arrears owed by the Florentines. In fact, of course, he was pursuing a quite different agenda; [385] he was laying plans to achieve his planned treason. But the marshal was shrewd enough to deny him the opportunity.

Nevertheless, in pursuit of his plans, [Gabriele] had already asked permission from the marshal to bring eight hundred horse through the city and across the river, saying that he needed to take them from Tuscany into Lombardy for reasons of his own, and the marshal had given him permission. But God, Who has so often – and long may it continue! – saved His servant the marshal from harm and loss, made sure that Gabriele's treachery would be made known, and by a strange means.

At this time the marshal was besieging a castle called Cremolino [Cromolin], held at that time by a wicked rebel called Tommaso Malaspina who was defying the king and the lordship of Genoa;[97] he belonged to the band around Facino Cane. At one point it happened, as God willed, that a particular Genoese who was part of the besieging army went into a tirade against this Tommaso who was up on the walls, saying that no good would come to him if he betrayed his king and lord, and that he would do better to listen to reason and surrender. Briefly, their exchanges became more and more heated and they exchanged more and more insults, until finally the Genoese said to Tommaso that he was looking forward to seeing his head cut off in the piazza in Genoa. Tommaso's anger and resentment [386] loosened his tongue, and he replied: 'And I promise you that in a very few days I'll be strutting along around the money-changers in Genoa!' His jibe caused much discussion among those who heard it, and they agreed that he would never have dared to say such a thing if he hadn't had reason to think it might happen. That made Gabriele distinctly

95 Letters of marque authorized acts of reprisal by individuals, to seize by force goods, chattels or even people as compensation for injuries that they had received. See M.H. Keen, *The Laws of War in the Late Middle Ages* (London, 1965), pp. 218–38.

96 Boucicaut granted the safe conduct in June 1408.

97 Cremolino is around twenty-five miles north-west of Genoa, and seventy-five miles south-west of Milan.

suspect because of his association with Facino Cane – but in order to smoke him out, they invented the following subterfuge.

A select body of good men-at-arms, known to be loyal to the king and his rule, were sent into the hills around Genoa to watch out for messengers passing between Gabriele and Facino Cane, and one day they were lying in wait when they saw a soldier coming on horseback. They drew their swords and daggers and ran on him shouting: 'Die, traitor! We can see from your badge that you're from the false traitor Gabriele, who is a friend of the marshal whom we hate because he's had us thrown out of Genoa. So you'll pay for our hatred of him!' Thinking that they were speaking the truth and that they had indeed been banished and did indeed hate the marshal, he told them that they should on no account kill him; he could tell them, since they were enemies of the marshal, that if they were willing to cooperate they could all be rich. The marshal's men pretended to be delighted, [387] and got him to lay bare his role in the plot: he was carrying letters from Gabriele to Facino Cane stitched into the soles of his shoes. They pretended that they would take him to safety, and instead brought him, much to his surprise, into Genoa; there he was questioned and very soon admitted everything. My lord Gabriele, having no idea of what was happening, was taken prisoner in the palace where the marshal lived; he had gone there to spy out the land so as to advance his plot. And he was persuaded to admit to the whole affair out of his own mouth: he explained that, on a particular day, Facino Cane was to arrive at the gates of Genoa with two thousand horse and three thousand foot, and shout: 'Long live the Ghibellines!' – at which point the marshal's men and the Genoese would issue from the gates to confront him; my lord Gabriele meanwhile, with his eight hundred horse, was to pretend to come to the marshal's assistance against Facino, but actually he would open the gates to Facino and they would merge their forces. They hoped that the Ghibellines of Genoa would make common cause with them, and that would have made the rebel forces so numerous that all the king's men would be killed; if the Ghibellines stayed loyal to the king, the rebels would ravage the city and then leave. Once Gabriele had made his confession, he had his head cut off, as he had richly deserved.[98]

98 Gabriele Maria Visconti was arrested on 16 November 1408 and beheaded on 15 December. Both Giovanni Stella and Pileo de Martini, archbishop of Genoa, accused Boucicaut of manufacturing an excuse to execute Gabriele in the reports that they sent to Charles VI in late 1409: A. Ceruti. 'Lettere di Carlo VI re di Francia e della Repubblica di Genova relative al maresciallo Boucicaldo', *Atti della società ligure di storia patria*, 17 (1886), p. 362 and Puncuh, 'Il governo genovese', pp. 676–7.

[390] I: Here begins the fourth and last part of this book, which will list the virtues, the good habits and the good disposition of the marshal, along with his good conduct; this first chapter deals with his appearance and physique.

I have now recorded in detail, thanks be to God, all the memorable deeds performed and achieved by my lord Boucicaut, marshal of France, [391] whose history I have been commissioned to write. As far as my memory serves, I have put them in chronological order; the importance of the history means that my record is imperfect, for I do not have the resources or the gifts to prevent this. I shall say no more, for the moment, as to his deeds, but rather proceed to talk about his appearance and conduct; now that we have talked of the richness of the treasure, and although his deeds speak for themselves, we should rightly turn to the treasure-chest itself. His steady conduct and his well-ordered life being such as to act as an example to all, it seems to me that we should describe them in detail; I shall begin with a few words on his appearance. He is not especially tall, but nor is he short. His physique is lean, but well built: he is athletic, and sturdy. He is broad in the chest, with wide and muscular shoulders; his hips, his thighs and his calves are sinewy; no-one could be more well developed. His face is uniformly handsome, lightly tanned, with a becoming flush, having a good beard, auburn in colour. His habitual expression is bold, self-assured, measured, and his countenance is composed and confident. [392] In particular, God has furnished him with an air of calm command such that he impresses and daunts everyone by his looks alone, so he is revered everywhere and by everyone, and even by those who are his superiors in rank. On the other hand, nothing in his appearance suggests pride or arrogance; these are things he particularly hates – although he might feel such emotions for an enemy, and in such a case he will show due pride and scorn. His garments are costly, but they are tasteful and stylish.

II: Here we describe the marshal's piety, and his charity.

Now that we have described the marshal's deeds and outlined his appearance and conduct, we must speak of his piety; we begin with his charity, this being, as St Paul tells us, the greatest of the virtues.[1] The marshal's compassion for the poor and his pity for them are so profound that he has sought out poor householders, without means of support [393] or with many children, poor young women who need to marry, women who are pregnant or widows, or orphans, and secretly sends them large

1 Romans 13: 8–10; 1 Corinthians 13: 1–13; Galatians 5: 14; Colossians 3: 14.

donations – and by this means he supports many of the poor. But he is not content to give alms on his own lands; rather, knowing for instance that there are many in Paris who are poor but unseen, he sends to agents of his, who are well informed, large sums to distribute. And I can bear witness – as can many others – that many poor households and indigent poor have been given assistance, and many young girls have been married.

Item, he often gives offerings to convents and churches, and pays for repairs to chapels and oratories; we can see this in many places, and notably at the [Cimetière des] Saints-Innocents in Paris, where his money has financed the building of fine charnel houses around the cemetery on the side facing the rue de la Draperie.[2] In addition, he donated a thousand écus to the church in Saint-Maximin[-la-Sainte-Baume] in Provence which houses the head of Mary Magdalene, to have a vaulted ceiling built in the chapel that holds the Blessed Head, and to restore the chapel itself which is now very beautiful.[3] He often gives donations to poor priests and clergy and to all those who serve God.[4] [394] In all, he never fails those who ask for charity in God's name. When he is out on progress, he happily hands out alms personally – and the sums involved are not small, but rather very generous. He is very supportive and liberal where he sees need, and especially for those who are deserving; he is caring towards those he believes live an honest life, and who love and serve Our Lord – after all, as the old proverb says, 'like attracts like'.[5] But I am very conscious of the fact that his unsullied nobility of soul and character might mean I owe him an apology: if ever this present book falls into his hands, he is likely to be embarrassed, as is so often the case with people of good faith when they hear the good works they do for God's sake made public. In which case I hope that the truth of my account will excuse me, and that it will not cause him displeasure; my account of his good works is not intended as vainglorious, but rather to make him a role model for those who hear them spoken of and who might read the present book. For the wise among the theologians consider that the embargo on revealing one's good deeds and the alms one gives is valid only insofar as the donor [395] must not himself seek praise by parading his own virtues; when on the other hand the donor is of such moral perfection that he takes no pride in the good that he does, the alms that he gives, or the prayers that he says, whether these things are privately or publicly done, but rather does such things for the love of God, then it

2 The Saints-Innocents was the oldest and largest cemetery in Paris. Because of the overcrowding of mass graves, arched structures called 'charniers' or charnel houses were constructed along the walls of the cemetery during the fourteenth and fifteenth centuries.

3 Saint-Maximin-la-Sainte-Baume, twenty-five miles east of Aix-en-Provence, was celebrated as the home of the sarcophagus of Mary Magdalene. The basilica was consecrated in 1316, and between 1404 and 1412 further work resulted in the construction of the sixth bay of the nave.

4 On 17 June 1406, Boucicaut founded the hospital at Sainte-Catherine-de-Fierbois, near Chinon.

5 See p. 38 above.

is best that he does so in public rather than in private, simply in order that he may set an example for those who contemplate his virtues.

III: Of the precepts that the marshal follows in God's service.

Not only is the marshal highly charitable, he loves and fears God above all things, and is very devout. Every day, without fail, he prays the liturgy of the hours, and recites other prayers to God and to the saints. Every day, however busy or preoccupied he is, he hears two Masses with every sign of devotion, kneeling on the ground; while he is at prayer or at Mass, no-one dares to disturb him, [396] and his prayers are suitably devout. Briefly, he sets so remarkably good an example of piety to onlookers, nobles and the general public alike, that the very serving lads in his house serve God with prayer and fasting, and he behaves in church so devoutly that one might imagine him to be a religious – and many to whom prayer was an unknown quantity have learned their hours from seeing him, and say them conscientiously.

Along with all this, in his wisdom and for the good of his soul, he has lived as all good Christians should with his afterlife in mind: he has made his will and lives by it every day.[6] When the marshal is at prayer, he prefaces his supplications with the phrase 'if it be thy will'; at all events, knowing his own frailty, he prays that God's will be done. Oh, who was it who taught him how to pray? It was not, I believe, human wisdom – which always risks slipping into vice; rather, it was the Holy Spirit that inspired him in such ways! In the manner in which he prays, he follows the doctrines of Socrates, whose wisdom was such that the ancients called him the divine oracle.[7] [397] Socrates told us that we should make no specific prayers to the immortal God, but rather pray that He be our help in whatever ways He thinks right. For, he said, God is better able to judge what is best for us than we are ourselves. Often, he said, we pray for things that would be injurious to us; our limited understanding means that we see darkly, and so we pray for what exceeds our need, for we cannot know what is best for us. 'You seek riches,' he said, 'which have destroyed so many. You covet honours, which inspire only envy, and which last so short a time. You long for thrones and kingdoms and lands, and yet such longings often lead only to sorrow. You hope, by making a noble marriage, to acquire a noble lineage, but such hopes are destructive of family and well-being, for if you nail your colours to the mast of Fortune, they will often be torn away. So,' he says, 'do not pray for such worldly things, but rather put yourself in the hands of the Creator Who knows better than you can what is best for you. Put all your wishes in His hands, for His wisdom will know how best to grant them.' These fine words of wisdom come from a pagan who knew nothing of the Word of God, and yet his reason alone allowed him to recognise

6 Boucicaut made his will on 18 July 1407.

7 This story of Socrates (470/469–399 BC) derived from Hesdin's translation and commentary upon Valerius Maximus, VII, c.2, ext. 1, in BNF MS fr. 282, fols 270b–271c.

godliness. [398] And another who did the same was Juvenal, at the beginning of his fourth book.[8]

And speaking of the pagans – who with no access to Holy Gospel manifested an innate understanding of God and of the divine – a case in point is Thales, one of the Seven Sages,[9] who gave a remarkable reply when he was asked if God knew all the deeds that man performed: 'Yes,' said he, 'and not only the deeds, but the thoughts.'[10] This saying shows us that we should ensure that our thoughts, as well as our deeds, are pure and innocent, since we must believe that God knows our innermost thoughts. If then the pagans, though ignorant of Divine Law, recognised that they should take a virtuous path for love of a God, how much more should we Christians do so when our knowledge of that Law comes to us from Holy Scripture, and when we are enrolled in the school of Jesus Christ, Who is both man and God? Should we transgress, we are the more deserving of punishment; as Boethius tells us at the end of his *Consolation*, we can but be virtuous, knowing that all we do is known to the Judge Who will reward us according to our deserts.

Item: on Fridays, the marshal follows all observances: he eats nothing living and wears only black [399] out of respect for the Passion of Our Lord. On Saturdays, according to custom, he fasts, and he observes all the fast-days prescribed by the Church, nor would he ever be tempted to break such a fast.

Item: he never swears by Our Lord, or by His death, or His flesh, or His blood; never does he utter detestable oaths of this sort himself, and nor will he permit them in any of his household. Not one of his men would swear in ways that deny God, or murmur against Him: woe betide them if they did so and it came to his attention, and he does not make distinctions in rank for transgressors. In the city of Genoa itself, and in all his lands, he has sent out an edict on the subject threatening serious punishment to anyone who would dare speak shamefully of Our Lord, or use blasphemous oaths. If only we had such a governor in Paris![11]

Item: he is eager to undertake pilgrimages to holy places, on foot and devotedly, and he takes a particular pleasure in shrines and sanctuaries; he also enjoys visiting holy men who serve God, as he has done several times in visiting the holy mountain in Provence where Mary Magdalene, to whom he has a particular devotion, lived

8 This reference to Juvenal (*Satires*, IV, c.10, verses 346–9), was taken from Simon de Hesdin's commentary upon Valerius Maximus, VII, c.2., ext. 1, in BNF MS fr. 282, fol. 270c.

9 Sometimes, in medieval France, called 'The Seven Sages of Rome', a cycle of stories circulating in many European languages. The Sages educate a young prince in the seven liberal arts; Thales of Miletus was responsible for philosophy.

10 This discussion of Thales of Miletus (c.624–c.546 BC), along with the reference to Boethius's *De consolatione philosophiae*, were drawn from Simon de Hesdin's translation and commentary upon Valerius Maximus, VII, c.2, ext. 8, in BNF MS fr. 282, fols 271d–272a.

11 For contemporary concerns about blasphemy, see J. Hoareau-Dodinau, *Dieu et le roi. La répression du blasphème et de l'injure au roi à la fin du moyen âge* (Limoges, 2002) and A. Kennedy, 'Christine de Pizan, Blasphemy and the Dauphin, Louis de Guyenne', *Medium Aevum*, 83 (2014), pp. 104–20.

out her days in penance.[12] [400] He donated some five hundred francs to search out beds and other equipment for a hospital for the poor, and to provide lodging for the pilgrims. He is particularly attracted to those who are said to lead good and holy lives, and he is eager to call on them and spend time with them. And when in command of a military expedition, he expressly forbids his army, on pain of hanging, from doing damage to any church or monastery, from harming any priest or religious; even in enemy territory, he will not have any fortified church attacked, whatever the treasures or other goods that have been stored there, and even if his own armies are suffering from food shortages or other deprivations: all this as evidence of his piety and his personal selflessness. And we can offer him as an example of such virtue, just as Valerius Maximus does Scipio Africanus whose habits were very like the marshal's: Scipio conqueror of Carthage, says Valerius, sent word across all the cities of the kingdom of Sicily [Cecile] that their citizens should come and identify the temple relics which had been looted from churches in Sicily and deposited in Carthage by Hannibal himself, formerly emperor of Africa and Carthage, [401] on his return from Sicily; they would repossess them and return them to their rightful places. And this, says Valerius, proves Scipio's piety, and his generosity, since some of those relics were of great value.[13]

IV: How the marshal refrains from breaking God's law, even in time if war, and of his restraint.

Anyone, of any rank, who loves and fears God must guard against breaking any of the commandments; whatever deeds he may be led to perform in the calling that he follows, he must nevertheless observe them. The marshal has been called by God to the exercise of arms, in pursuit of which many might imagine that such observances would be difficult to achieve; the marshal, however, has throughout his career, and even today, managed to follow the rule of justice, [402] thus following in the footsteps of many noble and valiant heroes of the ancient world whom I shall now name as being entirely comparable to him. But because God must be at the root of all things, and because indeed the marshal dedicates himself to the service of God, I shall first talk of his charity, and then of his piety, and finally, thirdly, of the ethical regime that he follows in the pursuit of arms and of the fine reputation that he has thereby acquired. In the pursuit of arms, then, he is particularly judicious and thoughtful: in other words, before engaging in war, he weighs up the pros and cons, considers if his cause is just, calculates the likely outcomes, assesses the men and finances he will need and

12 Medieval legend held that after the Ascension of Jesus, Mary Magdalene lived as a hermit for thirty years in a cave that was often supposed to have been located near Aix-en-Provence.

13 This is a loose paraphrase of Simon de Hesdin's translation and commentary upon Valerius Maximus, V, c.1.6, in BNF MS fr. 282, fol. 212a.

the strength of his adversaries, studies the seasons and the likely weather conditions: in short, he brings good sense to bear on the advantages and disadvantages of action. Once he has come to the considered conclusion that he should go to war, and once he has assembled his forces, he deploys them expertly, making those who have the most experience in arms captains of the others; his express command is always that all his men should obey their captains, failing which they will be punished. In addition, he operates a careful selection to choose those he will take with him, and makes sure that they are upright and well trained; on many occasions he has refused the services of men-at-arms – of whatever nationality – who are known to have acted wrongly in former wars, and who are ungovernable whatever punishments [403] they may incur. This is a demonstration of the good order and discipline that the marshal imposes, and which was in olden times, as their histories show, characteristic of the Romans, who inflicted grievous punishments on their own children and family members if they dared to disobey their commanders.[14]

Ah God! In insisting on such discipline, is not the marshal to be compared to the valiant Scipio Africanus whose virtues I have several times extolled here? When Scipio was put in command of a large army that the Romans were sending to Spain, he issued an edict that all superfluous or unnecessary items be left behind; by such an edict he was able to dismiss a large number of women camp-followers, and of merchants who lurked around the army selling all sorts of uncalled-for luxuries.[15]

Also on campaign, the valiant marshal forbade anyone from daring to waste his time on futile pursuits – gambling games such as dice – and from bringing into the host any item which might promote mindless amusements; [404] he also forbade the sale of luxuries and the use of blasphemous oaths,[16] and imposed serious punishments on those who transgressed.

That such measures are important is proven by Valerius, who points to a noble captain of Rome called Metellus who took over command of the army and of the legion of men-at-arms that had been under the command of a different captain; the command the latter had exerted had been so slipshod that the forces were of very little military value.[17] Taking charge, Metellus immediately followed Scipio in instituting measures to combat the bad habits that the men-at-arms had fallen into, and for good measure he forbade that any delicacies be brought into the army, forbade also that

14 See p. 103 above.

15 This story was taken from Simon de Hesdin's translation and commentary upon Valerius Maximus, II, c.7.1, in BNF MS fr. 282, fol. 114c. Christine de Pizan had also cited this story, via Hesdin, in *Le chemin de longue étude. Édition critique du ms. Harley 4431*, ed. and trans. A. Tarnowski (Paris, 2000), pp. 344–6 (vv. 4361–74).

16 See p. 191 above.

17 Quintus Caecilius Metellus Numidicus (c.160–91 BC) was chief commander in the Jugurthine War in Numidia. His story had been cited by Simon de Hesdin in his translation and commentary upon Valerius Maximus, II, 7.2, in BNF MS fr. 282, fols 107b–d. Christine de Pizan also made a brief reference to the comments by Valerius Maximus in *Le chemin de longue étude*, pp. 348–50 (vv. 4431–42).

any fighting man should load his armour onto a squire or a horse but rather ordered that he should carry his own; he also insisted that the army should be constantly on the move, and that they themselves protect their camp [with fortifications].

The marshal, then, is cautious about engaging in war, and well versed in warfare and leadership. On top of that, [405] he is expert in selecting his position on the battle-field, so that the enemy will be exposed to the wind and the dust, with the sun in his eyes and stationed at the bottom of a hill. If he believes himself to be well placed, he will not wait for an enemy attack; he chooses his moment for the advance with the intention of surprising them, if necessary, and if he thinks it best, by the use of a ruse. He remains cool and calm, never rushing out on the enemy, but rather waiting for a suitable time and place, very similar in this to Fabius Maximus, who, Valerius tells us, was once sent with a large army to resist the advance of Hannibal, prince of Carthage.[18] When Fabius – who was very shrewd – drew near to the enemy, he weighed up their military strength, but also the arrogance that they had developed from a victory they had won against the Romans. Fabius decided therefore not to attack immediately, in spite of his large army; he simply kept his army in battle-order, and followed the Carthaginians closely for many days. And day by day, Hannibal lost more of his men to desertion, and so his army was progressively weakened [406] and Fabius took possession of more strongholds; Hannibal, certainly, harried the countryside with fire when he could, but Fabius, whatever the provocation, waited for his opportunity. After some time had passed in this way, Minucius Rufus, Fabius's master of the horse, who was very brave, certainly, but not very wise, tried repeatedly to goad Fabius into launching an attack, and maintained that it was shameful to allow such damage to be inflicted without giving battle. But Duke Fabius was unmoved: eventually, Minucius, who thought he knew better than his master, went back to Rome and got permission from one of the Plebeian Council to give battle to Hannibal. At that Fabius's army was divided into two, so that Minucius was given half the men, and so that each half was commanded by one of them; Fabius, however, held to his strategy and would not allow himself to be swayed. Their mutual enemy Hannibal, his army by now so much weakened that he had been on the point of ordering the retreat, was delighted at these developments, for he knew that Minucius would be foolish enough to engage battle, and that Fabius himself would be much weakened by the loss of half his men. So Hannibal, who was very cunning, set an ambush; Minucius, determined on a pitched battle, went into the attack; Hannibal triggered the ambush, and Minucius was very soon defeated. The wise Fabius, on the other hand, who had foreseen this outcome, was determined not to abandon his men simply because of Minucius's folly; [407] he too had set an ambush; he launched an attack on the Carthaginians who were harrying those who fled, and had his

18 Quintus Fabius Maximus Verrucosus Cunctator (c.280–203 BC), as discussed in Simon de Hesdin and Nicolas de Gonesse's translation and commentary upon Valerius Maximus, III, c.8.2 and V, c.2.4 in BNF MS fr. 282, fols 169c–d and 218a–b.

trumpets sounded to rally them. In this way, Fabius's war of attrition was successful, and Minucius's impulsiveness was his undoing. All of which shows that the marshal's prudence should be extolled, by contrast with rash and hasty recourse to battle.

Let me give another example to prove that the wisdom and cunning in which the marshal is well versed are valuable assets in warfare, as is shown by his actions against the Saracens and elsewhere. Valerius tells us that while Hannibal and his brother Hasdrubal were in Italy and separately ravaging the countryside, two noble dukes were sent against them from Rome, and although they were far outnumbered by the Carthaginians, they followed a wise strategy whereby they prevented the forces of the two brothers from joining up; had this happened, there was no way that the Romans could have stood up to them, for the Carthaginians were far more numerous.[19] The two Roman dukes, meanwhile, managed to destroy Hannibal's army by taking him by surprise; [408] the two Roman armies joined forces one night by marching all night across a great distance; once they were united, they drew up in serried ranks as if there had been no reinforcements. Hannibal, who had issued a challenge to battle on that particular day, had no reason to suppose that he would be fighting a united army, and so he was defeated.[20]

V: How the marshal is brave and steadfast in all his enterprises.

As well as being wise and judicious in all matters of arms, the marshal is very brave, chivalrous and intrepid; never, when he has engaged with an enemy, has he emerged from the encounter other than with honour; never has he emerged other than to acclaim. He has been tried and tested in many such encounters, and has come out of the most seemingly impossible of them with success. Because of his great personal courage [409] and his tactical sense in the deployment of his forces, he has been able to manoeuvre as he wished. Indeed when he has found himself engaged in some testing and painful encounter, one from which he felt he would only emerge if he exerted all his strength and demanded great suffering from his forces, he would have it announced throughout the army that no-one, on pain of death, should dare to retreat or to withdraw; as a result of which his men, fearing his commandment and the inescapable punishments he would impose, came to prefer death in battle to a shameful death ordered as punishment. They were therefore so ready to expose themselves to danger that the marshal brought any enterprise in which he engaged to an honourable conclusion.

19 The Carthaginian armies of Hannibal (247–c.181 BC) and his brother Hasdrubal II (245–207 BC) were outwitted by the Roman consuls Marcus Livius and Gaius Claudius Nero in 207 BC, during the Second Punic War. This was discussed in Nicolas de Gonesse's translation and commentary upon Valerius Maximus, VII, c.4.4, in BNF MS fr. 282, fols 283b–d.

20 In fact it was Hasdrubal who was defeated and killed at the battle of Mataurus in 207 BC, as Valerius Maximus had originally noted.

On the grounds of this unusual and laudable performance in matters of war, I compare him to the most valiant of the ancients, and his deeds to those described by Valerius who singles out an instance which saw the Romans encamped on a river in Lombardy, not far from Piacenza [Plaisance], from where they were driven into retreat by their enemies.[21] When their consul – that is, their duke – learnt of this, he commanded his master of horse (who had been in command) and the whole army to return to their station, otherwise he would have them severely punished. [410] This was not because the consul had any expectation of success, but rather so that the army would not be dishonoured by retreat or flight. He sent out an edict saying that anyone seen to retreat, or to turn his back on the enemy, would be killed – and this brutal decree, Valerius tells us, left his men so despairing that they said they would prefer to die honourably, in combat with their enemies, rather than meet a shameful death. As a result, and although they were heavily outnumbered and poorly positioned, they carried off the victory. Those were precisely the tactics that the marshal favoured, as we suggested. And I have now, I believe, said enough about the marshal's valour: I have produced a wealth of examples to prove it. I do so because the record of valiant deeds serves as an example to noblemen to come in later generations.

VI: How the marshal is innocent of avarice and generous with his own.

It is a truth universally acknowledged that anyone wishing to accede [411] to the highest degree of honour must be without greed; after all, if he devotes himself to amassing a fortune, he will be distracted from the single-minded pursuit of arms which alone brings glory; to be known for avarice entails the loss of the friendship and companionship of his fellows, and leads ineluctably to the loss of reputation. The marshal is manifestly devoid of avarice, for never has he bought a lordship, lands, heritage; he is singularly uninterested in his own ancestral lands. Everything suggests that his thoughts and his attention are elsewhere.

We can thus say of him what is said of the wise philosopher Anaxagoras: that when he had been abroad for many years in pursuit of wisdom, he came back to his lands to find them uncultivated and barren. His friends condemned him for the way he had let them go to rack and ruin, but he replied: 'I prefer to improve myself, rather than my lands.' By which he meant that had he devoted himself to the cultivation of his lands, he would not have acquired the knowledge and wisdom that he had been able to do. And in terms of his own wisdom, he was perfectly right: [412]

21 This story of Quintus Caecilius Metellus Macedonicus (210–116/115 BC) was recounted by Simon de Hesdin in his translation and commentary upon Valerius Maximus, II, c.7.10, in BNF MS fr. 282, fols 113d–114a.

he had preferred to cultivate knowledge and wisdom rather than his lands and his patrimony, for had he pursued the latter, he would not have had leisure for study.[22]

Just as therefore the ancients called the wise philosophers knights of wisdom, so the good marshal could rightly be called a philosopher of arms: he loved to cultivate and to improve the science of arms, and preferred to nurture his own valour, courage and high reputation rather than to acquire lands, riches or mansions. He possessed, however, a great treasure, one of the greatest: sufficiency. Aristotle, we know, said that to be truly rich is not to covet anything; such riches cannot be stolen, for when thoughts are righteous they do not allow space to fear ill.[23] This is what creates great men, for they need spend no time thinking about acquiring wealth. That the marshal is uninterested in wealth is evident, for no nobleman could be more wisely and prudently generous: he is quick to be open-handed to knights and gentlemen from foreign parts or from home, [413] and he rewards everyone according to his deeds and his merit, and whenever the person does him good service; he wishes never to be in debt, so pays off any 'merchant' who supplies him. Briefly, then, anyone he has to do with gives him nothing but praise, and he himself is never happier than when showing his generosity. Of course, like any wise man, he does not give without careful inquiry as to the recipient, the amount, and the cause and occasion of the gift; he is not an advocate of foolish largesse – much to be condemned – but rather wishes his generosity to be freely given, carefully considered, and from his own rather than from another's purse: generosity, in other words, as prescribed by Saint Augustine.[24] He is careful to avoid appropriating riches from others, by extortion or by force, for his charity of soul would not permit it; he refuses all gifts and remuneration that might come his way, out of respect for the position of governor. [414] In this he follows the teachings of the wise duke of Athens called Pericles who, says Justin, maintained that anyone administering justice in public office should be temperate not only in hand and tongue, but also in eye – by which he meant that any man who is charged with governing others should refrain from accepting gifts, for such things pervert human judgement – and also be temperate in his speech and in his appetites, for the common people will look to him to set an example.[25] The marshal is noted for just such restraint, as I shall now explain.

22 This is a loose paraphrase of the discussion of Anaxagoras (c.510–428 BC) in Nicolas de Gonesse's translation and commentary upon Valerius Maximus, VIII, c.7, ext. 6, in BNF MS fr. 282, fols 322c–d.

23 This commonplace idea was expressed on many occasions by Aristotle, for example in his *Nicomachean Ethics*, pp. 56–8 (III, c.11 and 12) and 196–9 (X, c.8). Also see Oresme, *Le livre de ethiques d'Aristote*, pp. 195–200 and 510–12.

24 It is not clear whether the author was alluding to a specific passage by Saint Augustine. Simon de Hesdin had offered a lengthy discussion of generosity in his translation and commentary upon Valerius Maximus, V, c.1 praef, in BNF MS fr. 282, fols 208b–209a, which was used in turn by Christine de Pizan in *Livre du corps de policie*, pp. 24–5 (I, c.14). But neither Simon nor Christine referred to Augustine.

25 The discussion of Pericles (495–429 BC) was taken from Gonesse's translation and commentary upon Valerius Maximus, VIII, c.9, ext 2, in BNF MS fr. 282, fols 327b–c. Christine de Pizan

VII: How the marshal is a model of self-discipline and chastity.

That the noble man who is our subject here is abstemious and chaste is proved by his behaviour in general, for there are three principal signs that betray immorality. The first is an undue fussiness as to food and a preference for eccentricity in dress, the second is shown by particular expressions and glances, the third by ways of speaking: [415] as the old saying has it, 'The apparel oft proclaims the man', or as the Bible says, 'He that is of the earth, speaks of the earth'.[26] To prove how far he is abstemious, his unvarying habit is the following: although he is always copiously served, and although his table is very generous, he never eats more than one dish and that is the first that he takes – so it might be a dish of boiled meats, or one of roasted meats, or poultry, or beef, or mutton; he does not drink wine other than watered by at least a quarter; he drinks wine only at dinner or at supper; he has no interest in exotic foods or sauces or strange spices; he eats and drinks sparingly and soberly. Although his household is served on silver-gilt, and although he has plenty of plate, he himself is never served on gold or silver, but only on tin, or glass, or wood. He does not go for elegance or display in dress; he dresses neatly and tidily, but without self-consciousness. He takes no interest in or amusement from fashion: he does not have his clothes embroidered or adorned with gold in any way which would not befit his own standing – even though such ornament is increasingly common in France. His household is well staffed; he insists on a fine livery for each according to his function; he pays good salaries. He speaks little at table, [416] and indeed he speaks sparingly at all times; when he is moved to speak, he begins always by invoking God or the saints, and confines his speech to matters of virtue and charity, knighthood and heroism, or exemplary behaviour, or something on those lines. And never, at any time, whether in private or in public, will you hear him speak unworthily or inappropriately, or hear him speak ill of anyone; indeed he has no taste for tittle-tattle or malice, loose tongues or frivolity, and refuses to listen to unprofitable gossip. He takes great pleasure in pious books that talk of God or of the saints, and he much enjoys volumes like *Li Fet de Romains*, or other true histories.[27]

Item: he never lies, and his word is his bond; when he commands, he expects to be obeyed completely and promptly. He has a particular dislike of liars and flatterers and gossips, and dismisses them from his presence. He hates gambling, and never gambles himself. He possesses every virtue that is the opposite of lasciviousness – and if he gives every outward appearance of chastity and temperance, his inward and real

---

had also used this material in *Livre du corps de policie*, p. 38 (I, c.22).

26 John 3: 31.

27 *Li Fet des Romains* was an early thirteenth-century prose account of the life and deeds of Julius Caesar, written in Old French and largely based upon the writings of Lucan, Sallust, Suetonius and Caesar himself. *Li Fet des Romains compilé ensemble de Saluste et de Suetoine et de Lucan, texte du XIIIe siècle publié pour la première fois d'après les meilleurs manuscrits*, ed. L.-F. Flutre and K. Sneyders de Vogel, 2 volumes (Groningen/Paris, 1935–8).

self surpasses this: he keeps his marriage vows faithfully and lovingly. God indeed provided for Genoa just the governor that the city most needed, for the Genoese are a most jealous people, who fear profoundly that their wives might be led astray, [417] so they were fortunate in him; he remains stony-hearted whatever the temptation offered by Genoese ladies who are elegantly dressed and bejewelled, and often very beautiful. Moreover, he insists that his men also be temperate; if ever a complaint was made about one of them, the culprit might well wish that he had never come to the city. In addition to his preference for virtue, he wants – knowing Genoese customs and proclivities – to maintain peace among them; he is determined that no Genoese should have cause to complain of him or his men, and so does not wish there to be even a stealthy glance. On which subject I remember hearing from one of his gentlemen that once, when he was riding through the city, a lady was sitting by a window in the sunshine, as is surprisingly common there, combing her hair which was wonderfully blond. One of the squires riding in his escort saw her and said: 'Oh, what a beautiful head of hair!' and then as he rode on, he turned back in his saddle to admire her. But the marshal saw what was happening and said 'That's quite enough!' The marshal is therefore outwardly and inwardly immune to the sins of the flesh and to all excess, and this is the best proof of his chasteness, for the authorities tell us that immorality is most often provoked by little flirtations, or glances, or smiles, and is often associated with a liking for delicacies and knick-knacks, distractions that simply undermine virtue. [418] The marshal, as paragon of virtue, is well aware that fornication is a sin that leads the soul to damnation and, as Saint Augustine tells us, excludes virtue.[28] For that reason, he did everything to avoid it, even – to his great credit – in his early youth. After all, it is notoriously the case that any love of luxury, any succumbing to romantic desire, is damaging to the man-at-arms.[29] For Julius Caesar himself, valiant conqueror that he was, was deeply tainted by that sin when he was in Egypt; had he persisted longer in it, had he stayed in Egypt and given in to pleasure and sensuality, he would have lost all his reputation and all his military valour, for his knights and his men-at-arms were showing signs of insubordination and thought him lost.[30] As evidence of how foreign such things should be to any man of valour [419] because of their effect on his honour and reputation, Boccaccio, in the fifth book of his *De casibus virorum illustrium*, cites King Antiochus, after whom the city of Antioch is named: he was a prince of royal blood, rich and powerful, so much so that he could have conquered the whole world, and indeed had already subjugated many territories by force of arms: no-one could resist him and kingdoms

28 This was a commonplace idea in Saint Augustine, for example cited in *Civitatis dei*, I, c.30–3; XIII, c.13; XIV, c.1–5; XIV, c.16–20 and XXI, c.25.

29 For similar concerns, see Christine de Pizan, *Le chemin de longue étude*, pp. 344–6 (vv. 4349–84), and *Livre du corps de policie*, pp. 50–1 and 80–1 (I, c.30 and II, c.16).

30 The story of Julius Caesar and Cleopatra was recounted in *Li Fet des Romains*, I, pp. 656–7.

trembled before him.[31] But he was undone by fornication and by his taste for luxury, for, after conquering part of Greece, he returned to winter in Chalcedon [Calcidie], and there he was overtaken by a foolish love affair, and as he indulged in flirtations and extravagances, games and pleasures, so his pride and courage were diminished. He pursued this dissipated life for the whole of the winter, thus misleading not merely the princes of his army, but also his knights and even his men-at-arms into indulging in empty pleasure and recreation; they abandoned military discipline and the chivalric way of life that they had cultivated for so long, so that at their first encounter with an enemy – as it happened, a Roman army – they were overcome, and King Antiochus had to flee to Ephesus [Euphese].

Justin in his book confirms this history, saying that that winter the king participated every day in new orgies; [420] he was, says Justin, always attracted by the luxuries and trinkets which are a sure sign of the lustful:[32] the very nails on his shoes were made of gold, his kitchens used pans and roasting dishes made of silver, his garments were made of expensive fabrics and were richly bejewelled. Valerius says of such men that their possessions simply make them a more desirable conquest. And it is my opinion that those who write descriptions of such things, marvelling that such love of luxury should overtake kings and emperors, never in their own times saw anything to rival the excesses and the vices that nowadays run riot in France and elsewhere: not merely in royal or aristocratic circles, but also among the administrators and office-holders of their households: the flamboyance that holds sway is beyond anything that King Antiochus could dream of. We can deduce the causes of such corrosion from their results, and we can predict the results from the causes.

VIII: How the marshal always seeks to be just.

Along with all his other remarkable qualities we should count the marshal's love of justice: [421] no-one could be more scrupulous in its pursuit whenever it is necessary, and particularly in foreign parts; he is never unduly harsh or cruel to any living creature. As is right for anyone who dispenses justice, he is more inclined to mercy than to severity, although he seeks to balance right against might and to ensure that everyone receives justice according to his merits. This virtue of his is especially evident given the position he holds: it is remarkable that his judicious rule, stemming from his single person, can have imposed discipline and peace on a people so ill-disciplined, so rebellious, so unused to bowing to the principles of justice, and have done so so effectively that a man may walk through the streets of Genoa with a gold crown on his head or a treasure-chest under his arm without anyone stealing

31 Antiochus VII Sidetes reigned from 138 to 129 BC. This story was taken from Gonesse's translation and commentary on Valerius Maximus, XI, c.1, ext. 4, in BNF MS fr. 282, fols 353a–c. Christine de Pizan also cited this story in *Livre du corps de policie*, p. 81 (II, c.16).

32 Gonesse cites Justin (*Epitoma*, XXXI, c.6.3) in his commentary on the story of Antiochus.

it or attacking him; it is remarkable that in the course of a whole year, there was not one case of a man's complaining of fisticuffs or beard-pulling, where previously the citizens had killed each other every day like dogs, not one case of name-calling or abuse; on the contrary, under his rule, great and small developed the habit of saying to each other: 'Do me justice or my lord the governor will see it done.' And you can see how effective and beneficial the marshal's justice is, [422] in that the rich who would previously have walled themselves off out of fear of miscreants – as we said previously – now live openly and publicly, displaying their wealth fearlessly; in that their trading enterprises, which were often destroyed at sea and were in any case confined to a very small number of ships, are now very successful, and their merchant fleet – now trading all over the world – consists of some seven hundred large vessels; in that the malefactors who previously paraded the rich garments that were the fruit of their crimes are now reduced to earning a living digging in vineyards or leading a donkey. Oh people of Genoa! You should be so devoted to him who has brought you from annihilation to freedom, from poverty to prosperity, from sorrow to joy, from the shadows to the light; who has saved a hundred thousand of you who without him faced certain death; who has preserved your city from destruction (and that this threat was real cannot be denied, as all the evidence shows); the wings of whose protection spread henceforth over land and sea! How can you ever repay your good duke and governor, who has done you such favours, and advanced your cause day by day? Where will you find means to repay the favours he has done you? You do well to obey him, love him, care for him, pray God for his safekeeping; for should you lose him, [423] your glory will certainly decay: for the wicked among you are not dead, but hide their wickedness and remain quiescent only out of fear of him. Oh, how wonderful it would be for you if he could be immortal! All that threatens you is the marshal's mortality – and yet one day you will indeed lose him, and that will be to your great loss. But while you still have him, ensure that good customs and habits, and the ways of justice, become engrained in you; study to be like him! Leave your cruel ways, and the evil customs that once racked your city! How fortunate you were to fall under the rule of the king of France, who sent you such a governor! You should bless the day when you first set eyes on him who now protects and defends you, who now represents a true justice equal to that imposed by the Emperor Trajan, so acclaimed by historians, [424] who dismounted from his horse, in full battle armour, and brought his whole army to a halt to administer justice to a good widow who was demanding justice for a wrong done to her.[33]

33 This story of the Emperor Trajan (AD 53–117) had been reported in the anonymous French translation of Bernard Gui's *Flores chronicorum* in BNF MS n.a.f. 1409, fols 38r–v, and also Jean Golein's *Livre de l'information des princes* in Geneva, BM, MS 870, fol. 154r–v, as well as in Jacobus de Voragine's *Legenda aurea.* Christine de Pizan also cited the story in *Le chemin de longue étude*, p. 430 (vv. 5777–800); *Livre des fais de Charles V*, I, p. 61 (I, c.23) and *Livre de la paix*, p. 242 (II, c.9).

IX: How as well as pursuing justice, the marshal is also inclined to pity and mercy, and, with examples, how these qualities are necessary for any man of valour.

However, the marshal's commitment to justice does not prevent his being full of pity and compassion; these are qualities God has conferred on him, as is right in anyone who rules and governs. Many of his close associates have often heard him say that he would prefer to forget any injury done to him so that he would not be tempted to think of revenge; he has never been known to refuse mercy to anyone, whatever wrongs he may have suffered. His commitment to pity and compassion were demonstrated quite recently when he heard that a number of his servants [425] – those in charge of his treasury – were defrauding him in total to the tune of four or five thousand francs. He investigated and discovered the truth, not by means of torture or force, but by having the accounts verified by good men able to establish his true daily expenditure; this allowed the crime to be exposed. But in his goodness, Boucicaut did not wish any further punishment to be imposed; rather, he paid off the servants involved generously, according to length of service, and dismissed them with courtesy. And because they were afraid that they might be distrusted, having been dismissed from his service, he made sure that they were provided with well-written letters attesting that they remained in his favour, and that they had been given leave until he might recall them.

He is very indulgent towards simple folk, and towards those who are at fault not deliberately but because they are ignorant or naïve; he is quick to forgive anyone who is genuinely and pleasantly penitent if they offend him in some way. In this he echoes the leniency of the Emperor Octavian, [426] at that time ruler of the world, who became the target of excessive anger from a knight called Lucius Cuminus who subjected him to a tirade of insults and abuse – at which the emperor showed neither anger nor irritation.[34] We are told that the following day, when Lucius had cooled down and recovered from wine and anger, he remembered just how insultingly he had spoken to the emperor; he was then so ashamed that he wanted to kill himself. Hearing this, the emperor was moved to pity and went to his side. He found Lucius shamefaced and mortified at his own folly – but the emperor embraced him and comforted him, and said that he freely forgave him, and would not hold any sort of grudge against him.

Like the emperor, the marshal is particularly magnanimous towards veteran men-at-arms who were once valuable but are now infirm, and who, having failed to save money, are now poverty-stricken. So he does not behave as do many who realise

34 This particular story is unique to the biography of Boucicaut, though it closely parallels a story told by Christine de Pizan regarding the Athenian tyrant Philocrates and his friend Transippus, in *Livre du corps de policie*, p. 28 (I, c.16), drawn in turn from Simon de Hesdin's commentary on Valerius Maximus, V.1, ext. 2, in BNF MS fr. 282, fol. 214d.

that they have no more service to obtain from some aged or disabled man-at-arms, and therefore show him the door as if he were a greyhound for which they have no further use. This is not the marshal's way; on the contrary, he does them honour, and helps them with pensions, and sees them looked after in their old age. These are of course precisely the actions that are proper for a good captain or leader of men; seeing their leader exercise care of this sort, they will give him their love and affection, they will serve him with greater willingness, thinking: [427] 'That's how he'll treat us if we're wounded, or if we grow old in his service.' And by the way, we are told that this is just how King Alexander the Great operated: once, for instance, when he was on campaign in the dead of winter, he saw an elderly knight formerly from his own army out in the field, dying of cold and indeed almost stiff.[35] He was overcome by pity, remembering the old man's former courage, and admiring his stubborn pursuit of arms in old age. The king went and took the old man in his arms, helped him to his own tent, and sat him on his own chair; he had a good fire lit, and himself rubbed his hands and feet to bring them back to life – and in this way the emperor deigned to attend to him, through pity and compassion. These models of conduct should move today's princes and leaders to do likewise.

X: Of the marshal's outstanding eloquence.

I could give endless examples of the marshal's virtues, but to summarise and bring this biography to a close, I shall simply repeat what I have been told by so many [428] – basing myself on scripture which says 'the testimony of many is true'[36] – that there is no fault in him. Indeed, to sum up, there are so many who have been his associates who want to live a good life, and who therefore follow his example in everything, and do their best to follow his example. Not only is he virtuous and wise in all his deeds, not only is he loved, and feared for the rigour of his justice, but he attracts many because of the eloquence, the humanity, the lucidity and the candour of his speech, qualities which have moved the hearts of many, as I showed earlier in speaking of the affairs of the Church and of how he brought the Genoese to the path of righteousness; I could also point to other affairs where his wisdom and eloquence served to bring about a satisfactory ending. Now it is possible that some might think it unlikely that a layman, that is someone without great learning, might possess the gift of speech as eloquent as I have described. No-one sensible, however, should be surprised: there is no skill that cannot be acquired by someone who shows assiduity, provided that he is sufficiently intelligent – or indeed gifted; [429] as the proverb says, 'Practice makes perfect.' And because true eloquence is a great advantage to any

35 This story is taken from Simon de Hesdin's commentary on Valerius Maximus, V.1, ext. 1, in BNF MS fr. 282, fol. 214b–c.

36 The author is adapting John 8:17: 'It is also written in your law, that the testimony of two men is true.'

prince or leader of men, and to any ruler, and because it can have many good effects, and to encourage efforts in that direction, I shall give a number of examples which show that anyone, however unrefined his language, can learn eloquence.

Saint Jerome in his book bears witness that a valiant man named Demosthenes learnt the most fervent eloquence by sheer determination.[37] Saint Jerome says indeed: 'When he started out he had a terrible stammer and a very ugly voice, and could barely articulate. But he put such effort into the study of eloquence and into controlling his impediment that finally he learned to pronounce his words perfectly. By constant practice, in other words, he rectified the flaws in his speech.' Demosthenes was also an accomplished musician in spite of the ugliness of his voice, but again, with practice, he made a voice which had been ugly and discordant and unpleasant to listen to, melodious and rhythmic and a pleasure to hear. [430] Briefly, he who had started out so crude and unattractive in speech was so eager to better himself that, says Valerius, he overcame his natural disadvantages by sheer persistence, 'And thus,' says Valerius, 'his mother gave birth to a flawed and imperfect Demosthenes, who was reborn by effort and determination to become an unrivalled master.' For which he is often called a philosopher.

Another cogent example of the value of true eloquence and graceful language is furnished by Cicero, who shows that in the beginning men lived like beasts in the forests, incapable of reason and only understanding the brute force that was their sole means of survival. But then there came upon them a man of great authority who used eloquence and honeyed words to show them the value of a civilised life – the value, that is, of living in community, governed by laws and by reason. He exhorted them to this life so successfully that they took to living in communities and became capable of conversing.[38] [431] And it was in this way, by virtue of eloquence, that the first cities were founded. Which is echoed also by a fable recounted by Statius, who tells us that Amphion built the walls of Thebes by the power of song alone – by which we should understand that his remarkable eloquence drew a population to the city.[39] And we hear much the same of Orpheus: the poet tells us that with his harp he made even savage and untameable beasts, like snakes or lions, bow to him and do his bidding.[40]

37 The story of Demosthenes and the reference to Saint Jerome (*Epistola LIII ad Paulinum*) were taken from Nicolas de Gonesse's commentary on Valerius Maximus, VIII, c.7, ext. 1, in BNF MS fr. 282, fols 320a–c.

38 See, for example, Cicero, *De oratore*, I, c.8.3.

39 This echoes the *Silvae* and the *Thebaid* of Publius Papinius Statius (AD c.45–c.96), but Lalande suggests that the comparison between the stones and the people adds an original interpretation to the story.

40 The precise source for this reference is unclear.

XI: Of the marshal's way of life.

Some say that diligence is more important than intelligence – but anyone who possesses both will always achieve outstanding success. The marshal is one of those who do possess both, for he so loves endeavour and hates idleness that it would be difficult ever to find him other than engaged on some useful task. Here, having now listed his virtues, we shall describe his way of life and his occupations. [432] He gets up every day very early, for he likes to devote the larger part of the morning to the service of God, before turning to his more worldly duties. He spends about three hours at prayer. After that, he attends his council, which lasts until dinner. After dinner, which he takes briskly and in public (he never eats more than one meat dish, never eats spiced sauces or any flavouring other than verjuice and salt, and he never eats from gold or silver plate), he gives audience to all sorts of people who want to address him or ask him a favour. There is usually quite a press of people, enough to fill the entire room, some of them foreigners, some of them his own people bringing news from all over the country; he talks graciously to each of them, and his responses are so benevolent and so reasonable that everyone, whatever his request, feels satisfied; he deals with each of them quickly and dispenses justice and favours rapidly enough that they are not obliged to wait too long exhausting their funds. Thereafter he withdraws to his study, and composes any letters he wishes to send, and issues orders to his people; after that, unless he is really too busy, he attends vespers. After vespers he works for a while, or talks to those who need his attention, until he is ready to retire, [433] at which point he will issue his last directions and go to bed. Sundays and holy days he devotes to pilgrimages on foot, or to conversations with the godly, or listens to beautiful books concerning the lives of saints, or histories of the glorious dead, of the Romans, or of others. Such are his habits when he is in residence in Genoa, the city of which he is governor. When on the other hand he is on campaign, no-one could be more conscientious than he is in ensuring that everything is done suitably and correctly; it is only his enemies who complain. As the saying goes, 'Like master, like man':[41] he is careful to employ people in his service who lead godly and virtuous lives; should anyone, of any rank, show any sign of vice or degeneracy, he does not hesitate to get rid of them. On the other hand, he is very generous to those who serve him, and they are correspondingly devoted to him (as is right), and serve him diligently, obey him, fear his displeasure.

This valiant man, then, so determined to ensure that all his duties are entirely fulfilled, never takes time off or indulges in amusements; those who love him indeed, those who would wish him long life and the good health [434] which makes public duties manageable (and may God preserve it), ought rather to advise him to be a little less conscientious and to take at least some time for repose and recreation. The authorities, after all, say that such assiduity is very harmful to one's health, and that

41 See p. 120 above.

to be constantly at work is not advisable:[42] when the mind is constantly occupied dealing with one problem after another, then one's intelligence tires and becomes blind, and over a long period one can become melancholic, which in turn may create memory problems, and thence a number of other maladies. Many of the authorities say that it is dangerous to go to bed while in such a state of overtiredness, and without having spent some time in innocent recreation or enjoyment, for they say if one goes to sleep with the mind still exhausted from the day's problems, then one's spirit will be tormented by thoughts that are melancholy or painful. That is why the wise, to avoid troublesome thoughts, recommend that those who are permanently occupied in study, or any other occupation demanding effort from the mind, should give themselves at least an hour's rest to be spent in amusement or pleasure, thus bringing relaxation to their inner self [435] which can otherwise be damaged by unrelenting effort. And what is thought to be particularly relaxing is to listen to sweet singing or to harmonious instruments, to listen to merry conversation (if it does not involve bawdiness or impropriety), to watch something comic and restorative to nature – human nature being so frail that it can easily be harmed or depleted. I stress that I see no harm in amusements like these which enrich the soul and the mind and which are a comfort to the senses, provided that what is involved is neither sinful nor corrupt; things of that sort do not displease God, for is it not written that a holy hermit, after he spent a time in prayer, would amuse himself with the little birds that he would feed? Of the same hermit, it is said that one day a gentleman carrying a bow was passing his hermitage, and was incensed when he saw the holy man playing with the little bird perched on his finger.[43] The gentleman thought to himself: 'If this hermit was really as holy as they say, he would spend all his time in prayer, [436] and he wouldn't be playing around with birds!' The holy man realised what the gentleman was thinking; he took him to task and asked him to hand over the bow he was carrying, and the gentleman did so. The hermit then asked him always to have his bow strung, to which the gentleman replied that he couldn't: if the bow was kept permanently strung, it would soon weaken, and become so warped that its range would be reduced. To which the good man replied: 'My son, human nature is just the same: so weak that it cannot abide being constantly in contemplation without suffering damage. The spirit needs some moments of pleasure and amusement, so that the mind remains ready and eager for effort.'

42 Citing Aristotle and Seneca as authorities, Gonesse had expounded upon this point at some length in his translation and commentary upon Valerius Maximus, VIII, c.8.1–2 and ext. 1, in BNF MS fr. 282, fols 325a–326a. Christine de Pizan used Gonesse's discussion in *Livre du corps de policie*, pp. 53–4 and 99–100 (I, c.32 and III, c.5).

43 This story, in which the hermit is Saint John the Evangelist, appears in John Cassian, *Collationes patrum in scetica eremo*, XXIV.21, and Jacobus de Voragine, *Legenda aurea*. There are also parallels to a fable of Phaedrus in *Aesopus ludens*, vv. 10–13, and in a letter of Saint Bruno to Raoul Le Verd, provost of the chapter of Reims.

XII: To conclude, how a man of such high merit should be honoured.

From all that I have said, and I guarantee the truth of every word, it is clear that a man of such merit should be praised and honoured in heaven, and renowned here on earth – and such a man is he of whom we have been speaking. [437] Oh, what quality does he possess that might damage his reputation? Answer: none! Whatever the vagaries of Fortune – who, as we know, is often damaging to the good and the valiant – she is unable, in any adventure, to pervert his unyielding courage, and this in spite of the fact that we know Fortune to be eminently changeable and erratic, often withdrawing the honours and worldly advantages that she has bestowed and replacing them with misfortunes. Nothing could shake the marshal's unending and unbending acceptance of any such misfortune, as is right in anyone wise and valiant. Whatever harm Fortune may inflict – has inflicted – on any man of valour, she cannot rob him of his virtues, and, having his virtues, that man has lost nothing, for his virtues are all that he has. And that is just what our hero recognises. How many times – more often than I have been able to list here – has he risked betrayal, imprisonment, death and poisoning in Italy, from the wicked who detest the good! Had such people prevailed in Genoa, he would not have survived so long as governor – but he knew how to counter them. But no man alive can be far-sighted enough always to guard against treachery; it is not always easy to detect traitors, for those who harbour treachery are often those who flatter most obsequiously, who seem the most willing or the most obedient. May God protect the marshal from the machinations and plots of the traitor! [438] For his loss would be most damaging. And I say to the Genoese, do not harbour treachery: do not be ungrateful, do not forget the good that he has done you and is still doing you, do not allow him to be listed with those who are hated for their virtues: should you do so, it will forever be a blot on you and on your city!

XIII: Now, addressing the marshal himself: as shown by examples, let him not put his trust in fickle Fortune.

Oh noble marshal, I wish now to address you directly – and using, if you will allow me, the 'tu' form, not out of disrespect, but in order to adopt the forms that the wisest thinkers use in such circumstances. Of course, the wise, like yourself, have nothing to learn, but it can happen that a wise man is focused on great matters, and forgets [439] other essentials; it does no harm to remind even the wisest of what it is good to do or not to do, and they should not take offence even if the speaker is much less learned than they are.[44] As a man of valour, you may be tempted to put your trust in the deeds

44 Christine de Pizan had made similar statements in *L'Épistre Othea*, ed. G. Parussa (Geneva, 1999), p. 341; *Le livre de la mutacion de fortune*, II, p. 80 (vv. 6611–16); *Le livre des fais et bonnes*

you have performed, and still, thank God, perform, in France where you are marshal and have long shown your courage, in Genoa which you have rescued from ruin, in the lands of the unbelievers and the Saracens where you have sought to glorify the faith, in your efforts to bring peace to the Church, and in so many other fields. It may reasonably seem to you that your long service and your years of effort will have made you beloved of princes and nobles and subjects, and indeed of all Christians, and this may have meant that you have lowered your guard. Ah! Most valiant of knights, you must not allow this: although the proverb tells us 'Do right, and what will be, will be!', it has to be admitted that any man who provokes Envy is likely also to provoke Hatred. To remind you to guard against this and not to forget it, [440] whatever your present prosperity (which God preserve), whatever your merits, we cannot trust in Fortune; whatever the future may hold, and lest simple folk say that you have simply received your just deserts, I shall offer examples of good and valiant men that have incurred hatred and been cast from their positions – some even who have been killed out of the ingratitude and envy of those they have done good to.

The first example – showing that strength and reputation are no guard against misfortune – is that of Theseus.

The noble Theseus was king of Athens and companion to the mighty Hercules; he was at Hercules' side in all his valiant deeds.[45] Theseus freed the Athenians from the appalling servitude imposed on them by Minos, who demanded that every year they send him some of their children to feed the monster that he kept in a cage. The citizens of Athens drew lots, and those who lost had to send their children. [441] Theseus, however, saved them from this misery by his valour and his wisdom – and indeed he did more, for he rebuilt, repopulated and extended the city which previously had been in ruins, and it was this that kick-started its prosperity and led ultimately to its glory. But the Athenians repaid him by rebelling against him and sending him into exile on a tiny island called Scyros [Chiros]; and there he who had enjoyed such honour and such fame lived out his days.

That he was not alone in this, and that such miserable fates often attend those who are good and valiant, can be shown from Valerius's account of the life of a valiant knight and prince of Rome called Furius Camillus who possessed all the virtues.[46] But precisely because he was virtuous, and because he prevented the persecution of the good by the wicked, Envy made his enemies claim that he had not ensured a just division of the spoils from a great victory that he himself had had over the city of Veii [Veyox] which had long been the enemy of Rome, and which he had conquered. [442] But in spite of his triumph, the ungrateful Romans sent him into exile. The

meurs du sage roy Charles V, I, p. 192; *Livre du corps de policie*, p. 1 (I, c.1).

45 This is a summary of Simon de Hesdin's translation and commentary upon Valerius Maximus, V, c.3, ext. 3, in BNF MS fr. 282, fols 225b–226a.

46 The discussion of Marcus Furius Camillus (c. 446–365 BC) was taken from Simon de Hesdin's translation and commentary upon Valerius Maximus, I, c.5.2, I, c.8.3 and V, c.3.2a, in BNF fr. 282, fols 25c, 57a–58b and 220d–221a. Also see p. 109 above.

good, however, must not focus merely on the wickedness of their enemies; they must always pursue what is right, and, as Our Lord says, return good for evil. Accordingly, undaunted, this valiant and upright citizen, who sought the good of Rome above his own advantage, soon showed just how benevolent he remained, for it soon happened that the Gauls – now known as the French – sacked the city of Rome. Grief-stricken, he gathered all his friends and allies, equipped them with arms and armour, and went to the aid of the Romans who were fleeing the destruction. He rallied the Roman army and set up an ambush; he took the Gauls by surprise and defeated them, and recovered much of the booty that they had acquired during the sack. He gave everything to the rebuilding of the city, and forbade all citizens from fleeing into the countryside as they had intended. In this way the city was, as it were, refounded, and Furius Camillus became known as the second Romulus, for Romulus had been the first to found Rome, but Furius Camillus refounded it. [443]

On the same subject – that is, the way in which good deeds are not always rewarded, indeed are often repaid with evil – I shall cite another wise man called Scipio Nasica, who had devoted his life to the people of Rome and whose wisdom had often saved them from servitude.[47] But his selflessness and his benevolence were repaid by his downfall – for the citizens sent him on an embassy to Asia [Aise], where he was to stay, they said, until he was recalled. But he lived out his life there with no summons, for the Romans, feeling no gratitude for his benevolence, had no wish to see him return. And it is not unusual, says Valerius's translator, for those who are determined to live as they wish and with no controls to hate those who take them to task – which is why Scipio was hated for his good deeds and his good words. In your case, marshal, you might be confident in your own wisdom and prudence, but it is those qualities that make the Italians – by contrast the most treacherous and spiteful of all nations today – [444] believe that you are the wisest of statesmen. But know that Scipio was so wise that he is cited as an example by Saint Augustine in his *City of God*, and by Solinus in his *Collectanea rerum memorabilium*, who says that this Scipio was of the lineage of the earlier Scipios, and was held to be the wisest and the most virtuous of the Romans not by individuals, but by the Senate itself and the general populace – and look how they repaid him![48] And his fate shows how often men's judgements are unjust and false, when the city of Rome itself, whose citizens prided themselves on being the best educated and the most respectful of law, could be so blinded by Envy.

These examples show just how often virtue and wisdom generate hatred. Let no-one therefore believe that when Fortune brings down someone who has worked untiringly for the public good, who has punished the wicked and supported those whose cause is just, that he has simply got his just deserts, or received punishment

47 The story of Publius Cornelius Scipio Nasica Serapio (c.183–132 BC) was taken from Simon de Hesdin's translation and commentary upon Valerius Maximus, V, c.3.2e, in BNF MS fr. 282, fols 222d–223a.

48 The references to Saint Augustine (*Civitate dei*, I, c.30–2 and II, c.5 and 18) and to Solinus (*Collectanea rerum memorabilium*, I, c.115) were taken from Simon de Hesdin's commentary.

from God for hidden misdeeds. That this is not so is proved by the case of Job, whose patience God chose to test [445] by persecuting him in spite of all his virtues. Histories are full of accounts of goodness repaid with evil.

The valiant duke of Athens Miltiades was so valorous that he defeated six hundred thousand Persians that Darius, king of Persia, had assembled to destroy Athens.[49] Miltiades had under his command no more than eleven thousand men-at-arms – but he took the great Persian army by surprise, and saved the city from them. He did many other good deeds for Athens, but his reward was that the Athenians, eaten up by envy and wickedness, had him die miserably in prison.

The same fate befell, rather later, another of their dukes, a most valiant and upright citizen called Themistocles, who served the city of Athens so faithfully that he cleansed it of all its ills, and made it powerful, rich, and the pearl of Greece – but his reward was a hatred from the citizens so intense that he had to flee for his life.[50] [446]

Some might of course say that such hatred is inspired by a lord or governor or leader who extorts excessive taxes, or inflicts cruelty on the citizens, or who is insufficiently generous – but this is by no means always the case. This becomes obvious in the case of another valiant man killed by the Athenians, and who was called Phocion.[51] Phocion was generous, open-handed, liberal, the very opposite of avaricious – all the virtues which should normally make a ruler beloved – but the disloyal Athenians even refused him burial in the city. Valerius speaks of the great ingratitude of the Athenians, who were the most learned and the most well read, but who, nevertheless, in spite of all their learning, in spite of their worship of Minerva whom they believed to be goddess of wisdom and arms, although they were convinced that they were the wisest people in the world, and although their city which had given birth to so many great philosophers.[52] They nevertheless, he says, [447] repeatedly rejected those who had done most for them, and thereby diminished their own virtue; vices, he suggests, are more to be blamed in those who are great and learned than in those who know nothing. From this, Valerius concludes that the Athenians were more given to their evil habits than to their just laws. His overall conclusion is that a man who is ignorant of all the vices, but who nevertheless does not commit any of them, is more to be admired than someone who knows all about virtues but fails to follow them.

49 The story of Miltiades (c.550–489 BC) and the Athenian victory at the battle of Marathon in 490 BC was taken from Simon de Hesdin's translation and commentary upon Valerius Maximus, V, c.3, ext. 3, in BNF MS fr. 282, fols 226b-d. Christine de Pizan also cited the story in *Livre du corps de policie*, pp. 20–1 and 84 (I, c.12 and II, c.18).

50 The story of Themistocles (c.524–459 BC) was taken from Simon de Hesdin's translation and commentary upon Valerius Maximus, V, c.3, ext. 3, in BNF MS fr. 282, fol. 226d.

51 The story of Phocion (c.402–c.318 BC) was taken from Simon de Hesdin's translation of Valerius Maximus, V, c.3, ext. 3, in BNF MS fr. 282, fols 226d–227a.

52 Simon de Hesdin had referred to the Athenian worship of Minerva in his commentary in BNF MS fr. 282, fol. 227c.

XIV: The end of this book, where its author excuses himself to the marshal for having completed it without his knowledge or authorisation, and for its being less well written than it ought to be.

It is time now that I should draw to a close, although I could write much more. However, because it can happen that however pleasing the subject, the reader becomes overburdened with information, I shall bring this treatise to an end and bring an end to the marshal's life-story, even though he is still in his prime and will, I believe, achieve more and more. [448] Just as vice calls to vice, so virtue grows and burgeons. But all of us are mortal; should I die, or become incapable of noting additional material about the marshal's deeds henceforward, I beseech all writers to ensure that one of them completes his life-story as far as his demise (and may God grant him a good death). And I beg those noble and notable persons who commissioned this book to forgive me if I have not done justice to my subject, and if I have not written my account in good order; this was not, I assure them, because of reluctance, but simply that my information is not always complete. Let them remedy any faults, and welcome my work in spite of them.

I also humbly beseech the good knight who is its subject that if this book should fall into his hands, or come to his attention, that he forgive me if I have failed to do justice to his noble deeds and worthy way of life, and that he not hold it against me that I have dared to speak of his life without his permission and without his knowledge; I was charged and commissioned to do so with the best of intentions, in order that its glorious subject might serve as an example for all time [449] to those who aspire to do well and who seek a model. Let him not either be displeased at receiving in this way his just deserts, that is lasting fame and acclaim for his actions in this world. He should note that the great men of old whose true deeds were recorded did not resent it: Valerius says, on the contrary, as do many other authorities, that it was precisely because they hoped their deeds would be recorded and their fame perpetuated that these great men performed such deeds.[53] Aristotle says on this topic that praise and honour alone are not enough reward for the man who is virtuous.[54]

To prove that it is right that any prince or governor or general should receive praise, glory and honour such that they are revered, and feared, by their subjects, [450] Varro – a wise authority from Rome – tells us that it was expedient for kings and princes to claim to be descendants of the gods as many used to do, like Alexander,

53 Nicolas de Gonesse had made this point in his translation and commentary upon Valerius Maximus, VIII, c.14, in BNF MS fr. 282, fol. 336d.

54 Aristotle's discussion in the *Nicomachean Ethics*, pp. 68–72 (IV, c.3) was cited by Nicolas de Gonesse in his gloss to Valerius Maximus, VIII, c.14, in BNF MS fr. 282, fols 336c–d. Gonesse's text was also used by Christine de Pizan in *Livre du corps de policie*, p. 55 (I, c.33).

the emperors of Rome and others; Augustine mentions this in *The City of God*.[55] By which we are to understand that it is right for those who are in command to build their authority by any means available, not out of pride but because thereby they will be more readily feared and obeyed.

So let my valiant subject not resent the fact that with this book I have given birth to a new legacy, one so durable that it will last forever; books record the truth of a man as a son might record that of a father. Let him not resent it more than did Pompey the Great when he discovered that a wise poet named Theophanes of Mytilene had, without his knowledge, gathered up accounts of his accomplishments and his deeds [451] and recorded them in fine language and distinguished style.[56] He was not displeased, and when the volume was presented to him, he showed every sign of delight and said that to record his deeds for posterity was evidence of true love, and that anyone performing such a service should be well rewarded; Theophanes's reward was a generous pension which allowed him to live in good style. In addition, because the poet had done him honour and ensured by his writings that his name would live on, he paid him honour in return: he made him a knight and a citizen of Rome, in other words granted him the greatest honour known to man, and not something commonly granted to foreigners; such a station gave Theophanes a great position, and all the freedoms and privileges that it brought. Pompey himself was a great rhetorician, who wrote with elegance and produced a number of notable works; at that time, all the noble princes and knights were lettered and educated, as were Julius Caesar, Octavius Caesar and many other great lords – something that was very pleasing to God. Pompey accorded great praise to Theophanes, in lines well written and ornamented, and thanked him warmly for what he had said; ever after he was a close friend to the poet, and gave him many rich gifts. [452]

XV: Examples of valiant men of old who were grateful to those who had written their life-stories and recorded their deeds and their gallantry.

Similarly, Scipio Africanus was most grateful to the poet Ennius who had recorded his noble deeds, and accorded him much gratitude and reward.[57] So also did the noble and valiant knight Brutus Drusus who was most grateful to an excellent versifier

55 The advice of Marcus Terentius Varro (116–27 BC) was reported by Saint Augustine in *Civitate dei*, III, c.4. Christine de Pizan made a similar comment in *Livre du corps de policie*, p. 70 (II, c.9), without citing either Varro or Augustine.

56 Gnaeus Pompeius Magnus (106–48 BC) and Theophanes of Mytilene, who wrote an account of Pompey's expedition to Asia, were discussed by Nicolas de Gonesse in his commentary upon Valerius Maximus, VIII, c.14.3, in BNF MS fr. 282, fol. 337b.

57 This story of Publius Cornelius Scipio Africanus (236–183 BC) and Quintus Ennius (c.239–c.169 BC) was taken from Nicolas de Gonesse's translation and commentary upon

called Lucius Accius who inscribed at the doors of various temples elegant words celebrating Brutus Drusus's victories over his enemies, the spoils from which had brought riches to adorn the temples (that is, their churches). Brutus Drusus ever after considered Lucius Accius his friend, and gave him rich rewards.[58]

So also did Julius Caesar himself reward a number of writers and poets who had written in various ways about him, his deeds and his conquests; [453] he was most grateful, and showed it by his generosity towards them. If a book particularly pleased him, he showed his gratitude: on one occasion when he was undertaking the conquest of Egypt, Lucan tells us, and engaged in naval battles with his enemies, he found his flagship isolated from the rest of the fleet and was so beset that he had no choice but to disarm and jump into the sea. Of all the riches he could have taken with him, he saved only the book of his life-story, and held it above the waves in his left hand so that the water should not harm it; he swam with his right hand only, across a hundred yards of sea, as far as the rest of his fleet – a remarkable feat of strength! And also a sign of how much he valued the book.[59]

These examples show how delighted the heroes of such accounts were that their fame should be perpetuated, and this is not surprising: [454] everyone is eager for glory because, says Aristotle, everything in this world wants to perfect itself.[60] And truly, every man of valour wants to receive and should receive praise for his good deeds, not only for his spiritual good deeds and his service to God, but also for his successes in knighthood or in learning; that this is not something to be condemned but rather to be celebrated is endorsed by Aristotle himself, the great and incomparable philosopher and moralist: did he not wish to attain glory and honour? When he handed to his disciple Theodectes copies of all the books he had written on the art of rhetoric, then as Cicero bears witness he wanted his name as author to be perpetuated [455] so that no-one else would be able to claim authorship – as often happens – and appropriate the honour of having written the treatises that were his.[61]

The same might be said of Virgil, greatest and most accomplished of poets: he too wanted to have recognition and praise for his accomplishments, as he showed when he wrote: 'I have composed these verses, but another has claimed authorship, and that they are his work.' The same thing happened with Aristotle's *Rhetoric* – the work

---

Valerius Maximus, VIII, c.14.1, in BNF MS fr. 282, fols 336d–337a. Christine de Pizan had also drawn upon Gonesse for her discussion in *Livre du corps de policie*, pp. 82–3 (II, c.17).

58 The references to Lucius Accius (170–c.86 BC) and Decimus Junius Brutus Callaecus (180–113 BC) derived from Nicolas de Gonesse's translation and commentary upon Valerius Maximus, VIII, c.14.2, in BNF MS fr. 282, fols 337a–b.

59 This story came not from Lucan's *Pharsalia*, which actually ended before this episode, but rather from Plutarch and Suetonius via *Li fet des Romains*, I, pp. 654–5.

60 The reference to Aristotle derived from Nicolas de Gonesse's translation and commentary upon Valerius Maximus, VIII, c.14 in BNF MS fr. 282, fols 336c–d. Christine de Pizan also derived this reference from Gonesse in *Livre du corps de policie*, pp. 54–5 (I, c.33).

61 This story derived from Valerius Maximus, VIII, c.14, ext. 3, as translated by Nicolas de Gonesse in BNF MS fr. 282, fols 338c–339a.

I mentioned above: another writer claimed credit, much to Aristotle's annoyance, so he made sure elsewhere to set down that this was indeed his work, so that any praise due to him might not be misdirected.[62]

All this proves that any valiant man might reasonably want to have praise and honour and glory in this world for any good deed that he has done. For this reason, such men should be very grateful to anyone who sets down their noble deeds authentically and stylishly in books, in chronicles or in registers so that their fame will outlast them in perpetuity; were it not for such records, we would know nothing of the valiant dead. From which I conclude that the good knight who is my subject should bear me no resentment: [456] I have erected a monument so strong and so durable that it will survive fire, water, earthquake or any corruption, for nothing is more enduring, nothing more difficult to destroy than what is written in books once they are copied and distributed widely. And that of course is what any author would wish for any matter he thinks to be fair and well written – as I believe this book will be considered for the new and pleasing topic that it treats. I pray to Almighty God to grant long life to Marshal Boucicaut, my subject, to protect him from the envious and to grant him ever-growing good fortune, to give him grace to lead a life in this world so virtuous and so righteous that he may one day be taken to the kingdom of heaven and enjoy heavenly bliss. Amen

Here ends *The Book of the Deeds of the Good Marshal Boucicaut, Governor of Genoa*, completed to this date the 9th of April, in the year of Our Lord 1409.

62 The references to Aristotle and to Cicero were derived from Nicolas de Gonesse's commentary on Valerius Maximus, VIII, c.14, ext. 3, in BNF MS fr. 282, fols 338c–d.

Select bibliography

Unpublished primary sources

BNF MS fr. 282 (Simon de Hesdin and Nicolas de Gonesse's *Dits et faits memorables*, a French translation of and commentary upon Valerius Maximus's *Facta et dicta memorabilia*).

Published primary sources

Ainsworth, Peter, and Godfried Croenen, ed., *The Online Froissart*, version 1.5 (Sheffield, HRIOnline, 2013), <http://www.hrionline.ac.uk/onlinefroissart>.

Aristotle, *Nicomachean Ethics*, trans. Roger Crisp (Cambridge, 2000).

Cabaret d'Orville, Jean, *La chronique du bon duc Loys de Bourbon*, ed. A.M. Chazaud (Paris, 1876).

Chandos Herald, *La vie du Prince Noir [The Life of the Black Prince], by Chandos Herald. Edited from the Manuscript in the University of London Library*, ed. D.B. Tyson (Tübingen, 1975).

Chronique de Du Guesclin, collationnée sur l'édition originale du XVe siècle, et sur tous les manuscrits, avec une notice bibliographique et des notes, ed. F. Michel (Paris, 1830).

Chronique du Religieux de Saint-Denys contenant le règne de Charles VI, de 1380 à 1422, ed. M.L. Bellaguet, 6 volumes (Paris, 1839–52).

Cuvelier, Jean, *La chanson de Bertrand du Guesclin de Cuvelier*, ed. J.-C. Faucon, 3 volumes (Toulouse, 1990–3).

Faits et gestes de Guillaume de Meuillon, publiés d'après le manuscrit original, ed. E. Maignien (Grenoble, 1897).

Froissart, Jean, *Oeuvres de Froissart*, ed. K. de Lettenhove, 25 volumes (Brussels, 1870–7); *see above* Ainsworth.

Froissart, Jean, *Chroniques*, ed. S. Luce, G. Raynaud, L. Mirot and A. Mirot, 15 volumes (Paris, 1869–1975).

La Sale, Antoine de, *Oeuvres complètes d'Antoine de La Sale*, ed. F. Desonay, 2 volumes (Liège/Paris, 1935–41).

Le livre de bon messire Jean le Maingre dit Boucicaut, Mareschal de France et gouverneur de Genes, ed. C. Petitot (Paris, 1819).

Le livre des faicts du bon Messire Jehan le Maingre, dit Boucicaut, mareschal de France, in *Collection complète des mémoires relatifs à l'histoire de France*, ed. C.B. Petitot, 52 volumes (Paris, 1822–6), VI, pp. 375–513 and VII, pp. 1–324.

Le livre des fais du bon messire Jehan le Maingre, dit Bouciquaut, Mareschal de France et gouverneur de Jennes, ed. D. Lalande (Geneva, 1985).

Le songe véritable, pamphlet politique d'un Parisien du XVe siècle, ed. H. Moranvillé (Paris, 1891).

Les cent ballades, poème du XIVe siècle composé par Jean le Seneschal avec la collaboration de Philippe d'Artois, comte d'Eu, de Boucicaut le jeune et de Jean de Crésecque, ed. G. Raynaud (Paris, 1905).

Li Fet des Romains compilé ensemble de Saluste et de Suetoine et de Lucan, texte du XIIIe siècle publié pour la première fois d'après les meilleurs manuscrits, ed. L.-F. Flutre and K. Sneyders de Vogel, 2 volumes (Groningen/Paris, 1935–8).

Machaut, Guillaume de, *La prise d'Alixandre (The Taking of Alexandria)*, ed. and trans. R.B. Palmer (London, 2002).

Mézières, Philippe de, *Une epistre lamentable et consolatoire adressée en 1397 à Philippe le Hardi, duc de Bourgogne, sur la défaite de Nicopolis (1396)*, ed. Philippe Contamine and Jacques Paviot (Paris, 2008).

Mézières, Philippe de, *Le songe du viel pèlerin*, ed. J. Blanchard, 2 volumes (Geneva, 2015).

Oresme, Nicole, *Le livre de Ethique d'Aristote. Published from the Text of MS 2902, Bibliothèque Royale de Belgique with a Critical Introduction and Notes*, ed. A.D. Menut (New York, 1940).

Pizan, Christine de, *Les oeuvres poétiques de Christine de Pisan*, ed. M. Roy, 3 volumes (Paris, 1886–96).

Pizan, Christine de, *Le livre des fais et bonnes meurs du sage roy Charles V*, ed. S. Solente, 2 volumes (Paris, 1926–40).

Pizan, Christine de, *Le livre de la mutacion de fortune*, ed. S. Solente, 4 volumes (Paris, 1959–66).

Pizan, Christine de, *Le livre du corps de policie*, ed. A.J. Kennedy (Paris, 1998).

Pizan, Christine de, *The Love Debate Poems of Christine de Pizan*, ed. B.K. Altmann (Gainesville, FL, 1998).

Pizan, Christine de, *L'Épistre Othea*, ed. G. Parussa (Geneva, 1999).

Pizan, Christine de, *Le chemin de longue étude. Édition critique du ms. Harley 4431*, ed. and trans. A. Tarnowski (Paris, 2000).

Pizan, Christine de, *Le livre de l'advision Cristine*, ed. C.M. Reno and L. Dulac (Paris, 2001).

Pizan, Christine de, *The Book of Peace*, ed. and trans. K. Green, C.J. Mews, J. Pinder and T. van Hemelryck (Philadelphia, PA, 2008).

Seneca, *Moral Essays, Volume III: De beneficiis*, trans. J.W. Basore (Cambridge, MA, 1935).

Songe du vergier: édité d'après le manuscrit Royal 19 C IV de la British Library, ed. M. Schnerb-Lièvre, 2 volumes (Paris, 1982).

Valerius Maximus, *Memorable Doings and Sayings*, ed. and trans. D.R. Shackleton Bailey, 2 volumes (Cambridge, MA, 2000).

Secondary sources

Ambühl, R., 'Le sort des prisonniers d'Azincourt (1415)', *Revue du Nord*, 89 (2007), pp. 755–88.

Benes, C.E., *Urban Legends: Civic Identity and the Classical Past in Northern Italy, 1250–1350* (University Park, PA, 2011).

Boulton, D'A.J.D., *The Knights of the Crown: The Monarchical Orders in Later Medieval Europe, 1325–1520* (Woodbridge, 1987).

Bozzolo, C., *Manuscrits des traductions françaises d'oeuvres de Boccacce. XVe siècle* (Padua, 1973).

Bozzolo, C. and Loyau, H., *La cour amoureuse, dite de Charles VI*, 2 volumes (Paris, 1982–92).

Çeçen, Z.K., 'Two Different Views of Knighthood in the Early Fifteenth Century: *Le Livre de Bouciquaut* and the Works of Christine de Pizan', *Journal of Military History*, 76/1 (2012), pp. 9–35.

Ceruti, A., 'Lettere di Carlo VI re di Francia e della Repubblica di Genova relative al maresciallo Bucicaldo', *Atti della società ligure di storia patria*, 17 (1886), pp. 349–64.

Charras, C., 'La traduction de Valère-Maxime par Nicolas de Gonesse', PhD dissertation, McGill University (Montreal, 1982).

Châtelet, A., *L'âge d'or du manuscrit à peintures en France au temps de Charles VI, et les heures du Maréchal Boucicaut* (Dijon, 2000).

Contamine, P., '"Les princes, barons et chevaliers qui a la chevalerie au service de Dieu se sont ja vouez". Recherches prosopographiques sur l'ordre de la Passion de Jésus-Christ (1385–1395)', *La noblesse et la croisade à la fin du Moyen Âge (France, Bourgogne, Bohême)*, ed. M. Nejedlý, J. Svátek, D. Baloup, B. Joudiou and J. Paviot (Toulouse, 2009), pp. 43–67.

Cotton, W.T., 'Teaching the Motifs of Chivalric Biography', *The Study of Chivalry: Resources and Approaches*, ed. H.D. Chickering and T.H. Seiler (Kalamazoo, MI, 1988), pp. 583–609.

Croenen, G., Rouse, M. and Rouse, R., 'Pierre de Liffol and the Manuscripts of Froissart's *Chronicles*', *Viator*, 33 (2002), pp. 261–93.

Curry, A., *Agincourt: A New History* (London, 2005).

Delaville Le Roulx, J., *La France en Orient au XIVe siècle: expéditions du Maréchal Boucicaut*, 2 volumes (Paris, 1886).

Delisle, L., *Recherches sur la librairie de Charles V*, 2 volumes (Paris, 1907).

Delogu, D., *Theorizing the Ideal Sovereign: The Rise of the French Vernacular Royal Biography* (Toronto, 2008).

DeVries, K., 'The Effect of Killing the Christian Prisoners at the Battle of Nicopolis', *Crusaders, Condottieri and Cannon: Medieval Warfare in Societies Around the Mediterranean*, ed. D.J. Kagay and L.J.A. Villalon (Leiden, 2003), pp. 157–72.

Di Stefano, G., 'Ricerche su Nicolas de Gonesse, traduttore di Valerio Massimo', *Studi francesi*, 9 (1965), pp. 201–21.

Di Stefano, G., 'Nicolas de Gonesse et la culture italienne', *Cahiers de l'Association internationale des études françaises,* 23 (1971), pp. 27–44.

Di Stefano, G., *Multa mentiere poetae: le débat sur la poésie de Boccace à Nicolas de Gonesse* (Montreal, 1989).

Epstein, S.A., *Genoa and the Genoese, 958–1528* (Chapel Hill, NC, 1996).

Famiglietti, R.C., *Royal Intrigue: Crisis at the Court of Charles VI, 1392–1420* (New York, 1986).

Famiglietti, R.C., *Tales of the Marriage Bed from Medieval France (1300–1500)* (Providence, RI, 1992).

Ferris, S., 'Chronicle, Chivalric Biography and Family Tradition in Fourteenth-Century England', *Chivalric Literature: Essays on Relations Between Literature and Life in the Later Middle Ages*, ed. L.D. Benson and J. Leyerle (Kalamazoo, MI, 1980), pp. 25–38.

Fuess, A., 'Prelude to a Stronger Involvement in the Middle East: French Attacks on Beirut in the Years 1403 and 1520', *Al-Masaq,* 17 (2005), pp. 171–92.

Gardiner, R. and J. Morrison, eds, *The Age of the Galley: Mediterranean Oared Vessels Since Pre-Classical Times* (London, 1995).

Galderisi, C., ed., *Translations médiévales. Cinq siècles de traductions en français au moyen âge (XIe–XVe siècles). Étude et répertoire,* 2 volumes (Turnhout, 2011).

Gaucher, E., 'Les proverbes dans une biographie du XVe siècle: *Le livre des fais de Bouciquaut*', *Le Moyen Âge: Revue d'histoire et de philologie,* 99 (1993), pp. 61–81.

Gaucher, E., *La biographie chevaleresque. Typologie d'un genre (XIIIe–XVe siècle)* (Paris, 1994).

Gaucher, E., 'Deux regards sur une défaite: Nicopolis (d'après la *Chronique de Saint-Denis* et le *Livre des faits de Boucicaut*)', *Cahiers de recherches médiévales,* 1 (1996), pp. 93–104.

Gaucher, E., 'Les joutes de Saint-Inglevert: perception et écriture d'un événement historique pendant la guerre de Cent Ans', *Le Moyen Âge,* 102 (1996), pp. 229–43.

Hedeman, A.D., *Translating the Past: Laurent de Premierfait and Boccaccio's De casibus* (Los Angeles, 2008).

Hoareau-Dodinau, J., *Dieu et le roi. La répression du blasphème et de l'injure au roi à la fin du moyen âge* (Limoges, 2002).

Hoornstra, D.S., 'Boucicaut fils and the Great Hiatus: Insights from the Career of Jean II Le Meingre, Called Boucicaut', *The Hundred Years War (Part III): Further Considerations,* ed. L.J. Andrew Villalon and D. Kagay (Leiden, 2013), pp. 105–44.

Housley, N., 'Le Maréchal Boucicaut à Nicopolis', *Annales de Bourgogne,* 68 (1996), pp. 85–99.

Housley, N., *The Crusaders* (Stroud, 2002).

Housley, N., 'One Man and His Wars: The Depiction of Warfare by Marshal Boucicaut's Biographer', *Journal of Medieval History,* 29 (2003), pp. 27–40.

Huizinga, J., *The Autumn of the Middle Ages,* trans. R.J. Payton and U. Mammitzsch (Chicago, 1996).

Jarry, E., *Documents diplomatiques et politiques. Les origines de la domination française à Gênes (1392–1402)* (Paris, 1896).

Keen, M.H., *The Laws of War in the Late Middle Ages* (London, 1965).

Kennedy, A.J., 'Christine de Pizan, Blasphemy and the Dauphin, Louis de Guyenne', *Medium Aevum*, 83 (2014), pp. 104–20.

La Roncière, C. de, 'La domination française à Pise', *École française de Rome: Mélanges d'archéologie et d'histoire*, 15 (1895), pp. 231–44.

Lalande, D., 'La naissance d'un sobriquet: Boucicaut', *Revue des langues romanes*, 85 (1981), pp. 115–23.

Lalande, D., *Jean II le Meingre, dit Boucicaut (1366–1421): étude d'une biographie héroïque* (Geneva, 1988).

Lalande, D., 'Nicolas de Gonesse est-il l'auteur du *Livre des fais du Mareschal Bouciquaut*?', *Miscellania Mediaevalia: Mélanges offerts à Philippe Ménard*, ed. J.-C. Faucon, A. Labbé and D. Quéruel, 2 volumes (Paris, 1998), II, pp. 827–37.

Lecourt, M., 'Antoine de La Sale et Simon de Hesdin: une restitution littéraire', *Mélanges offerts à M. Émile Châtelain* (Paris, 1910), pp. 341–53.

Lecourt, M., 'Une source d'Antoine de La Sale: Simon de Hesdin', *Romania*, 76 (1955), pp. 39–83.

Lehoux, F., *Jean de France, duc de Berri: sa vie, son action politique (1340–1416)*, 4 volumes (Paris, 1966–8).

Luttrell, A., *The Hospitallers in Cyprus, Rhodes, Greece and the West, 1291–1440* (London, 1978).

McLean, W., '*Outrance* and *Plaisance*', *Journal of Medieval Military History*, 8 (2010), pp. 155–70.

Margolis, N., *An Introduction to Christine de Pizan* (Gainesville, FL, 2011).

Masson, C., 'Gouverneur royal ou chevalier croisé? Boucicaut à Gênes, une administration intéressée', *Faire la guerre, faire la paix. Approches sémantiques et ambiguïtés terminologiques* (Paris, 2012), pp. 181–91.

Masson, C., *Des guerres en Italie avant les guerres d'Italie. Les entreprises militaires françaises dans la péninsule à l'époque du Grand Schisme d'Occident* (Rome, 2014).

Millet, H., 'Nouveaux documents sur Nicolas de Gonesse, traducteur de Valère-Maxime', *Romania*, 102 (1981), pp. 110–14.

Millet, H., 'Qui a écrit *Le livre des faits du bon messire Jehan Le Maingre dit Bouciquaut*?', *Pratiques de la culture écrite en France au XVe siècle*, ed. M. Ornato and N. Pons (Louvain, 1995), pp. 135–49.

Murray, A.V., 'The Saracens of the Baltic: Pagan and Christian Lithuanians in the Perception of English and French Crusaders to Late Medieval Prussia', *Journal of Baltic Studies*, 41 (2010), pp. 413–29.

Nobilleau, P., *Sépultures des Boucicault en la basilique de Saint-Martin (1363–1490)* (Tours, 1873).

Palmer, R.B., 'Guillaume de Machaut's *Prise d'Alexandrie* and Late Medieval Chivalric Ideals', *Chivalry, Knighthood, and War in the Middle Ages*, ed. S.J. Ridyard (Sewanee, TN, 1999), pp. 195–204.

Paviot, J., 'Boucicaut et la croisade (fin XIVe–début XVe siècle)', *La noblesse et la croisade à la fin du Moyen Âge (France, Bourgogne, Bohême)*, ed. M. Nejedlý, J. Svátek, D. Baloup, B. Joudiou and J. Paviot (Toulouse, 2009), pp. 69–83.

Phillpotts, C.J., 'The French Battle Plan During the Agincourt Campaign', *English Historical Review*, 99 (1984), pp. 59–66.

Picherit, J.-L., 'Christine de Pisan et le *Livre des faits du bon messire Jean Le Meingre*', *Romania*, 103 (1982), pp. 299–331.

Puncuh, D., 'Il governo genovese del Boucicaut nella lettera di Pileo de Marini a Carlo VI di Francia 1409', *Mélanges de l'École française de Rome. Moyen Âge, Temps modernes*, 90:2 (1978), pp. 657–87.

Puncuh, D., 'Il maresciallo Boucicaut e l'arcivescovo Pileo de Marini', *Il maresciallo Boucicault, governatore di Genova tra Banco di San Giorgio e Magistrato della Misericordia* (Genoa, 2002), pp. 15–31.

Richard, J., 'Les prisonniers de Nicopolis', *Annales de Bourgogne*, 68 (1996), pp. 75–83.

Rollo-Koster, J. and T.M. Izbicki, eds, *A Companion to the Great Western Schism (1378–1417)* (Leiden, 2009).

Schnerb, B., 'Le contingent franco-bourguignon à la croisade de Nicopolis', *Annales de Bourgogne*, 68 (1996), pp. 59–74.

Schnerb, B., *Enguerrand de Bournonville et les siens. Un lignage noble du Boulonnais aux XIVe et XVe siècles* (Paris, 1997).

Schullian, D.M., 'A Revised List of Manuscripts of Valerius Maximus', *Miscellanea Augusto Campana: Medioevo e Umanesimo*, ed. R. Avesani, G. Billanovich, M. Ferrari and G. Pozzi, 2 volumes (Padua, 1981), II, pp. 695–728.

Setton, K.M., *The Papacy and the Levant (1204–1571). I: The Thirteenth and Fourteenth Centuries* (Philadelphia, PA, 1976).

Taylor, C.D., *Chivalry and the Ideals of Knighthood in France during the Hundred Years War* (Cambridge, 2013).

Taylor, J.H.M., *The Making of Poetry. Late-Medieval French Poetic Anthologies* (Turnhout, 2007).

Tuchman, B.W., *A Distant Mirror: The Calamitous Fourteenth Century* (New York, 1978).

Tyson, D.B., 'Authors, Patrons and Soldiers: Some Thoughts on Four Old French Soldiers' Lives', *Nottingham Medieval Studies*, 42 (1998), pp. 105–20.

Valentini, A., 'Entre traduction et commentaire érudit: Simon de Hesdin "translateur" de Valère Maxime', *La traduction vers le moyen français*, ed. C. Galderisi and C. Pignatelli (Turnhout, 2007), pp. 353–65.

Valois, N., *La France et le Grand Schisme d'Occident*, 4 volumes (Paris, 1896–1902).

Wright, C., 'An Investment in Goodwill: Financing the Ransom of the Leaders of the Crusade of Nikopolis', *Viator*, 45 (2014), pp. 261–97.

Wright, C., *The Gattilusio Lordships and the Aegean World 1355–1462* (Leiden, 2014).

Index